OUTDOOR LIFE
DEER
HUNTER'S
YEARBOOK

Grolier Book Clubs Inc.
Danbury, Connecticut

Cover photo: Leonard Lee Rue III

Copyright © 1989 by Grolier Book Clubs Inc.

Published by
Outdoor Life Books
Grolier Book Clubs Inc.
Sherman Turnpike
Danbury, CT 06816

Distributed to the trade by
Stackpole Books
Cameron and Kelker Streets
Harrisburg, PA 17103

Book design: Jeff Fitschen

ISSN 0734-2918
ISBN 1-55654-056-6

Manufactured in the United States of America

Contents

Me and Joe
Are Alive and Well

Much has been written about backwoods balladry, but the frontiersman's characteristic form of artistic expression was not the ballad but the prose episode. As in all interesting episodes, they were compounded of strict factuality. If the facts sometimes seemed unusual, it was up to the raconteur to show by a weaving of circumstantial logic that it could not have happened otherwise." This quotation from *The Alamo,* a book by John Myers Myers, describes the storytelling tradition of the frontiersman.

Above all, the art form was a story because it was oral. In the early days, this was about the only casual form of entertainment people had. Storytelling around a campfire or during a quiet night watch in the saddle was the sole thing anyone could do to drive away boredom and, sometimes, fear of what the dark woods or unending prairie had in store.

The same storytelling arose among sailors. They were short on books and letters from home and did not dream of the day when storytelling would be replaced by television watching. Indeed, most frontiersmen and long-voyage sailors could not read, even if a stray almanac or book did find its way to them.

Frontier tales and seamen's yarns, at first quite factual, were soon overtaken by stories by embroiderers and outright liars, who fabricated tales that were often devoted to self-glorification. The tradition grew that tall tales and fantastic yarns were acceptable as long as they were internally consistent and, above all, interesting. The listener was willing to surrender veracity for good entertainment.

The new tradition soon graduated into published fiction with the objective of making money, not the entertainment of friends. Fiction soon overcame fact in many supposedly factual magazines and books. Thus, Davy Crockett, the frontier statesman, Indian fighter, and martyr at the Alamo, lived to see books and magazine stories exaggerate his exploits, even though his life included enough real adventure to fascinate anyone. The trouble was that one life could not meet the needs of money-hungry writers.

But the older tradition of truthful storytelling lives on, and it is strong among hunters. During the deer-hunting season, you will hear many prose narratives told in camps or over a drink or two at the day's end. The hunter who has just taken a trophy buck is anxious to tell all who will listen how it happened, and his listeners are anxious to hear his story because they might pick up a clue on how to hunt or where to hunt whether for meat or a trophy. Also, they just plain love a good story about their favorite sport. But if the storyteller embroiders even the least bit and is detected, all faith in his character vanishes and he is often punished by jeering or other persecution.

"Liar!" is the ultimate insult when it comes to hunting and fishing "oral episodes." Of course, the big buck or big fish that got away is another matter. Since the hunter or fisherman is making no claim to proficiency or any other form of superiority in a

1

"got away" story, everybody understands that the buck deer, bear, muskellunge, or trout might have been a smidgen smaller than the storyteller allows. One cannot use a tape measure on something that is still in the woods or water.

The prose narrative is still alive and well among American hunters and fishermen because they tell such stories themselves and usually like to read them. These narratives were the backbone of "hook-and-bullet" magazines for many years. *Outdoor Life*, founded over 80 years ago in Colorado, lived on these stories (never called articles) for many years, and so did many other outdoor magazines. When I joined the staff of *Outdoor Life* in 1964, the magazine had for many years contained 13 features every month. Of these, well over half were narratives about hunts or fishing trips, some dramatic, some mostly informative, some humorous. Still others consisted of a blend of all three elements, but that type of story is difficult to write and is therefore rather rare. It is beyond the skills of most hook-and-bullet writers.

But in the 1940s and 1950s, a prejudice arose against what were sneeringly termed "Me and Joe" stories. Where this prejudice arose is a question, but I have my theory. I think it arose mostly among editors, not among readers. By that time, one had to have a college degree, usually in English or journalism, to land a job as an editor on a magazine, and that included the hook-and-bullet magazines. Having taken all those courses, the young editor considered himself a sophisticate and disdained the simple prose narrative told in a hunting camp or some other quiet place where TV and the latest issue of a picture magazine were not available.

Because of the prejudice against storytelling in print, the outdoor magazines were suddenly flooded with "service articles"—never called "stories." Where-to-go and how-to-do-it informational material suddenly almost overwhelmed the outdoor magazines, and good old "Me and Joe" were largely banished to those places from which they had sprung—the hunting and fishing camps and other places where hunters and fishermen meet.

Nowadays, however, Me and Joe stories are back again, and the reason for their return is reader dissatisfaction with instructional material that reads like a poor high-school textbook. The results of endless reader surveys forced the editors of outdoor magazines to acknowledge that their publications had a unique mass audience. Sure, the readers liked well-written, useful informational pieces, and they would read them, provided they weren't too long and boring. Introduce some humor and color, and an information piece did get a fairly good readership score. But that's hard to do if you're writing an illustrated article about how to skin a catfish or tie dry flies, typical how-to subjects. And if the editors ran a good hunting narrative, the readership score in the survey hit the ceiling.

I well remember the shock at *Outdoor Life* when the stories of Peter Hathaway Capstick achieved over 90 percent "read-all" scores in our regular readership surveys. Since Capstick was writing about hunting dangerous game in Africa, the high scores clearly told us that the modern hunter is still interested in narratives, even narratives involving overseas hunting in which the vast majority will never participate. It's sometimes called "armchair adventure," but that term is often really a sneer. When Jim Carmichel, *Outdoor Life*'s inimitable shooting editor, writes a good hunting narrative, the readership score is almost always twice as high as it is for one of his informational articles. The same was true of Jack O'Connor, Jim's predecessor as shooting editor. These astonishing scores clearly proved that if the narrative is interesting enough, even a fisherman who doesn't even own a gun will read a hunting story. Such high scores are impossible if nonhunters (fishermen) in the audience do not read the hunting story.

It is possible to combine narrative material with information. This is done simply by inserting short action anecdotes about actual occurrences into the informational material. Often, the writer uses an action incident as the attention-getting lead of his story and then goes on with straight information. The other extreme is to piece together a whole series of anecdotes and intersperse information sparingly. The nature of the subject determines how much narrative is used. In fact, these combination or "hybrid" stories, as I call them, form the single largest class of material published in *Outdoor Life* and many other outdoor magazines. Hybrids work quite well. The incidents illustrate the information and the information makes the incidents clear.

Though pure narratives have not regained their former dominance, Me and Joe are alive and well and living in the pages of the outdoor magazines. This fact would astonish those who take an interest in journalism or "communication." The conventional wisdom comes from advertising and the electronic media, and the message is to keep it short and hit the audience with a single incisive message. Above all, we are told, use pictures rather than words, if you can possibly do so. Ignore the demises of weekly picture magazines, of course. Look in any "communications" or advertising textbook, and you'll soon find that message. It is reinforced by commercial TV, which airs very few narratives other than endless soaps. Communications people have often said that the printed word would inevitably vanish and be replaced by televised pictures and dialogue. So far, that confident prediction hasn't even begun to come true.

What do most of these communications practitioners think of a readership consisting of millions who will sit down in silence and read a narrative of 3,000, 4,000, or even 6,000 words? The answer is that they don't think about it. Most such people are born and bred Easterners who inhabit large cities or their suburbs. They have never hunted or fished, or if they ever did during their younger days, they have largely forgotten. In addition, most modern

The William Faulkner story concerns the magnificent big buck that seems untouchable by any hunter. Leonard Lee Rue III photo.

"communicators" actually have a distaste for the "primitive" or even "barbarous" outdoor sports, particularly hunting. They are also overwhelmingly in the anti-gun camp. As far as hunters are concerned, they are the enemy. Believe it or not, we once had one of these people as editor-in-chief of *Outdoor Life* magazine.

Most "communicators," including professors of English, would never think of taking the hook-and-bullet magazines as serious purveyors of literature. Most of them have treated Garrison Keillor *(Lake Wobegon Days)* with the same disdain, and for much the same reasons. Keillor *told* his books before they were published, don't you know, and he's a rural person. He couldn't possibly appeal to us modern sophisticates. But he appeals to millions of other people, and the hook-and-bullet magazines do too.

If you're reading this, you are almost surely a sportsman, and I think you should be proud of what you and your fellow sportsmen have achieved—the survival of the narrative in print in American magazine journalism. It's a great feat, even though it's unintentional, and you should be honored for it. But you won't be, at least not on TV, in most classrooms, or in the publications that most people read nowadays.

In American outdoor publications, what are these narratives about? As far as hunters are concerned, the answer is deer hunting by a big margin. The insatiable appetite of hook-and-bullet readers for deer-hunting narratives is demonstrated by the fact that *Outdoor Life* publishes more narratives about deer hunting than they do about any other kind of game. *Outdoor Life* also publishes many how-to and where-to-go articles on deer hunting, but they seldom achieve high readership scores because few hunters read them unless they intend to do what the author did. A good hunting narrative, on the other hand, will be read by almost every hunter. One reason is that a deer is almost always the first big game killed by a youngster. He remembers every detail of that hunt with Uncle John 20 years ago when he took his first buck, a fork-horn that weighed all of 110 pounds on the hoof. He wants to know how others felt when they got that first big buck or that unusually clever buck, or had some unusual and interesting experience during a deer hunt.

That kind of reader may also vividly remember a particularly good duck hunt, a remarkable day of quail hunting, or a fine trophy squirrel that he got with his first .22. But such experiences are more difficult to turn into narratives than an exciting or even just an interesting deer hunt. Big game is inherently of greater interest to most hunters than small game, and small game is more difficult to write about in narrative form. That is why it is so extremely difficult for editors to find a really good story (narrative) about a rabbit hunt. Few people ever think of trying to write such a story.

This edition of the *Deer Hunter's Yearbook*, therefore, appropriately includes stories (narratives), articles, and "hybrids" in about the same proportion as they appear in *Outdoor Life* magazine and two of its offshoots, *Deer and Big Game* and *Hunting Guns*, both published once a year, as well as a chapter that I wrote for *The Outdoor Life Deer Hunter's Encyclopedia*. I hope you enjoy them all and find them useful.

Among the stories and articles, some deal with other big game—elk and moose hunting. These stories are appropriate here because most deer hunters eventually hunt the larger members of the deer family. These appear, logically enough, under the heading "Bigger Game."

One story comes from an outside source. It is "Race at Morning," a short story by William Faulkner, the great American novelist, prose poet, and winner of the Nobel Prize for literature in 1949. Though the story is drawn from Faulkner's own experiences, it is fiction.

For many years the "requirement sheet" for authors provided by *Outdoor Life* stated: "We do not publish fiction . . ." Why, then, is the Faulkner story included in this yearbook?

Every effort was and still is made to prevent the publication of whole-cloth fiction disguised as unvarnished truth in *Outdoor Life*. In the sleazy days of some outdoor magazines, it was common for money-hungry writers to palm off fiction as fact purely for the sake of the money. The profit was tidy since you didn't actually have to spend money on a hunting or fishing trip. It was done all too often, and there were many protests from readers. They can smell a liar a long way off, and in a few cases, people on the scene of the fictional events wrote to editors and denounced the fictioneer. These frauds largely disappeared when the outdoor magazines switched mainly from line drawings and paintings to photographs. If an author said he had killed a large, ferocious grizzly bear but his only photograph showed an inoffensive half-grown cub, the story was, and is, rejected. The same thing happens when somebody writes about the magnificent buck he shot, and his photographs do not show a suitable animal in his possession. Nevertheless, a fly-by-night fictioneer sometimes borrows or even buys supporting photographs from someone else and tries his luck. Fortunately, most of these guys are such poor writers that no one would buy their material, and there are other ways to check out the authenticity of a story. Every effort is still made to detect fiction masquerading as fact and reject it with extreme prejudice against the writer's future submissions. All this has built up a strong anti-fiction feeling among hook-and-bullet editors.

Nevertheless, *Outdoor Life* did knowingly publish one fiction story in recent years. It was titled, "The Invincible Grouse Hunter," and was written by Joel Vance, the well-known outdoor writer. It appeared in the November 1984 issue. It is a first-person narrative. A grouse hunter gets lost in the woods and comes to an old farmhouse with his dog. There he meets an old-timer, who asks him to take his old dog grouse hunting for a while because the dog wants to go and the old-timer is too crippled to hunt. To sweeten the request, the old man brings out a magnificently engraved Parker shotgun. With the fine gun, the hunter makes his first double on grouse over the old dog. He says good-bye to the old man and makes his way home by following his directions. From a gun-nut friend he finds out that the fine shotgun was undoubtedly a Parker Invincible, only two of which were manufactured, but the serial number of the gun, which he noticed, does not match the known numbers, so there must have been an unknown third. He goes back and finds that no one has lived in the old farmhouse for many years. The old man, the gun, and the dog have vanished. The old-timer was a ghost. Maybe the gun was, too. This is one of the most effective stories I have ever read, and I rate it as the finest ghost story ever put on paper, superior even to "The Turn of the Screw," by Henry James. But there is probably little chance that the Vance story will ever enter mainstream literature. Literary critics do not read hook-and-bullet magazines and so may never become aware of it. And even if they did run across it, almost all of them would reject it because it is about hunting, and, land sakes alive, guns!

All the *Outdoor Life* editors read the Vance story and liked it, but there was doubt about publishing it. I said that it should be plainly labeled *"Outdoor Life* Fiction" in order to avoid confusion and preserve our reputation for strict veracity. Another editor said that such caution wasn't needed since a ghost story is obviously fiction. My reply: "That isn't true if you believe in ghosts, and a lot of our readers do. I believe in hants myself." In the end, the story was published without the fiction label.

I believed that the publication of the Vance story would open the floodgates and that we would soon be wallowing in thousands of fiction manuscripts with no time to read a tenth of them. It's one thing to do something or learn enough about something to write a story or an article. Anybody can make up a tall tale. But the floodgates did not open. To the best of my knowledge, we did not receive a single additional fiction story. I asked one of my knowledgeable friends about this, and he said: "Maybe most folks realize they just don't have enough imagination to make up a really good fiction story, and maybe they know they can't write well enough to put it across if they did." That about sums up the fiction front to date.

Why then is the William Faulkner story included in this yearbook? In the first place, it is an excellent narrative. It is also a portrayal of deer hunting that is very adventurous and extremely dangerous —horseback hunting with hounds and shotguns. That form of hunting is legally possible nowadays only in three or four southern states. It's even more dangerous than riding to hounds in pursuit of the red fox, in which sport several people are killed or severely injured every year in the United States, Scotland, England, and Ireland. As such, the Faulkner story is a fine portrayal of hunting that is extremely novel to most modern American hunters. It is also a story that is concerned with a universal theme among hunters—the magnificent big buck that seems untouchable by any hunter. In this story, the big buck does get away, and the hunters are quite happy that he does. They look forward to running him next year and for years after that. The basic theme has formed the basis of many stories that have appeared in many outdoor magazines. In fact, the theme has been used so many times that some editors shy away from it.

It is Faulkner's writing style that transforms the narrative into a wondrous tale, and his concern with the people in it makes it a telling portrayal of human emotions. The story is more about people than about hunting, which is often true of great hunting stories.

It is interesting to compare the Faulkner story with the majority of *Outdoor Life* deer-hunting narratives. If you make this comparison, you'll find that nothing that faintly resembles the author's style has ever appeared in the magazine. Faulkner was a unique writer. He deliberately induced what I call "reader doubt" by using vague words and constructions. The reader has to search deeply for the inner meaning, and if and when he does discern it, that meaning comes as a rewarding revelation. The writing is very skilled, but it does include this element of intentional murk. For instance, there is the author's characteristic unwillingness to tell the reader the time sequence of the events in his novels and short stories. He even skips back and forth between generations of his families without telling you that he has done so. You have to figure out the sequence of things for yourself more often than not. This stylistic device puzzles the reader and lends the material an otherworldly quality that many readers find eerily attractive.

"Race at Morning" is well worth reading if you are a typical reader of hunting stories because it shows what a great author can do with an overworked theme. But if the manuscript had come to me as a submission to *Outdoor Life*, I would have rejected it, and I would have done so even if the byline had been "By William Faulkner." I don't think the vast majority of our readers like hunting fiction. Reality is more attractive to them. I also know that most of them unhesitatingly reject stories and articles that are difficult to understand. When a writer, even a Nobel Prize winner, is *deliberately* unclear, I really doubt that his work should appear in a hunting and fishing magazine. How about a hunting story by Franz Kafka, the famed Viennese fabulist? He concealed his inner meaning so perfectly that scholars are still arguing about it 65 years after his death.

In this *Deer Hunter's Yearbook*, however, the Faulkner story serves a useful purpose. Those who do enjoy Faulkner's unique writing will enjoy the story, if they have not read it before. Those who like good narrative writing, clear as a freshly washed windowpane, may want to contrast it with the very best nonfiction narratives that appear in *Outdoor Life*. Although I would have rejected Faulkner's story for *Outdoor Life* publication, I enjoyed reading it. How about you?

George H. Haas
Consulting Editor
Outdoor Life **magazine**

PART 1

HUNTING WHITETAIL DEER

Whitetails Every Way

By Gary Clancy

Larry Boughten is the most patient hunter on a deer stand I have ever known. Once he selects his stand site, he stays put until it is time to drag out the object of his vigilance. For the 15 seasons we have shared the warmth of a deer camp, only once has the drag rope remained coiled in his pocket.

Another friend of mine is a stillhunter. Like a dusk-shadow, he drifts through the woods. He slinks and sneaks. Peeks and peers. I've lost count of the number of whitetails that have fallen to his brush-scarred, short-barreled, fast-handling pump gun.

Up in the big-woods country of northwestern Wisconsin, near the quiet, little town of Solon Springs, is a hunting shack tucked back in the dark pines that is the headquarters and deer season home of a group of hunters known as the Dirty Dozen. Their preferred deer hunting tactic is driving. Off to one side of the weathered shack is a rope-polished meat pole. Folks thereabouts use the number of bucks hanging from that pole as a barometer to indicate how well (or poorly) the season is in general.

"Saw six bucks hanging at the Dirty Dozen Camp," someone in the bar and grill will announce.

"Yep, that's better than last year. Course, I knew it would be," comes the reply.

Hunting from a stand, stillhunting and driving—the trio of methods by which most whitetails end up packaged neatly in hunters' freezers. It has been my privilege to hunt with men who have been proficient at each of these time-honored methods. I would never bet even money against any of them not filling their tag. But as successful as these specialists are, they must play second fiddle to the versatile whitetail hunter when it comes to consistently scoring.

The versatile whitetail hunter is not strictly a stand hunter, not purely a stillhunter and certainly not convinced that the drive is the best method for putting bucks on the ground. Rather, the versatile whitetail hunter is a student of all three schools. The versatile whitetail hunter lets the weather, the season, the hunting pressure, the terrain, the habits of the local whitetails and his gut feeling dictate which method he will use from day to day, and often from hour to hour.

No, I have never met the versatile whitetail hunter with the patience on stand of a Larry Boughten. Nor one who can slip through the woods with the quiet ease of my friend the stillhunter. None of the versatile whitetail hunters I know can duplicate the record of the Dirty Dozen when it comes to driving deer. But the versatile whitetail hunter is proficient enough at all three methods to get the job done. Like the three-letter high-school athlete who may not be a superstar in any one sport but who can sink that clutch free-throw, deliver the key base hit or catch the third-and-long pass, the versatile whitetail hunter is proficient enough to be confident using whichever method he chooses.

Nearly every hunter in the woods has the makings to be a versatile whitetail hunter. It takes no special talent to determine where deer have been or will go and then to plant your butt on the bark of a tree limb and stay put. It requires even less woodsmanship to walk from point A to point B as directed by the drive captain. Even stillhunting, which requires a certain amount of grace and a large dose of patience, is not beyond the physical capabilities of most hunters. No, I am convinced that it is not howto that stumps the would-be versatile hunter, but rather the when-to.

When should I sit on stand? When would I be better off stillhunting? When is a deer drive my best bet for action? These are the questions which confuse so many hunters.

WHEN TO SIT ON STAND

More whitetails are downed by hunters hunting from stands than by any other method. The biggest reason for this is senses—the whitetail's and our own. A whitetail can smell our stinking hides at a half-mile. Most of us couldn't smell a whitetail at arm's length.

Then there is the whitetail's sense of hearing. Compared to our own incessant-racket-assaulted flappers, the whitetails oversize, independently operated, fine-tuned, extremely sensitive ears are the envy of even the Bionic Man.

And although the whitetail's vision is not much better than yours and mine, the whitetail is quick to pick up the slightest movement.

From a properly situated stand, a hunter has an excellent chance of remaining undetected by any of

You've got to know when to get on stand but must also know when it's time to leave.

those senses. Naturally, this leads to more deer seen, more deer shot and the popularity of hunting from a stand.

The best time to occupy a stand for whitetails is any time the deer are on the move. Whitetails move about within their loosely defined home areas for a variety of reasons. Food, sex, comfort, security and evasion are the main reasons for whitetail mobility.

I can tell you that the average-size whitetail needs to consume eight to nine quarts of food to fill its paunch, but until you have the opportunity to dress a buck with a full belly, you really cannot appreciate just how much brown and green stuff that really is.

To make sure that all four of the whitetail's stomach compartments are kept busy, the whitetail feeds heavily twice each day and grabs a snack or two between meals.

The main feeding period begins about twilight and continues until the deer has the rumen section of its four-compartment stomach filled. Under good conditions when food is plentiful, this will take less than two hours. With its belly full, the deer will lie down, often right where it is, and rest for a few hours. It will then rise about midnight to top off its stomach before bedding down again. An hour or two before dawn, the deer will again feed heavily and then vacate the feeding area for more secure cover. Though does, fawns and young bucks may linger around the feeding area after first light, the bigger bucks are in cover by good shooting light.

Positioning yourself between the bedding and feeding areas during the first and last hours of light will put you in good position to intercept any deer that may be traveling between the two areas.

I prefer to hunt from stands overlooking trails leading between feeding and bedding areas in the evening rather than in the morning. By shooting light in the morning, a buck has already had two feeding periods and, even if not quite finished with breakfast, he will usually head for cover at the first hint of day. In the evening, however, deer are hungry. They have been chewing their cuds all day, and by late afternoon their stomachs are complaining. That need for food becomes greater as the weather becomes colder.

In many parts of the whitetail's range, deer are dependent upon crops for a good share of their diet. Corn, soybeans and alfalfa are three of the favorite but by no means the only crops upon which the whitetail dines. It is easy to fall into the habit of hunting from stands overlooking fields; after all, the tracks show that is where the deer are feeding. But remember, most of those tracks were made at night. Such stands are good bets for the early-season bowhunter who hunts where competition from other hunters is limited, but they are poor choices for the rifleman.

Sex really puts whitetails on the move, and a good share of the big bucks harvested in this country each season had procreation of the species in mind when they made the mistake of ambling by a hunter on stand. A call to the game manager in the unit you hunt will inform you of the dates that the rut peaks in your area. But you don't have to hunt the peak of the breeding season to get in on the action. The bucks are ready to breed long before the first doe come into estrus. Now, the bucks spend their time making and tending scrapes, beating up saplings, picking fights with other bucks and checking out every doe they encounter just in case they get lucky. The two weeks prior to the peak and the week after are all good times to be on stand.

Comfort and security go hand in hand. Though a whitetail will nearly always pick a place to bed where the shade keeps it cool in warm weather and the sun warms it in cold weather, it will quickly sacrifice all comforts for security once hunters invade its turf.

Although I have found plenty of bucks using out-of-the-way, skimpy parcels of cover where few hunters ever look, most of the deer will head for the meanest tangle of timber and brush your area has to offer once the guns start popping on opening day. A stand in or on the edge of that cover is a good bet any time other hunters are active in the area.

A whitetail spends much of the gun season evading hunters. Any time a whitetail is busy staying out of the crosshairs of another hunter's scope, there is an excellent opportunity for you to settle him in yours. There are a couple of tricks to putting yourself in the right place to take full advantage of the whitetail's evasion tactics.

One is to locate the points where most of the hunters enter the land you hunt. Most hunters are reluctant to venture more than a half-mile from their vehicles. Get up early and be on your stand beyond that half-mile line before the other hunters begin to enter the woods, and there is an excellent chance that they will push a buck under your tree or at least close enough for a shot.

My friend, John Tidemann, has the ideal situation to illustrate this concept. John hunts the Mississippi River-bottom country, a hardwood-studded, 3-mile-long chunk of ground carved up in ravines and gullies and thick, bramble-littered flats. On each end of the valley is public hunting land and a state parking area to accommodate the hunter's vehicles. John sought and was granted permission to hunt on private land, which puts him smack dab in the middle of the valley. With hunters approaching from either direction, John has taken a half-dozen huge bucks from his well-located escape routes.

Funnels are any area, natural or man-made, that constrict the movement of whitetails. The more that movement can be confined, the better the location. The hourglass configuration, where a narrow band of cover connects two larger parcels, is the classic example, but there are many others. Search your memory for areas where funnels exist in the places you hunt. A good topo map will give you some clues. If you really want to find the best funnels, spend a few dollars and hire a pilot to fly you over your area in a light plane. If possible, do it when there is snow on the ground, and every bottleneck in the woods will be plainly visible.

Funnels are so effective that whenever I hunt new country, the first thing I look for when scouting are areas where the movement of whitetails will be compressed.

STILLHUNTING

Stillhunting is a poor word to describe the act of hunting slowly on foot and stopping often to look and listen for game. Sneak hunting would have been a better choice. Pussyfooting is the way I like to describe this tactic that so closely resembles the movements of a hunting cat. But regardless of what you call it, stillhunting is an exciting, challenging and extremely satisfying method of hunting whitetails. Unfortunately, there are hundreds of thousands of whitetail hunters who are under the mistaken impression that they do not have the ability to become a stillhunter. That's not true. It takes no special talent to stillhunt—what it takes is the knowledge of when stillhunting is possible, and when it is little more than a walk in the fall deer woods.

I prefer to hunt in rolling terrain where I can use the lay of the land to close on deer before they spot me. Stillhunting in flat terrain is very difficult, because a whitetail quickly perceives the slightest movement, even the fluid moves of a stillhunter.

Naturally, I prefer to hunt with the wind in my face, but that is not always possible, and I have no problem with hunting with the wind quartering from either side. I have even stillhunted effectively with the breeze at my back, although conditions must be perfect before I will attempt to do so. One condition that allows me to hunt with the wind is when it is raining. Rain, and to a lesser degree snow, tends to beat down and dissipate scent. In a light rain, I never hesitate to hunt with the breeze at my back if that is the direction from which I can most effectively hunt a piece of ground.

The other condition when I will hunt with the wind is when the wind is howling at 30 mph or better. A wind of that velocity scatters scent so quickly that a downwind whitetail has little chance of picking up your scent until it is too late.

But as important as it is to take every precaution against being seen or smelled by the whitetail, it is the whitetail's ears which most often detect the intrusion of the stillhunter.

A whitetail's ears are always working. Even a deer in its bed, contentedly chewing its cud, will have those ears twitching and turning to pick up every scrap of sound. Most of the sounds a whitetail hears are interpreted by the brain as normal—the chirping of birds, the scampering of a squirrel, and falling leaves, for instance. But let the brain register a "suspicious-noise" signal, and the whitetail goes on full alert until it can identify the source of its alarm or until it forgets what alarmed it in the first place. Fortunately for the hunter, the whitetail's memory span is about like my own, and in five minutes the deer will forget what it heard. The trick is to stand still for a timed five minutes every time you make one of those suspicious noises.

What constitutes a suspicious sound to a whitetail? The brush of hard fabric on bark will do it. So will the clink of coins in your pocket or the clunk of binoculars banging against your rifle. Don't worry about the occasional snapped twig or crunched leaves—those are common sounds in the whitetail's world.

The best way to avoid detection by those sensitive ears is to hunt when the footing is in your favor, and that means quiet. No one can hunt on foot effectively when the leaves are crisp and dry, or when a crusted snow blankets the forest floor. My stillhunting friend, the shadow, just pouts and sulks on such days.

Stillhunt when the woods are damp. After or during a rain shower or snow squall are excellent times. After the morning sun has melted the frost from the leaves, but before they have dried out, is one of my favorite times to be on the prowl.

A good strong wind will mask your inadvertent steps, but be forewarned that whitetails are jumpy when the wind blows. They know that the wind will foil all of their senses, and they are constantly on full alert. Use those binoculars even more than usual when stillhunting in the wind—it's important to spot the deer first.

And don't worry about what time of the day you are stillhunting. I know that tradition dictates that we hunt from stands morning and evening during the prime movement times, but I've taken plenty of bucks by stillhunting while others sat and then sitting when others moved. Stillhunt any time the conditions allow, and you will discover that stillhunting is not beyond your woodsmanship skills.

DEER DRIVES

You can drive deer anytime. Weather makes no difference, but hunting pressure does. It makes little sense to waste your energy driving deer past hunters other than those in your own party. That's why most of the successful groups who depend upon deer drives opt to stillhunt or hunt from stand individually for the first day or two of the season, and begin to conduct drives after the bulk of the hunters have gone home.

Actually, you cannot drive deer as you can drive cattle from winter to summer range. What a deer drive really does is move deer, and the most successful drives are those where standers have been posted along the routes that these disturbed deer take. You cannot make a whitetail go where you want him to go; you must position yourself where he wants to be.

The best (and safest) drives have a single person designated as the drive captain. He is normally the one most familiar with the area being driven. He assigns standers to their positions and spaces the drivers. Strategy is plotted on tattered maps or sketched out with a stick in dirt or snow.

And don't think you need a big gang to drive deer. Many times, two or three hunters working a small area with which they are intimately familiar can move deer by each other with excellent results. The key is to pick areas to work that match the size of your group.

Stand hunting, stillhunting and driving—the versatile hunter is proficient at all three, not because he is some kind of a superhunter, but because he chooses his methods to meet the conditions.

Did You Get Your Buck?

By Tom Huggler

Any good deer hunting magazine contains articles by or about the experts. These are the hunters who score year after year because of their superior woodsmanship, a new tactic they have discovered or their uncanny knowledge of whitetail ways. Accompanying photos show the expert in his den, surrounded by enough buck racks to keep a team of Boone and Crockett Club scorers busy all day. We'd like to be like these whitetail wizards, and so we read the stories and copy the techniques, and another season goes by and we don't tag a buck. Skunked again.

Why didn't *you* get your buck last fall? What will you do differently this year?

A couple of years ago, I spoke to more than 1,200 deer hunters who attended a clinic at a high school in southern Michigan. As *Outdoor Life*'s Michigan Editor, I passed out a form asking which questions about deer the hunters would like answered in the magazine. Then, in last year's *Deer and Big Game Annual,* we ran a special seven-page article on those questions and answers. The survey I took also revealed that 24 percent of the hunters had shot 10 or more bucks, and 20 percent had never killed a buck. A startling fact was that many of these unlucky hunters had been following their sport for years. One man with 40 years of experience wrote: "They [his partners] tease me in deer camp, but I'll show them this fall."

He didn't show them, however, and his dubious record now stands at 42 consecutive years without a buck. He asked that I not use his name.

Major reasons for this lack of success are obvious.

Some hunters, for example, make no preparations at all: They don't scout their territory, show up in camp on the eve of the opener without a clue as to where they'll hunt in the morning, and neglect to sight-in their rifle. Others heed no precautions: They don't choose a good stand where the wind is favorable, they cough and make other noises, constantly squirm on stand, or wander off on little adventures all day. Their hunting clothes are too warm or too cold, so they are never comfortable. Sometimes, their clothing reeks with the odor of mothballs, bacon grease, motor oil or other foreign smells. And some of them aren't at all serious about hunting deer, spending more time at the poker table, in the truck cab with the heater running and the football game on, or at the local tavern telling deer hunting stories.

This article is not about those hunters. It is about those who are trying to kill a deer but not succeeding.

What about bad luck, then? Is bad luck a valid excuse—especially when it dogs a hunter for years—or is there some truth to the statement that successful hunters make their own luck? I thought about that and other possible common denominators when I telephoned a few of the unlucky Michigan hunters for follow-up interviews. I learned that these were serious sportsmen who are trying to improve their score. Most of them are avid readers of deer hunting literature, and they attend seminars and clinics and rent videos to learn as much as possible. Another common thread: To a hunter, they are not at all pleased with their performance.

Everyone's got to start somewhere. Consider taking any legal buck. Richard P. Smith photos.

Dave Dunkel of Millington has yet to tag a buck in 24 years of hunting.

"It makes me sick when I come home from hunting to find out that my neighbor or a friend has killed a nice buck," he said. "I want one, too, and in the worst way. I'd like to think it's just bad luck. I mean, I see deer, but they're usually moving and I can't seem to get a shot."

Dunkel said that he always hunts the first four or five days of the season. He is in the woods before

dawn, and he stays there until dark, remaining on his stand in the morning and late afternoon and walking at midday. He has taken up bowhunting in recent years to improve his skills at reading sign and understanding whitetail behavior, and last fall he added a 4× scope to his .30/30 lever-action rifle. So, why is his freezer empty of venison?

"We've always hunted state land between Hale and Gladwin [in mid-lower Michigan]," Dunkel said, "and there are just too many hunters. My brother, brother-in-law and I recently bought 50 acres that was timbered off about 10 years ago. It contains a creek and a lot of brush, and there is plenty of deer sign. Because I'm a part-owner, I take a lot of interest in the property. I'm going up this weekend [late March] to begin scouting for next fall. Call me again, and see whether I've broken my jinx."

Switching to private land should improve Dunkel's odds considerably. According to Ed Langenau, deer specialist for the Michigan Department of Natural Resources, 75 percent of the statewide firearms deer kill occurs on private land. Another sobering statistic is that private-land hunters enjoy success rates that are three times higher than that of their counterparts on public property. The same is likely true for other states, too. That is not to say that a hunter can't score on state or federal land. Michigan has nine million acres of it, for example, more than any other state east of the Mississippi River. But the distribution of hunter to public parcel is unbalanced. In some counties of the northern Lower Peninsula, where about 65 percent of the statewide annual harvest occurs, hunter densities run as high as 50 or 60 per square mile. But in remote regions of the Upper Peninsula, there may be fewer than one hunter per square mile.

Bill Vasilides of Rochester admits that the main reason why he has killed only one deer in 25 years of hunting is that his reflexes need honing. "I've got to learn to respond faster," he told *Outdoor Life*, "and take the shot when it presents itself. Many times, deer have suddenly appeared when I wasn't ready. It's a question of being ready all of the time, because most deer don't give me a second chance."

I can relate to Vasilides' experiences. The largest buck I ever saw in 25 years of hunting deer was a big-beamed animal with more points than I could count. It was 4:30 P.M. on an opening day many years ago. The ground was frozen, and there was no wind. My rifle lay in my lap, and I was reading a book, my back nestled against a tree trunk. Suddenly, I heard a measured crunch, like someone walking on cornflakes across kitchen linoleum. I expected to see a hunter in Blaze Orange; imagine my shock when a magnificent buck stepped into the opening 25 feet away.

The deer turned toward me, took two steps, looked up suddenly and froze. We stared each other down for several minutes, while my unblinking eyes watered and my lungs screamed for a deep breath. I tried to control my racing heart while ever so slowly lifting the gun from lap to shoulder. I got it halfway there when the buck was gone, like gun smoke on a windy day. I was in the right place at the right time, but I wasn't ready.

Many of the unsuccessful hunters I interviewed said that they are always in the wrong place at the wrong time. For example, a buck crosses the only part of a trail you can't cover or makes an appearance at the most unlikely location. To be sure, such scenarios happen to every deer hunter, but when

Getting to know your hunting area is crucial for consistently successful hunting.

they repeat themselves year after year, it is time to analyze the problem. Ralph Waite of Lapeer has shot one doe and no bucks in 17 years of hunting prime farmland in southern Michigan. There are two reasons—one obvious and one not so obvious—why his living-room wall is devoid of antlers.

The obvious reason is a poor choice of gun. Years ago, Waite bought an old 20-gauge pump shotgun (rifles are not permitted in southern Michigan). On four occasions since then, either his shells have misfired or the gun has jammed, including one incident involving a 16-point buck at handshaking range. "I've had several people take the gun apart and try to fix it," Waite said. "But it's just too old and worn out, so I'm retiring it and buying a 12-gauge single-shot. Why? I figure that a single-shot can't jam."

The other reason is Waite's choice of a place to hunt. He hunts a 160-acre farm containing some woods surrounded by open fields. The farm lies next to a youth camp where Waite once worked as a caretaker. That 300-acre wooded property, which is closed to hunting, acts as a refuge for many deer, including some big-racked bucks that Waite has seen frequently. For 10 years, he tried to waylay one from blinds he built and maintained on the adjacent farm. "I saw plenty of deer," Waite said, "but they always seemed to know where I was, plus they were totally unpredictable. I learned that they moved at all different times of day and in different locations. I couldn't pin them down. Finally, I gave up and changed hunting locations."

Deer are predictable except when gunning pressure seems to make them disappear, but even then they usually head for security habitat, such as river-bottom tangles or open farm fields. The deer Waite was hunting were not pressured because only he and a handful of others had permission to hunt next to the camp. He simply had not observed the whitetails' habits closely enough to be in the right place at the right time.

Knowing your hunting area is crucial to year-in-year-out success. In a research paper called *Deer Hunting Success: Skill or Luck?*, Ed Langenau documented 10 years of hunter behavior and success on 72 square miles of heavily hunted public land in northern Michigan. In a typical year of sampling successful hunters, he found no major discrepancies in age, education, sex, occupation, residence, number of days hunted, or size of hunting party. He learned, however, that 82 percent of successful hunters were in the woods on opening day (other studies show that most of the deer taken in Michigan are bagged during the first two days of the season), and that those with prior experience on the property—either as bowhunters or small-game hunters—scored highest.

Langenau also divided his hunters into categories of high success (those with a lifetime success rate of at least .30 deer per year), average success (.29 deer per year or lower), and those with no success (had never shot a deer). The average age of the unsuccessful hunters, who comprised 25 percent of the survey, was 32 years. The average age of the other two groups was 42 years. Again, he found no major variations in education, party size, or occupation. A major difference, however, showed up among those who permanently lived or owned property near the study area. Langenau concluded that hunters who know their terrain are more likely to tag a deer. He also found that successful hunters stayed on their stands longer and tended to hunt edge areas and cuttings rather than mature timber or swamps.

Another reason why some hunters fail to score is because they continue to hunt an area long after it has stopped producing deer. Even the best areas, normally young-growth forest that has recently been cut, begin to slip after 10 or 12 years. According to Langenau, 15 years is the maximum for which hunters should expect their favorite hunting spot to produce. Of course, there are exceptions. Farmland habitat, for example, may continue to grow deer for generations, but even in those instances, crops are often rotated and some fields are probably reverting to weeds or even brush in later stages.

Most deer hunters are like ice-fishermen in that they choose a place to go from hearing or reading about it. Once everyone goes there, however, the quality drops fast. Even if you're lucky enough to find an unpressured hotspot, odds are that it won't remain a hotspot forever. That is why mobile hunters, those that pull up stakes every few years and find new places to hunt, are often the most successful.

Impatience is another reason why some hunters go buckless. The inability to stay motionless on stand is one kind of impatience. Refusing to take antlerless animals and spike bucks is another. More than half of Michigan gun hunters (about 400,000 out of 700,000), for example, do not apply for some 300,000 hunter's-choice permits that are available each fall. Many of these hunters perpetuate the myth that the only whitetail worth taking is a boss-racked buck. Consequently, because they don't kill deer, they never get the chance to sharpen their skills, including how to place killing shots and track wounded animals. When the once-in-a-lifetime chance comes to kill a big buck, they blow it.

While checking hunters over a 10-year period for his survey, Langenau came to know several who went buckless year after year. One of these hunters flagged down Ed's car one day to ask for help in checking out a deer that he had shot. "It was a 60-pounder," Langenau said. "We all have to start somewhere, and this was the beginning for him. Two years later, he proudly showed me an eight-pointer on his buck pole."

According to Langenau, the typical hunter takes six to seven years to gain confidence in a new area and to improve his skills sufficiently to tag a buck. That got me thinking about Mark Freigruber, a young hunter who indicated on the *Outdoor Life* survey that he had not shot a deer in six years of effort. I called Freigruber, who is 21, to see whether his luck had improved in the two years since I had seen him.

"I'm still looking for my first one," he told me over the telephone. "All of my friends get deer, but I don't. In fact, I get teased about it. I'd like to shoot a buck, but I don't know what I'm doing wrong."

How about you? Do you know why you didn't score last year? If so, you have already solved half of the problem.

Sit Still for Whitetails

By Gary Clancy

We are a nation of people on the move. Rushing here, hurrying there, working our tails off to make our jobs, our families and our personal lives mesh into an elusive goal called The American Dream. With all of this racing around and jockeying for position in our daily lives, it is little wonder that our nervous systems often refuse to stop those revving internal engines when we climb into a deer stand.

Why is it so important to make as little movement as possible on a deer stand? After all, there is nothing really outstanding about a whitetail's eyesight. Many game animals have the whitetail beat hands down in the vision department. A whitetail cannot distinguish colors, as the wild turkey can; cannot duplicate the pronghorn's ability to spot you from a mile away; cannot instantly recognize you as "man" simply by your shape, as a coyote or fox can. What the whitetail can do, though, is instantly detect any movement within the 310-degree arc it constantly scans with those bulging, side-mounted optics. Once a whitetail detects movement—your movement—your chances of killing him have decreased dramatically.

Yet, hunting from a stand remains the most consistently successful method for getting a whitetail. The bulk of this nation's whitetail hunters spend more time on stand than they do stillhunting or driving. Stands overlooking trails between feeding and bedding sites are favored locations. During the rut, a stand overlooking a string of fresh scrapes is hard to beat. Stands near funnel areas, places where the natural lay of the land or man's hand have shaped the terrain in such a manner that the whitetail's movements are restricted, are always a good bet. Where hunting pressure is not a factor, hunting over fields, where whitetails often feed, also is commonplace.

More whitetails are taken by hunters on stand than by any other method, and yet for some, success on stand remains elusive. After 25 years of hunting, photographing, and studying whitetails and the people who hunt them, I am convinced that most hunters who are unsuccessful from stands owe their lack of success to their inability to *sit still*.

The most graphic example of this that I have ever seen occurred several years ago when I hunted during a special muzzleloader season in a northern state. An early December blizzard had dumped 3 feet of snow on the hardwood valley I was hunting, hampering the movements of both deer and hunters. Just before noon one day, I saw a hunter descend the sidehill across the valley from where I was hunting; he took a stand in the upper branches of a fallen tree that had wedged in the crotch of another tree a third of the way down the steep hillside. A half-mile down the valley, another hunter dropped down off the ridge and began to walk the sidehill toward the first hunter. A one-man drive was in progress. Under normal conditions, such a tactic would have been useless in a valley of that size, but under the prevailing conditions, with the deer sticking to established trails, I figured that the pair had a chance, so I brushed off a log and sat down to watch the show.

Through my 8×42 binoculars, I watched in

Many whitetail hunters prefer to make their stands on the ground because it is more comfortable.

amazement as the driver not only walked the sidehill but also zigged and zagged up and down the steep slope, plowing through knee-deep snow with every step. This guy was in shape.

The first group of deer came out of a brushy gully ahead of the driver, looked back over their haunches and, when the driver got too close, ambled down the trail ahead of the driver. There were four deer, three does and a small basketracked eight-pointer. Through my binoculars, I could easily follow the line of the trail to where it passed just below the hunter in the windfall. With the wind in their favor, I figured that the pair had a good chance of scoring.

Two more deer joined the first four somewhere along the way, just suddenly materializing as whitetails so often do. The six would stop often to stare at their backtrail, ears cocked forward, nostrils sucking for scent. When the driver got too close, the deer would walk another 100 yards and stop again. The big buck came trailing the six out of the thick stand of dogwoods. I heard myself suck wind when the glasses settled on him. He was one of those bullbodied, heavy-racked, corn-country bucks, common enough in the nation's breadbasket but not so everyday commonplace that just seeing one doesn't get me excited. As I watched the small herd, with the big buck in the rear, march toward the hunter in the windfall, I felt like a New Yorker watching the Mets and Yankees play in the World Series; part of me was siding with the big buck, the other part was rooting for the hunters. Then, I swung my glasses over to the hunter on stand, and I knew that the deer were going to win this game.

The hunter was on his feet, shifting his weight from one side to the other. His muzzleloader hung from a broken branch alongside him, and his hands were tucked deep in his coat pockets. It was cold, and I couldn't blame the hunter for trying to get a little warmth circulating through his body, but I knew that no whitetail was going to walk under a deadfall with an orange blob doing the two-step in its branches.

And they didn't. With the driver a couple of hundred yards behind them and the stander an equal distance ahead, the long-legged doe in the lead of the whitetail procession suddenly stopped, stretched her long neck and stared hard and long straight ahead, her tail twitching nervously. The rest of the deer did the same. When the driver had closed the distance to slightly more than 100 yards, the herd moved uphill and followed a hazel-brush-littered washout, the big doe breaking trail for the rest of the string. I watched them until the last deer, the big buck, disappeared over the top of the ridge.

The driver came along a few minutes later and cut the trail where the herd had left the well-defined sidehill path and plowed their way uphill. I could almost see his shoulders slump, almost feel the dejection and disappointment in his tired body, as he plodded along the path to his buddy on stand.

There is a big difference between sitting in one place for a couple of hours and sitting still.

I know many hunters who have no trouble spending the best part of the day sitting in one location, yet they rarely see deer because their movements while on stand allow any approaching deer to detect them and take evasive action. Ironically, most of the movements that a hunter makes on stand are so natural to our everyday lives that the hunter does not even consciously know he is making them. My friend Jack is a good example.

I have hunted whitetails with Jack for the past 17 seasons. Each fall, we hunt the same rolling valley, not far from the sluggish waters of the Mississippi River. After that amount of time, we have naturally become intimately familiar with "our" valley. Jack knows where the deer feed, where the best bedding sites are located, which ridges have the most white oaks and the best acorns, where the deer go when hunting pressure is intense, and where they hole up when tough weather slides in from the north. Jack chooses his stand with attention to detail, paying particular notice to the wind. Yet, in an area that has averaged nearly 20 deer per square mile in the years we have hunted there, Jack sees few deer and rarely kills a buck.

Jack's problem is a common one; he has never learned to sit still. More than once, I have taken a position where I could watch Jack on stand without his knowing I was anywhere around. For a minute, maybe two, Jack would be still, then he would suddenly lunge for his thermos and pour a cup of coffee, or hastily unwrap a sandwich, or dig in his pocket for a cigarette and then in another pocket for his lighter. When he turned his head to look right and left, he turned it abruptly, as he would if a friend had hollered his name on the streets back home. If he itched, he scratched. If his muscles grew tired of being in one position, he quickly stood, stretched, stomped around a bit and then plopped back down on his stool. Every movement Jack made was with the same quick, herky-jerky motions he is accustomed to performing during the other 51 weeks of the year. Jack has never learned that to be successful at hunting from a stand, each of those moves must be made in *slow* motion.

Squirrel hunting is the best practice there is for the whitetail hunter. When I was a boy, my father and I spent every Saturday morning of the season hunting squirrels. My father insisted that only head shots could be taken, so it was necessary to have the squirrel motionless and within 30 or 40 feet to ensure consistent hits to the head with our iron-sighted .22 rifles. We would move into position as quietly as possible and sit down with our backs resting against the morning-wet hides of stout oaks, drawing our knees up before us, rifles resting comfortably over one knee. No matter how stealthily we crept into our stands, though, the squirrels would detect our presence and nothing would be visible when we first sat down. That was one of my very first lessons in patience—sitting there motionless, looking at nothing but tree branches, while just over the next ridge I could hear a gray squirrel cutting, a squirrel I just *knew* I could sneak up on and pot. But Pa had said, "If we sit and wait and don't move, the squirrels will come back out and go on about their business, and then we will get our chance." He was right.

Ten minutes after sitting down, the lifeless woods in front of my eyes would spring to life. The birds always came first: flitting chickadees, nuthatches walking upside-down on the trunks of maples, tapping downy woodpeckers and noisy blue jays. If I could be still for long enough without fidgeting, there would suddenly be a flicker of gray in the upper branches of a hickory as the first squirrel checked things out. I believed then, as I believe now, that the first squirrel was a scout, the point man. If the first squirrel found things in order, the rest soon popped out of hiding.

I continue to hunt squirrels that way, the old-fashioned way, a little .22 with iron sights resting over my knees, taking only sure head shots. It is exciting hunting in itself, and great training for the whitetail hunter.

There are three rules that make for successful and enjoyable stand hunting.

One we have already discussed: to put forth a conscious effort to make every movement on stand in slow motion. It takes years before this comes naturally; doing it consistently demands thinking about it. This slow-motion movement holds over to the moment when you raise your gun or bow. More than one buck owes his life to the hunter who quickly raised his rifle for the shot and discovered in the process that a whitetail can jump from an open trail to heavy brush quicker than the best snap shooter can get off a well-aimed shot.

The best advice is to do as the turkey hunter does; make your move when the deer's head is behind a large tree or heavy brush, but even then make that move slowly and smoothly. If there is no time to raise your gun or bow while the deer's vision is obstructed, wait until the deer has walked by your stand and make a smooth move as he quarters away from you.

The second rule for consistent success from stands is to choose your stand sites carefully. Notice that I said "sites," not "site."

In my younger days, I stubbornly stuck to my

stand even after I was bored silly, and well after I had given up all hope of seeing, much less killing, a buck. But deer hunting should be enjoyable, not some macho test of stamina and resolve. These days, I no longer commit myself to any one stand. I sit in one stand for as long as I feel like sitting, for as long as I feel confident about my chances of scoring from that location. When I become bored, or find my concentration slipping, I move. Sometimes, I stillhunt for an hour or two if conditions are right. But I often just make a short hike to another stand, one I have chosen carefully during preseason scouting or while hunting in previous seasons. A new stand offers me a whole new perspective. Not only is the scenery different, but there are those new stumps that look like deer and must be checked out, and there are squirrels hopping through leaves in new directions, momentarily causing my heart to lodge in my throat. There is that feeling that this is the place.

The hunter who can sit still in one location for one hour will see more deer within range than the hunter who spends the entire day fidgeting on stand.

My final rule for successful stand hunting is to make yourself comfortable. There is no need to suffer while on deer stand. The hunter who is not cold, hungry, tired and thirsty, or so sore and stiff that his mind is occupied with pain rather than concentrating on looking and listening for approaching deer, will see more deer.

Getting cold has probably forced more hunters to fidget on stand, or to vacate good stands prematurely, than any other factor. An entire article could be devoted to the subject of how to stay warm, but the basics are this: Take precautions against getting sweated up when walking to your stand. Dress in layers of clothing rather than one heavy overgarment. And eat right.

To avoid perspiring heavily on the way to your stand and then spending the next hour slowly freezing to death in your own sweat, dress lightly for the walk to the stand, carrying extra clothing in a daypack.

Now, I know that polypropylene underwear is supposed to wick away all of that nasty perspiration and take care of this problem. I use polypropylene underwear, and it works up to a point. But I have yet to find the underwear that will keep me dry when I wake up 20 minutes after the alarm has sounded and do a mad dash through a half-mile of woods to reach my stand before daylight.

Ideally, I prefer to leave camp early enough to allow for a slow walk to my stand; I dress in only the aforementioned underwear and a wool shirt and pants, and carry the rest of my clothing in a daypack.

Never before has the hunter had so many choices when it comes to choosing clothing for keeping warm on stand. It doesn't really matter whether you choose to go traditional and stick with wool or go modern and try the array of new synthetics, so long as you depend upon *layers*, not *bulk*, for warmth. My own deer hunting duffel is a good example. I pack two pairs of polypropylene/wool underwear, tops and bottoms. One pair is heavyweight, the other is medium. I also take along two pairs of wool pants—again, one heavyweight and one lighter—a wool shirt, wool sweater, down-filled vest and an uninsulated Blaze Orange shell. By choosing my underwear bottoms and my pants according to the weather forecast and the morning weather conditions, my lower torso is set for the day. On top, I usually wear only the underwear and wool shirt under the Blaze Orange shell. At the stand, I can add the sweater or vest, or both. When the day warms up, I remove a layer or two and put it into the daypack. It is a simple solution to the chills, one that has served me well on hunts across the whitetail's range.

The relatively new "heat pouches," available at any sporting-goods department, have made cold hands a thing of the past. I keep one in each pocket of my coat, or if I am hunting from a stand where a deer may suddenly appear within range, I use the smaller size and tuck one in the top of each of the fingerless wool gloves I normally wear. They work.

For all but single-digit temperatures, a good pair of pac boots with leather uppers, rubber bottoms and removable felt liners will keep your feet warm. It's a good idea to purchase an extra set of liners, switching daily so that dry ones are always in your boots. When the bottom drops out of the thermometer, insulated overboots, often called "boot blankets," work well.

Just because it is called "stand hunting" does not mean that you have to stand the entire time you wait. Sitting is less tiresome and will allow you to remain still for longer. If you use a portable tree stand, make sure that it has a seat. My brother-in-law always hunts from a tree but never uses a portable stand, instead selecting trees that offer him the option of standing or sitting.

There is nothing wrong with hunting from the ground, either. Many people are not crazy about heights. It is hard to concentrate on hunting when you are constantly concerned about slipping and falling. If you hunt from the ground, a folding stool makes good sense. There are some excellent ones on the market that double as a daypack.

Even if you return to camp for a midday meal, bring food along to the stand. A hungry hunter will have trouble staying put. I like hard candy for a snack in the tree. One piece of hard candy lasts longer than chocolate or a candy bar. Avoid gum; chewing it interferes with your ability to hear.

If you eat lunch in the woods, wrap your food in soft paper or plastic, not wax paper, which is noisy to unwrap. If it is cold, I take a break and build a fire when I have lunch. A hot cup of soup, warmed sandwiches and some of the most gosh-awful-boiled-in-a-can coffee make sitting still a few more hours a pleasure rather than torture.

Scrapes . . . the Real Dirt

By John Weiss

Analyzing the scrapes made by whitetail bucks could probably result in terminal exasperation if you let them get the best of you. The problem is that scrapes occur under so many different circumstances that they sometimes seem like disjointed puzzle parts that simply won't fit together into a meaningful whole.

For many years, I wrestled with the enigmatic field problem of learning to properly identify the five different types of scrapes commonly made by bucks. There were primary, secondary, boundary, unclaimed-estrous and community scrapes. Yet, as so often happens, the more I learned, the more confused I became.

Then one day, Larry Marchington, the heralded deer biologist at the University of Georgia, dropped a bombshell on me. In an almost nonchalant tone of voice, he said that there was conclusive evidence that does also make scrapes. Does!

Right then and there, I was overwhelmed with mixed feelings. On the one hand, this revelation answered many questions, such as why I had sometimes waited long days on stand overlooking certain scrapes and had seen nothing but female deer. Yet, at the same time, I had that sinking feeling that one experiences when his stock portfolio takes a devastating nosedive and he begins wondering whether it's time to step out onto the ledge. I mean, buck scrapes were themselves perplexing enough, and now I had been told that some of those dug-out places in the woodlands were indeed *not* the work of bucks at all!

Nevertheless, though there still is a plenitude of missing information pertaining to whitetail mating habits, enterprising hunters should avail themselves of every opportunity to study the most recent findings. In this manner, one's hunting success gradually becomes far less a matter of simply "being lucky enough to be in the right place at the right time," and instead hinges increasingly upon the acquisition of knowledge and the application of skills.

Scrapes, of course, are the catalysts that serve to unite male and female deer. And because we now know that whitetails make at least six different types of scrapes—each with its own significance and level of importance—understanding which specific scrapes should be discounted and which others should be diligently hunted can go a long way toward helping a hunter consistently hang up nice bucks.

With only one exception, every scrape that a buck makes begins its life as a so-called secondary scrape. It is only after forthcoming events begin to unravel that a secondary scrape may become elevated in status to either a primary or a community scrape, or reduced in status to a boundary scrape.

The exception is the estrous-response scrape, which is the least likely to produce a buck sighting. When a doe begins to approach her estrous cycle, there is a chemical change in her endocrine system. Hormonal secretions indicating that she is nearing sexual readiness are then duly transferred to the ground whenever and wherever the doe happens to randomly urinate. When a buck chances upon one

18

*Scrapes are the catalysts that serve to unite male and female deer.
Mike Biggs photo.*

ever, that a hunter's success in such an instance is usually the result of watching a general travel corridor that is occasionally used by deer; the scrape itself is merely a happenstance.

Boundary scrapes are also unlikely to produce buck sightings for the simple reason that they are visited only infrequently when a buck occasionally ventures around the outermost extremities of his home range. Because these particular scrapes randomly dot the periphery of the buck's territory, knowing how to recognize typical home-range boundaries of deer will in turn help you to identify such scrapes.

Although it sometimes seems as though whitetail bucks are inclined to go anywhere they darn well please, radio-tracking studies have shown that they actually spend as much as 90 percent of their time in an approximate 40-acre "core area," in which they have the best combination of food, water and security cover at their immediate disposal. Furthermore, when they do periodically leave the safety of their core areas to venture into surrounding or outlying regions, they are reluctant to go beyond major man-made or natural barriers that they come upon (assuming, of course, that they are not being chased by dogs or being subjected to intense hunting pressure). Because these obstacles tend to restrict the bucks' travels, the obstacles, in large part, serve to establish the irregularly shaped home ranges (usually no more than 2 square miles in size) in which the bucks are destined to live out their entire lives.

Just a few examples of home-range boundaries, or barriers, include superhighways (especially if they are bordered by fences), wide river courses, lakeshores, sheer rock bluffs, steep mountain ridges and even those particular woodlot edges that yield to wide expanses of prairie or open ground. There is a great likelihood that scrapes found along any of these types of well-defined edges are boundary scrapes, even though they may be characterized by overhanging tree branches and other signs of authenticity. You may wish to mark each of their locations on your scouting map in the hopes of gleaning more meaningful insight regarding the terrain as a whole, but unless you're one of those individuals who is always blessed with an inordinate amount of good luck, I wouldn't hunt them.

A third type of whitetail scrape that is not worth hunting, and one that we've only recently begun to learn about, is the doe scrape. Interestingly enough, though bucks typically make scrapes by pawing the ground alternately with their two front hoofs, does more commonly use their rear hoofs.

If you've ever observed the peculiar behavior of a dog as it vigorously clawed and scratched grass and sod in a backward direction with its rear paws—most often, shortly after it had defecated—you can understand how does create scrapes in almost exactly the same manner. Upon only a few occasions—while observing penned deer at wildlife

of the places where an estrous doe has voided herself, he instinctively makes a scrape right there on top of the urine-dampened earth.

There are several telltale signs that these are not meaningful scrapes. They average only 7 or 8 inches in diameter. They are very often discovered in open feeding areas, such as meadows, or in thickets where matted ovals in grass and leaves reveal that does have been bedding. There is the distinct absence of a mutilated tree branch hanging over the scrape. And upon periodically rechecking the scrape, a hunter will find that it has not been cleaned and freshened, but is gradually drying out and becoming weathered.

Of course, there always is a slight probability that one might take a buck in the vicinity of an estrous-response scrape. It should be emphasized, how-

experiment stations since speaking with Marchington—have I seen does make scrapes with their front hoofs.

To date, we don't know why does make scrapes. Likely as not, these scrapes have some type of communicative significance in the social order of local deer. In any event, the only two values to the hunter in knowing about these scrapes are as follows: The hunter knows that a doe was standing in the scrape location at one time, and so possibly he can discern a trail that other deer might also be using from time to time, and of far greater importance, the hunter can identify the scrape for what it is and therefore not invest long hours in sitting nearby with mistaken expectations that a buck will return.

There are several ways to distinguish between a doe scrape and a buck scrape. First, a doe scrape will reveal the appearance of having been crudely and superficially scratched away. As an analogy, imagine taking a garden rake and dragging it only two or three times through a small spot in the grass on your front lawn. Such doe scrapes just aren't nicely cleaned away to bare soil or manicured around their perimeters, as are buck scrapes; in many instances, they are not even round in shape. Sometimes, such a scrape will have a long tubelike or oval shape because the doe scratched a few times with her hoofs, walked forward a step and then scratched again. Other times, when a doe doesn't place her rear hoofs close together and then uses each hoof alternately to scratch backward, the result is what appears to be two small scrapes side by side. Finally, with regard to any type of doe scrape, you will not find the scrape in association with an overhanging tree branch.

I've just described three types of whitetail scrapes (estrous-response, boundary and doe) that the hunter should know how to identify so he won't waste time hunting near one of them. Now, it's time to take a look at the three types of scrapes that the hunter's attention should indeed be riveted upon because they are premier locations to collect nice bucks.

Recall that I said earlier that all buck-scrape types except one begin life as secondary scrapes. It is not until many weeks later that a small percentage of these secondaries will become elevated to either primary or community scrapes. Therefore, early in the season—up until early November in the northern states and up until about mid-December in the southern states—all scrape hunting will be done in the vicinity of secondary scrapes. There simply are no primaries in evidence at this time.

Studies have shown that any given mature buck of 2½ years of age or older will make an average of 20 to 35 scrapes throughout his home range, and I've already indicated that some of these will be outlying boundary scrapes that aren't worth hunting because of their infrequent revisitation. I also noted that each buck has an approximate 40-acre core area in which he spends up to 90 percent of his time.

Consequently, the secondary scrapes you'll want to begin hunting early in the season will be those located within the buck's core area.

Ascertaining buck core areas is a relatively easy matter that simply involves wearing down a good deal of boot leather. What a hunter particularly wants to watch for is an abundance of concentrated sign in the form of tracks, beds, droppings, rubbed saplings and scrapes themselves. And especially with regard to tracks, beds and droppings, a hunter should hope to find some sign that is very old, some that is moderately old and some that is very fresh, as this combination is the best indicator of the almost continuous presence of the buck in his core area over long periods.

In reconnoitering the terrain and deciding where to build a blind or install a portable tree stand overlooking secondary scrapes, I would strongly caution against hunting too close to the deer's bedding area. To a buck, a bedding area is the single most important place within his core area because it's where he feels safest during the daylight hours. Therefore, if a hunter gets too close, the intrusion will quickly become evident, and it will quite often result in the buck abandoning the immediate area in search of better hiding elsewhere.

As a result, if I could set the stage for hunting secondary scrapes early in the season, here are the circumstances I'd want to sketch into the picture: I'd be in a buck's core area, and I'd be in a tree stand at least 200 yards from the buck's bedding area. Moreover, that tree stand location would be on the downwind side of one of the many trails filtering to and from the bedding area and upon which at least one secondary scrape is to be found. With this setup, I could quietly slip into my stand and then simply wait for the buck to make an appearance as he returns to his bedding site in the early morning or as he leaves his bedding site in the late afternoon.

It should be mentioned that hunting secondary scrapes early in the season is basically a hit-or-miss proposition in that all of the scrapes in the core area are of relatively equal value. This means that the buck in question does not specifically favor one scrape over another, and his revisitation is random. About the only way for a hunter to tip the odds slightly in his favor is to situate his stand in the vicinity of concentrated numbers of scrapes.

In the following weeks, a small percentage of the buck's secondary scrapes will begin warranting his special consideration and attention. They will suddenly become primaries that he can be counted on to return to time and again.

How and why any particular secondary scrape suddenly becomes a primary involves an intriguing bit of biology. First, understand that whitetail bucks are not at all territorial; many bucks commonly share the same home range and, in many cases, even have overlapping core areas. As a result, the many secondary scrapes littering the woodlands in a several-square-mile region may be the products of perhaps a dozen bucks or more. These scrapes serve to inform the local does that these bucks are around, but more important, the does can smell the scrapes and determine the current state of health of the individual bucks in residence.

That's right—it is each doe that decides which particular sire she wants to breed with. Understandably, she instinctively knows that the successful propagation of her species depends upon her successful impregnation by a virile, healthy male, and nature has given her a way to determine this. In smelling a buck's urine in one of his secondary scrapes, a doe is able to recognize certain chemical byproducts. Virile, healthy, mature bucks metabolize fats and carbohydrates, and they release the byproducts of this in much greater concentrations than do equally healthy but immature bucks. Furthermore, bucks that are old and beyond their reproductive peaks, or that are experiencing declining health, metabolize proteins, and this is equally evident in their urine.

In effect, then, each doe may investigate a number of scrapes made by different bucks before deciding both which buck she wants for her sire and where she will allow the mating to take place. She urinates in that appropriate scrape, depositing her own unique glandular secretions, and then remains in the general area, waiting for the buck to return.

Upon making his rounds and randomly checking his secondary scrapes, the buck will suddenly come upon the doe-scented scrape, recognize it for what it is, and elevate this scrape immediately to primary-scrape status. The buck then proceeds to scent-trail the doe until he eventually catches up with her, whereupon copulation usually takes place in short order.

This apparently well-ordered plan, however, quickly turns into pandemonium as the rutting period intensifies toward its peak. This is because not every doe experiences her estrous cycle at precisely the same time. Furthermore, in any given several-square-mile region, there may be upward of 50 or more males and females, all healthy and capable of reproducing. As a result, a buck may conclude the impregnation of one doe only to immediately thereafter take up the trail of another and then still another as he continually checks and rechecks his few primary scrapes.

Identifying these primary scrapes is not difficult because they will seem to be in perpetual "muddied" states as they are repeatedly cleaned of wind-blown debris and freshened with new urine deposits. Conversely, the recently abandoned secondary scrapes will quickly become hard and dried out and partially covered with leaves and other forest duff.

From this point on, areas around primary scrapes are *the* places to hunt, at least until the rutting period is over and the deer return to their former activities.

Yet, a hunter should keep in mind that after he's ascertained the annual rutting dates in his particular region (which can be determined by talking with local deer biologists), there is a second rutting season that occurs about a month later. If a given doe does not conceive during her initial estrous cycle, she'll lose heat but then experience a follow-up estrous cycle 24 days later, whereupon she again goes through the entire ritual of selecting a mate. Although no studies have been conducted on this subject, it's logical to assume that former primary scrapes would be reopened, so to speak, for the secondary rutting period, unless the buck that had made those particular scrapes was harvested in the meantime, in which case the doe would have to search elsewhere for service.

So, a hunter shouldn't give up scrape hunting for the year just because the first, formal rutting period is over. Once the first period has ended, several weeks should be spent trail watching or hunting known feeding grounds. Then, the hunter should return to the scrapes that were discovered previously to determine which are being used again as primaries for the second rutting period.

The fifth and final type of scrape created by whitetail bucks is perhaps the most fascinating of all. It is known as the community scrape. In scientific literature, there is, to date, no explanation for the occurrence of community scrapes, but hunters' theories abound.

In essence, a community scrape is a secondary scrape that is simultaneously used by several bucks that share overlapping core areas within their home ranges. The most logical explanation is that the bucks are of the same age, have nearly equivalent racks and therefore all rank about the same in the local pecking order. Because there is no rigid hierarchy distinguishing the animals, a given scrape does not become the personal property of one buck or another, and it therefore enjoys revisitation by different bucks, each hoping to eventually discover a doe's estrous urine. While there, the buck will clean the scrape, hook at the overhead branch with his antlers and leave his own scent.

Consequently, if a hunter stays well attuned to the scraping activity in the region he's hunting, various members of his hunting party may all take nice bucks over the very same scrape over a period of several days. The initial requirement is that someone must first take a buck near a scrape. Then, each day someone must return to that very location to examine the scrape. The very instant it is recognized that the scrape has been visited and freshened, a hunter should get back on that same stand fast! If the second hunter takes a buck, the scrape should again be checked daily in the hope that still a third hunter can successfully occupy the same stand.

As I have tried to demonstrate, a scrape is obviously not just a scrape, but may actually fall into one of six different categories of significance. If the hunter learns both how to identify these scrapes and how to determine which are worth hunting and which are not, he'll be well on his way to more filled tags than ever before.

Rub-Ways to Whitetails

By Greg Miller

There is a way of absolutely predicting the travel pattern of a mature whitetail buck throughout his home core area during the pre-rut.

What would you think if someone made that statement to you? Well, believe me, after spending hundreds of hours doing actual in-the-field research on whitetails and their habits, I have come to the conclusion that patterning a big buck is not quite as difficult as most people think. All it takes is just a little of your time and the ability to read and decipher one of the most obvious pieces of information left behind by a whitetail buck. No, I'm not talking about scrapes. In fact, I believe that scrape hunting may be the most overrated, overhunted and over-publicized system of hunting whitetails to come along in the last two decades. My system of hunting whitetails deals with something other than scrapes. It centers around one of the most highly visible bits of sign left behind by a buck—antler rubs.

For years, I was under the impression that a buck rub meant nothing more than that a whitetail buck had been at that spot at one time. In fact, I was even told by one knowledgeable hunter that buck rubs meant absolutely nothing. To me, this hunter's word was like gospel, so I went on believing that rubs were useless as far as being included as a valuable part of my scouting data. How wrong I was for all of those years!

In my home state of Wisconsin, whitetail bucks normally shed the velvet from their antlers around the first week of September. From that time on, not a day goes by that a buck doesn't rub his antlers on

something. Trees, bushes, shrubs, fence posts and even an occasional high-line pole will be used as a sparring partner by a whitetail buck during this time. The thing to keep in mind here is that, other than sparring matches with other bucks, the only way a buck has of building up his neck and shoulder muscles is to continually rub on trees. This is probably where one of the most misunderstood parts of buck antler rubs comes into focus.

The actual process of antler velvet removal takes only a few hours. In actuality, a lot of the velvet is scratched off with a hind foot or simply falls off by itself. The first real flurry of rubbing by a buck takes place *after* the buck's velvet has already been shed. It is from this time on that a whitetail buck becomes more easy to pattern. The first rubbing activity often coincides with the opening of the bowhunting season.

Why hunt rubs and rub lines? The most important reason is that by hunting a rub line where I find nothing but huge antler rubs, I know that I am dealing with a very big buck. All of my research has shown me that small bucks just don't seem to make really big rubs. Therefore, I'm usually able to stay away from the concentrations of does and fawns. That's fine with me. I often have more trouble with does and fawns seeing me up in my tree stand than I do with bucks spotting me. You know how disastrous it is if a doe blows the whistle on you just about the time that Mr. Big walks into view—end of game.

Much has been written about using scrapes and scrape lines to accomplish the same things that I use

22

A whitetail buck creates rubs along an established route called a rub line. Erwin and Peggy Bauer photo.

territory and make a rub on a tree. My findings indicate that those rubs are not on particularly big trees but rather on smaller saplings. The reason why a buck seems to choose small trees is anyone's guess. Perhaps it is simply a means of working the kinks out of his muscles after being bedded for the better part of the day. He will rub much bigger trees (depending upon the size of the buck) later in the night. After making this first rub or rubs, the buck will then get on the runway and mosey along to his final destination—most often a source of food, water and does. At various points along this runway, the buck will stop and make more rubs. Some of these rubs will be on fresh trees while others are made on trees that the buck has rubbed on previous nights or, in some cases, previous years. Bucks do seem to have preferred rub trees. The closer to the rut it gets, the less important food and water become and the bigger the does' role in the bucks' daily movement patterns.

The runway that a whitetail buck prefers to use, and therefore makes his series of antler rubs along, is called a rub line. For the most part, these rub lines will originate in or very near a buck's bedding area and will end near a food source. The distance between these two points will vary. I have seen rub lines that twist and turn their way through about 2 miles of country. I have also found rub lines that were less than 500 yards in length. Rub lines can vary due to the lay of the land or the temperament of the particular buck. Each individual buck has his own style of rubbing. Some bucks prefer to rub a lot of trees along their route while some will only rub an occasional tree.

In my area of the country, there is a lot of pine, popple and red willow. A buck will often select a certain type of tree and then rub on that same type of tree all the way along his rub line. For example, I kept track of an extremely large whitetail buck for the last couple of years simply by using his rubs as an identifying trait.

This big buck continually selected pines in the 4- to 6-inch diameter class. His rubs were always very clean, with no unusual scratches or gouges to indicate that the buck had any sticker or non-typical points on his rack anywhere. In another area, I plotted another big buck's rub line. I suspected that this buck was at least slightly non-typical because of the unusual scratches that always appeared on his rubbed trees and because most of these buck's rubs were only about a foot off the ground. I guessed that the shape of his rack made it tough for him to rub his antlers. In both of the above-mentioned cases, my suspicions were confirmed. We found the shed antlers of the first buck that spring. He was a very "clean" and massive 10-pointer that was very close to making Boone and Crockett. In the case of the second buck, there was a confirmed visual sighting of a huge non-typical buck seen crossing the road in that area.

As you can tell by now, there is more to buck ant-

rubs and rub lines for; however, I've found scrape hunting to be far less effective. A whitetail buck will begin rubbing his antlers during the first week of September and continue to rub right until he eventually sheds his antlers, which is usually sometime in late January or early February in Wisconsin. So, for roughly 20 weeks, bucks will leave behind evidence of their passing. Scraping, on the other hand, is something that the bucks do with real gusto for only a few weeks. In addition, bucks using the areas I hunt do very little, if any, scraping. That's why I had to come up with a system that I could count on year after year. When I hunt those big rubs, I know that I'm hunting a big buck. And he may be a big-bodied deer as well as big in the antler department.

To understand how my system works, it's best to first take a look at the habits of big bucks. When not disturbed by hunting pressure, a whitetail buck will follow a specific routine each day beginning around dusk. Upon leaving his preferred bedding area, the buck will stop somewhere along the edge of his core

ler rubs than meets the eye. Not only can they be used to determine the travel routes of whitetail bucks, but they can also aid you in identifying certain bucks just by their rubs. Pay close attention to the height of the rub off the ground, unusual scratches or gouges, a preference for a certain kind of tree or maybe even a certain size of tree. Any of these things either alone or in some sort of combination may be enough to tip you off that the same buck is making a series of antler rubs. Once you are able to identify certain bucks in your hunting area and learn more about their travel patterns, your success rate as a hunter should go up.

My favorite time to locate and figure out rub lines is in the spring. As far as I'm concerned, there is no better time to be in the woods scouting for the upcoming season. What good is scouting in the spring with hunting season a good six or seven months away? The chief advantage is that you can go into a hunting area with complete confidence that the bucks will be there year after year, rubbing in almost the exact same spots as before. Even if a big buck is harvested from an area, you can continue to hunt that area and the dead buck's old rub line.

During one bowhunting season in Wisconsin, for example, I found an active rub line in an area that up until that time I had never before hunted. Rather than stumble around in the locale and take a chance on spooking the bucks out of their bedding area, I did just enough preliminary scouting to find a suitable ambush point and then vacated the area for a week. The very first evening that I sat in the stand, a bowhunter's dream came true. I watched five different whitetail bucks parade by me at a range of 12 yards in less than five minutes. I shot the fifth and largest of those bucks. He was a 175-pound, 10-pointer with about a 16-inch spread. The very next year, an acquaintance of mine shot a very respectable eight-point buck off that same rub line. This is only one case where I have seen several different bucks using the same rub line. And in almost all of my hunting areas, the bucks seem to use the same rub lines year after year.

The most important reason why I prefer to spend so much time in the woods in the spring is that I am able to *thoroughly* scout a buck's rub lines from one end to the other. I don't have to be overly cautious about spooking deer and can walk from one end of the big buck's rub line all of the way up into his bedding area. If I happen to spook a big deer out of his bedroom at that time of the year, I know that he will eventually return and forget about the whole incident long before the hunting season opens in the fall. Run a big, mature buck out of his bedding area while scouting in the fall, and you can almost forget about killing that deer that year. One thing that big bucks will not tolerate is the presence of humans near or inside their bedding areas. It will almost assuredly be enough

to send them into a strict nocturnal pattern. A bonus of spring scouting is the possibility of finding shed antlers. There is no more positive indication of just what caliber of bucks you have in a certain area. Most of the sheds that I find are usually found right on or very near an active rub line.

In the spring woods, I constantly look for spots that could be considered for stand locations. If brush and branches need to be trimmed, this is the time to do it. By preparing my sites at this time of the year and by finding a good, quiet approach into my area in the spring, all I have to do is carry my portable stand into the preselected tree during hunting season and I'm all set. The least amount of disturbance you make, the better.

So, all you have to do to get a big buck is find a hot rub line. Right? Well, nothing is that easy when it comes to deer hunting. The first thing that any deer hunter must realize is that the whitetail understands his nocturnal advantage over his number-one enemy (man) as he understands no other. And, my research has shown that a lot of rubbing activity does take place at night—especially by the big boys. Another negative factor of hunting rub lines is that you are very probably going to see fewer deer. There definitely are doe/fawn runways and buck runways. The buck runways are where you will find the rub lines.

And that is where to place your stand. I like to place my portable stand close to a buck's bedding area, 12 to 15 yards off the runway if bowhunting, farther if hunting with a gun. It is crucial that the wind direction be perfect before hunting the bedding area. I'll head to a spot when the wind is right and then not hunt it again for up to a week. Use every precaution when heading into a stand site—rubber boots, gloves, etc. Also, get into your stand at least 30 minutes before shooting light. Remember, the buck will be heading back into his bedroom before first light, and you must beat him there. If you are one of those hunters who has to see deer every time you go out, I would suggest that you not try my system of hunting. When you hunt an active rub line, the deer you see will almost assuredly be bucks. But as far as seeing a lot of deer while hunting rub lines, forget it—unless you happen to be hunting an area that is overrun with bucks. So far, in 24 years of hunting whitetails, I haven't run into this "problem."

There are other problems associated with rub-line hunting. One of these is wind direction. Another is hunter competition. Or, maybe other deer are "picking you off" before the big bucks get to you. These are just a few of the things that may interfere with your success and need to be taken into consideration before you climb into your tree stand to hunt a particular rub line.

Yet, despite the "flaws" in the system, rub-line hunting for big bucks works no matter where you live and no matter when you hunt during the hunting season.

Bucks and B.O.

By Greg Miller

I had been watching the same three deer use the same approach into the alfalfa field for about a month. The order of their appearance was always the same. The big old doe would emerge first, followed a few minutes later by her fawn from that year. These two would feed for about 10 or 15 minutes before the third deer would walk out into the open. This third deer was the one that interested me. He was a very respectable eight-point buck.

The time of year was very late summer, and I could only hold my breath and pray that no one else would discover "my buck" before the beginning of bow season. Opening day was fast approaching, and I was confident that if nobody interfered, I would be able to take that nice eight-pointer on the first evening of the bow season.

My plan of attack was not complicated at all. Because the three deer had been observed using the same approach to the field, and because the buck was in the alfalfa well before dark every evening, I figured that I'd be able to get away with setting up just inside the treeline. That way, if the deer were bedding close by, I'd stand less chance of spooking them when I put up my tree stand. It all seemed a little too easy.

I didn't even bother to hunt on opening morning of bow season. I was confident that come about 6 P.M., I would be drawing down on a very nice whitetail buck. So, along about 9 A.M. on that first day of the season, I took my portable tree stand and drove my pickup to the alfalfa field that the three deer were frequenting. I also took along a good

friend of mine and my younger brother. The decision to do that eventually proved disastrous.

There were a few other bowhunters out and about that morning, so in order not to be spotted by anyone who was traveling the road, I decided not to walk across the open alfalfa field on the way into my hotspot. Rather, I walked just inside the treeline bordering the field, with my brother and my friend tagging along behind me.

When we arrived at the spot where I had been seeing the deer walk out of the woods and into the field, my heart skipped a beat. Even as early as it was in the season, there was buck sign everywhere. Fresh rubs, a couple of scrapes and a runway worn deep into the ground told me that there was no need to look further for an ambush point.

I carefully jumped over the runway to get to a tree on the other side, as wind direction dictated that I place my stand there. But I figured that even if I left some footprints in the area, the scent from those prints would be long gone by the time the three deer came to feed in the alfalfa. That time was a good eight hours away.

I was busily preparing the tree I had selected when I noticed that my friend and my brother were no longer standing quietly below me. I took a quick look around and saw both of them walking on the runway that the deer were using for an approach. They were heading back toward the area where I suspected the deer were bedding! I let out a sharp, quick whistle, and both of them stopped in their tracks and looked at me. I motioned that they

25

If this buck catches a whiff of "eau de man," he'll be gone like the wind. Len Rue Jr. photo.

should come back, and when they were once again standing at the base of my tree, I suggested that they not walk around too much in the area. They agreed that it was probably wise not to. I then quickly finished preparing my stand site, and as we drove away from the alfalfa field at about 9:30 A.M., my expectations were very high.

At 5:45 P.M. that same day, I had been on my stand for 1¾ hours, and I was just beginning to get a slight case of the "fidgets." But just as my mind was beginning to wander a bit, I thought I heard something. I slowly turned my head in the direction of the suspected noise, and there came the old doe, walking on the runway that passed by my stand. Looking beyond her, I saw the fawn walking along about 20 yards behind. Both deer seemed to be very relaxed. I imagine that it had something to do with the fact that they had been using the same runway to enter the field for well over a month without being disturbed.

The doe steadily continued toward my position, but just as she neared the point where my friend and my brother had been when I had whistled them back earlier in the day, she suddenly stopped. She then started intently to sniff the ground, and her behavior changed almost at once. Now, instead of being relaxed, she was tense and on guard. She would alternately sniff the ground and then jerk her head up and scan the area. She then began to slowly continue on, "tracking" my two companions along the path they had followed earlier in the day. Although the tracks were more than eight hours old, the doe never made a mistake. She walked right by me, turned, and followed the scent trail until she was out of sight.

I assume that the doe followed those tracks all the way out to the road because she had been gone for about five minutes before I saw her making her way back toward me. When she reached the runway going to the field, she stopped, as if deciding what to do. Looking first out into the field and then back toward the fawn (which, I might add, hadn't moved a muscle all this time), the doe quickly made up her mind. She turned and walked back to the fawn, stopped, sniffed noses with her young one, then continued on in the direction she had originally come from, no doubt taking the unseen buck right with her. I sat until dark that evening and never saw another deer. In fact, I kept an eye on that field for the better part of the fall and never saw a deer eating there before dark again.

Although this incident took place almost 10 years ago, I haven't forgotten any of the details. I was so impressed by the sense of smell that the old doe displayed that I have made it a point to be extra careful about not leaving human odor around my stand areas ever since. But even with all of the precautions that I still take today, I continue to see whitetails—both bucks and does—exhibit an unbelievable ability to sniff out threatening odors.

There have already been an untold number of articles written about how to try to keep yourself "odor-free" while in the woods in pursuit of whitetails and other big-game animals. There are also many widely publicized products on the market that are designed to help you achieve this supposed scentless state. This article was not written to try to explain to you yet another way of trying to fool a deer's nose. Rather, I'm going to relate to you a couple of incidents in which I have witnessed deer using their noses to warn them of impending danger. I'll also tell you how I prepare to hunt big bucks, as well as how a lack of preparation on the parts of some other hunters has been the reason for their lack of success on trophy-size whitetails. If you happen to learn something along the way, that's great.

This past fall, while on an October bowhunt in northern Wisconsin, I watched as a small forkhorn buck approached my position in a tree stand about 14 feet off the ground. Because I had no intention of shooting the forkhorn, I sat back and waited to see what he'd do when he hit the walking trail by which I had entered my area that morning.

As I continued to watch the little buck, I noticed that he was beginning to become more and more nervous. He wasn't smelling the ground on which I had walked in my knee-high rubber boots or the bushes that my pant legs might have brushed against. Rather, he was sniffing the places where I had pushed branches and brush aside with my bare hands when I had walked in an hour earlier. Because of the warm temperature, I had neglected to wear gloves, and every place that I had touched, the buck was smelling.

Fortunately for me, the last 10 yards to my stand was relatively brush-free, so at that point, he lost my trail. Seemingly confused, the forkhorn stood looking for the man that he knew had to be close by. After a few minutes, he gave up and continued on to his bedding area. There's no doubt in my mind that a bigger, more mature buck would have been long gone at the first hint of human odor. Another lesson learned.

Just recently, I was talking to a man whom I have known for many years. This fellow, whom I'll call Fred, has been hunting whitetails for more than 30 years. Fred has the reputation of being one of the area's most consistent bowhunters. He is very proficient at taking a deer every year with bowhunting gear. But for all of the deer that Fred has taken, I can't remember any that could be considered "bragging-size." In fact, many times when an unsuccessful season has neared its end, Fred has shot a doe. Now, don't get me wrong. We need to harvest antlerless deer, too, and there is nothing belittling about doing so. However, Fred has complained to me that he has trouble even seeing a good buck from his stand, let alone getting the opportunity to kill one. I know from my conversations with him that he is dying to knock over a bruiser of a buck. I also know that if he does, it will probably be due more to luck than to skill. I'll tell you why I feel this way.

During my latest conversation with Fred, he berated the general theme of most articles written about the problem of human odor. "All this garbage about washing your clothes in baking soda and using odorless soap on yourself makes me laugh," he said. "When I come home from a hunting trip, I throw all of my clothes in the washroom and I let my wife take care of them. I'm lucky to have her wash them at all. I'm not going to press my luck and tell her that she has to wash them in baking soda and pack them in plastic bags. Sometimes, I spend as many as nine days in a row at my cabin without a shower, so why should I worry about how my clothes smell?" Fred went on to say. "By the end of those nine days, I smell like an old bear, but I always manage to fill my tag."

I wasn't about to argue with Fred on his last statement. He does manage to fill his tag every year. Spikes, forkhorns and an occasional small six-pointer are the usual victims of Fred's arrows. When confronted with human odor, the behavior and general attitude of this class of bucks should in no way be compared to what a mature, trophy-size whitetail buck will do. Though the smaller, more inexperienced bucks may become somewhat confused and even curious when confronted with human scent in the woods, the big boys will almost never

show such confusion or curiosity; they'll just skedaddle.

As far as Fred having his wife do his laundry for him, that's fine, especially if he wants to continue to smell like a box of detergent. I don't care to smell like detergent, nor do I prefer to smell like a dryer-type fabric softener. And that's exactly how I'd smell if I let my wife wash my hunting clothes. You see, I have no problem running the washing machine or the dryer at my house, so I take care of my own laundry. I know that a big, macho hunter like Fred would probably have trouble dealing with having one of his friends catch him in the family washroom loading up the washing machine, but I don't have that problem. I also don't have any problem seeing bigger-than-average bucks from my stand, either.

In November 1984, I got to see firsthand what happens when a big whitetail buck gets an unexpected nose-full of man-smell. The rut was going strong at the time—in fact, while climbing the tree up to my stand before daylight that morning, I could hear three different bucks grunting nearby—and I just knew that something was going to happen. I was right. I had been in the stand for about a half-hour when the soft crunching of steps in the frozen oak leaves told me that a deer was approaching. I grabbed my bow off its hanger and got into a position to shoot just as the deer walked into

STOP MAKING SCENTS

As an added precaution for achieving an odorless state, today's hunters have available to them products that actually destroy human and other man-made odors, including tobacco and petroleum smells. These products are not to be confused with cover scents, such as essence of acorn, skunk or fox, which are applied to *mask* human odor; these products actually eliminate man-smells on the molecular level.

Scent Shield (Robinson Laboratories, 2833 15th Ave. S., Minneapolis, MN 55407) is one example of a product offering this type of odor protection. It is said to stop the process whereby human odor molecules form a gas. And when there is no gas, there is no scent. Scent Shield is said not only to destroy human scent on contact, but also to continue working all day as a shield on clothing to keep body odor from escaping.

A similar product that kills human odors on contact and continues to eliminate smells as they are produced is No Scent Spray (James Valley Scents, HCR 1, Box 47, Mellette, SD 57461). With this product, "all odors are 'bound' together and broken down molecularly to the point where they cannot be detected by the olfactory system." But in addition to simply working from the clothing in, No Scent Spray is said to "carry out" to offer blanket protection by surrounding the entire body. What this means is that instead of the hunter having to completely cover himself with the product, he need only apply the spray at three or four heights to cover his whole body area. Also available from James Valley Scents is its longer-lasting No Scent Gel and its Scent Stopper Boot Creme, which is specially formu-

lated to eliminate odors from leather boots.

Tink's Non-Stink (Tink's Safariland Hunting Corp., Box 69, Trapp, MD 21673) works similarly by chemically bonding odor-causing molecules into a ring-formation lattice structure and thus preventing the molecules' escape from within clothing. Also, because this bonding is not as effective in clothing already contaminated with odors, the company recommends that this product be used in association with its NonScent Camo Soap as a pre-treatment for hunting gear to prevent odors from being absorbed into the clothing in the first place.

Other products that serve to eliminate human odors are also available. Scent Eliminator Spray and Protective Wrap (Game Tracker, 3476 Eastman Drive, Flushing, MI 48433) are two parts of a scentless system in which hunters wash their clothes and themselves with the Protective Wrap and then apply the spray to all of their hunting equipment. Scent Destroyer (Whitetail Disguise Scent Co., Box 22187, Chattanooga, TN 37422) is sprayed on clothing or even directly on the skin.

Of course, no hunter should consider any of these products to be foolproof, and wind direction should always be a major consideration when planning any hunting strategy. But should a hunter find himself upwind of a circling buck or the victim of a sudden change in wind direction, having taken these extra precautions just might mean the difference between the sweet smell of victory and the foul odor of defeat.

view. A doe. I relaxed a little and watched as the doe walked nearer and nearer to my walking trail. When she got to the spot where I had walked in that morning, the doe stopped and smelled the ground. She twitched her tail a couple of times, did a few head bobs, looked back over her rump, then continued on her way.

The old doe had just walked out of sight when I heard another deer coming along on her trail. My suspicions that it was a buck were confirmed when I heard a deep, piglike grunt break the early morning quiet. The buck walked into view following the exact route that the doe had taken a few minutes earlier. He was a dandy 10-pointer, and judging from his action, I guessed that the doe was either very close to or already in estrous. When the buck reached the spot where I had walked in, he exploded into action. Unlike there had been with the doe, there was no hesitation this time. That big buck vacated the area as if he had just been poked in the rear with a fully charged cattle prod. I didn't have time to even draw my bow back. The interesting thing was the type of reaction that the buck had by just smelling human tracks. I normally wear rubber boots on all of my hunting and scouting trips, but unfortunately, I had neglected to do so on this day. I should have known better. And if a big buck shows the above described behavior when smelling tracks, I can just about imagine what one will do if he gets a direct whiff of a hunter.

In the fall of 1986, I shot a 10-point, 186-pound whitetail buck with my bow in Wisconsin. After I had the buck loaded in the back of my pickup, I drove to a local "nectar parlor" to show the deer to some acquaintances of mine who I knew would be there having a few post-hunt cocktails. Everybody in the joint filed out to admire my buck and to offer congratulations. When the crowd began to retire back into the bar, one of my acquaintances sidled up to me and, under his breath, said "You have got to be the luckiest son of a gun alive. I have never had a buck like that walk by me when I was hunting."

I just looked at the fellow and smiled. "Yup, I guess I'm just lucky," I replied. For some reason, I didn't feel that the time was right for me to tell the guy that I might have a few suggestions to help him become "lucky," too.

Later that same night, while lying in my bed and feeling a little euphoric about my success, my thoughts drifted to what the guy at the saloon had said to me about being lucky. His statement that he had never had a good buck walk by him hadn't surprised me at all because for as long as I'd known this man, his routine during his weekend hunting trips had always been the same. He would arrive at his cabin on Friday evening, unload his gear, and then drive to a nearby tavern to meet his hunting group. The whole bunch would then sit and talk strategy for the weekend's hunt amid the smoke and cooking odors. Invariably, each one would be wearing a part of his hunting clothing to the bar. It's bad enough for a hunter to let his hair and skin become contaminated with vagrant scents, but when he allows any part of his hunting clothing to become saturated with the smells, I'm afraid he's committed one of the worst sins that a deer hunter can commit. Unbelievably, when the weekend hunt would end, these guys would pack all of their hunting clothes away for a week, not bother to wash them, and then unpack them the following weekend and wear them into the woods once more.

Believe me, through the years I've tried to talk to some of the fellows in this hunting group about their bad habits, but I'm afraid that my comments and suggestions are viewed as being completely worthless information. I can only imagine what they must smell like to any deer that passes downwind of them, and how badly the areas that they hunt must continue to smell long after they've left their stands. I imagine that it's enough to make a wise old buck, or any buck for that matter, either limit all of his wanderings to strictly a nocturnal pattern or vacate the area altogether.

The impression that I get from most of the deer hunters that I talk to is that they seem to think that once they leave the woods, all human odor goes with them. That's just not the case. How careful a hunter is when he *walks into* his hunting area, how careful he is *while* he is hunting, and how careful he is when he *walks out* of his area may all have a direct bearing on his success on future hunts in that particular spot. It pays to remember that man-made smells strike fear in the hearts of whitetails. These smells could be perspiration odors or the smell of cigarette smoke, gasoline or diesel fuel, boot oil, after shave lotion, laundry detergent or maybe even alcohol. It makes no difference. The whitetail deer has learned that the smells of these things and many others add up to mean that a human is or was near. And that means danger.

Because of this, I have developed my own system for trying to stay as odor-free as possible. And for me, this system has worked well so far. First, as I mentioned previously, I wash all of my own hunting clothes. It gives me tremendous peace of mind to know that my clothing, from my underwear all the way out to my camo clothing, has been washed in baking soda and stored in sealed plastic bags. By the way, when I'm done with the day's hunt, the clothing goes back into the plastic bags until I wear it again. And if possible, I try to wash my clothing every two or three days. All of it!

I happen to perspire quite heavily. It's just the way I am. So, because of this, I have to be very careful about my own personal body odor, too. Luckily, my cabin is equipped with a shower. Before going out on a morning hunt, I shower and wash my hair with an odorless soap. Phisoderm liquid soap works well, and Ivory makes an odorless shampoo. After drying off, I immediately pull on the light layer of my hunting outfit and my rubber

Man-made odors strike fear in the hearts of whitetails. Leonard Lee Rue III photo.

boots and head out to my hunting area, carrying my outer camouflage and any heavier clothing items in a daypack. By only wearing the light layer, I avoid getting overheated en route to my stand. Once I arrive at my stand, I then take any necessary heavier items and my camouflage clothing out of the pack and put them on.

Most of the time, I wear a pair of light cotton gloves that have also been washed in baking soda. These gloves help immensely if I have to push brush and branches aside as I walk through the woods. Bare hands are "collectors" of foreign odors, and when they touch branches or bushes, they pass that odor on. Gloves are a very important item that many hunters often forget.

I've already mentioned that I wear rubber boots. Mine are knee-high pullovers that I can wear over the top of my insulated leather boots. Not only is this combination odorless, but it is extremely warm.

Being careful in and around your hunting area is something that a lot of hunters forget about, too. The number-one problem is: "Where do I go to the bathroom?" I've read those articles where the author says it's okay to walk 100 yards away and take care of business, but this will never work if you're hunting wilderness bucks. You won't get away with doing that in the areas that I hunt. For just this purpose, I carry a plastic bottle with a screw-on cover in my daypack. My daypack goes up the tree with me and is hung on a branch within easy reach. When I have to urinate, out comes the bottle. It's that simple.

The only time that I get out of my stand is when it's time to leave. And leave I do. This is not the time to dillydally and walk around to check out runs and scrapes that should have been investigated during the scouting process. I leave my stand site as I entered it—quietly and cautiously along the same path on which I walked in. If I plan on hunting that spot again, I don't want to let any big buck in the vicinity know that I was there, whether it be from a cracking branch or a fistful of man-smell on an overhanging limb. I sneak out with rubber boots and gloves in place, and I take my camouflage clothing off after a short while so that if I do work up a sweat, I don't contaminate the outfit.

Last of all, I would like to address the subject of treating unforeseen odoriferous accidents or problems. One that comes to mind happened a couple of years ago during the best time to bowhunt here in Wisconsin—the first week in November. A guy who was hunting with me had taken off his camouflage clothing and thrown it into a box in the back of his pickup—a box in which he had forgotten that he had a can of gas for his chain saw. You guessed it. The gas spilled and got on the hunting clothes. Not knowing what else to do, I suggested he run some water in the bathtub at my cabin and soak his clothing in a strong baking soda solution. First, though, I had him scrub the "infected" area with a baking soda paste. I loaned the fellow some clothing to wear for the rest of the day with the promise that he wouldn't throw the items in the back of his pickup. When his camo clothing had dried the next morning, we were surprised to learn that we couldn't detect even the slightest hint of gasoline odor.

Undoubtedly, occasions will arise where an exposure to smoke (either from a cigarette or a wood fire) may be unavoidable. If there is no place to wash and dry the clothing, my best tip would be to hang the items out in the open air overnight or throughout the day. This should certainly help. If a hunter's person should be contaminated, I would suggest that he wash his hair and his body with an odorless shampoo and soap. Prevention is really the best cure. If at all possible, a hunter should try to stay away from situations where he might jeopardize his "odorless" state.

The whitetail deer is, without question, the most popular big-game animal today. Because of this fact, thousands of articles have been written about different subjects concerning whitetails, including their keen sense of smell. Many hunters, at some point in their careers, will get to experience this smelling ability firsthand. Yet, a large number of hunters still regard the whitetail deer as just another dumb animal. Well, I'm here to say that this isn't even close.

Big, trophy-size whitetail bucks are not invincible creatures, although, at times, it may seem that way. The big defense that a deer has is its nose. Its eyesight isn't the greatest. Its hearing is a little better than average, maybe. But a whitetail trusts its sense of smell like no other sense it possesses. All deer hunters, whether they be totally obsessed fanatics or just weekend warriors, would be wise to keep this in mind when in pursuit of a trophy buck.

From Bucks to Nuts

By Jeff Murray

When the computer kicked out a hunting buddy's number for a special muzzle-loader hunt at Fort McCoy in Wisconsin, I put myself in his shoes. His home was a long drive away, and he only had one day to scout unfamiliar terrain. Where would he start, and what would he look for? Because we're both full-time nuts when it comes to hunting whitetails, I expected a phone call shortly after his return. But the season was long over, and I still hadn't heard a thing.

Finally, he called. The inflection of his voice gave the story away. It was the greatest hunt of his life, he said. There was a super acorn crop, and the place was crawling with whitetails. In one spot, he found so many deer droppings that he had a hard time keeping his footing. He went on to tell about the 20 deer he saw in the pin oaks by noon, and how he had no trouble sneaking up on what proved to be his nicest buck to date.

At first, I was really excited. But after hanging up the phone, I thought about my own experiences with deer and acorns. In all honesty, it sounded more like a fluke than a new way to hunt whitetails. Deer in association with any food source, as a basis for practical hunting strategy, can only be described as an iffy proposition—especially for big bucks. After all, everyone knows that breeding bucks don't eat much during the fall.

My prejudices were reinforced the following year when my buddy drew another muzzleloader permit at Fort McCoy. What happened? His acorn connection bombed. The mast crop was way down, and he had a hard time filling his tag. To make matters worse, this time around he didn't have any time to scout and ended up wasting precious hours of the opener on the oak ridges, when he should have been down on the bottomlands. He was very fortunate to eventually kill a young buck.

Since then I've been forced to rearrange my thinking on how deer foods can affect overall hunting success. I've done a flip-flop. I now believe that acorns may indeed hold the key for consistent deer hunting action. And not just for yearlings and does, but for real bruisers as well. Unfortunately, it isn't as simple as it may sound. For sure, you have to know a few things about oaks and acorns. More important, there are a number of interesting quirks that whitetail deer display when it comes to feeding on acorns in the fall. But first, the fundamental question: How is it that a food source can aid a hunter in bagging a mature buck when it's a given that breeding bucks are more interested in sex than food throughout the fall?

The answer comes from Jim Byford, dean of the School of Agriculture and Home Economics at the University of Tennessee at Martin. In completing a radio-tracking study a few years ago, Byford proved conclusively that deer shift their range in response to changing food supplies. Further—and here's what hunters ought to know—daily movements "were very concentrated when food was concentrated, but dispersed when the food supply was dispersed."

Prior to this study, there had been little documen-

31

tation showing that deer migrate for reasons other than weather. Most of the animals in Byford's study, however, were females. So, what about the bucks?

"It's relatively simple," Byford said. "Bucks are going to be where the does are. No food source can offer as much nutritional value as acorns, and does of breeding age know it. You can bet that whenever and wherever acorns become available, the does will absolutely key on them to the exclusion of just about everything else."

Now, the light bulb should be turned on. As my buddy says, you'd have to be nuts to ignore anything so significant as to cause a major shift in a deer's range.

This acorn phenomenon is not limited to the South. Jerry P. Duvendeck, a former Michigan Department of Natural Resources biologist, studied deer on acorn diets for three years at the Houghton Lake Wildlife Experiment Station. The results of this work were published in the *Journal of Wildlife Management* in a paper titled, "The Value of Acorns in the Diet of Michigan Deer." Duvendeck was primarily interested in determining the food value of acorns to see whether they could help increase deer survival in years of harsh winters. Control groups of deer, separated in pens, were fed a variety of foods. Included were balsam fir, jack pine, white cedar, oak browse, and an acorn supplement consisting of 50 percent Hill's oak, 42 percent northern red oak and 8 percent white oak.

Among other things, Duvendeck found that deer in captivity, and in the wild, preferred white oak acorns over the others; that only one of the 18 deer involved in the study would not eat all of the acorn, including the shell; that if insect-infested acorns were inadvertently offered, the deer would not eat them; and that deer eating only 1½ pounds of acorns per 100 pounds of body weight daily would easily survive a 90-day winter.

This study is but one example of how finicky deer can be when they decide which acorns to zero in on—a fact that many hunters will sooner or later encounter.

Byford, who is also an avid bowhunter, has noticed a number of equally peculiar feeding traits that deer sometimes exhibit. For instance, in years of super-abundant mast crops, deer will not only pass up red oak acorns in favor of white oak acorns when both are available in a given area, but they will also stick with a specific kind of white oak acorn.

"It's the craziest thing," he told me. "I don't know how they do it, but when acorns are in the process of falling to the ground in heavy bearing years, most of the deer will only feed on those nuts that have just dropped. I've seen years when the entire countryside was carpeted with acorns, but only those ridges with fresh-fallen ones attracted deer consistently."

This is one of the best clues for hunting during years of outstanding mast crops. It is during these times that patterning deer movement becomes a game of Russian roulette. Trails seem to be leading every which way, and getting a handle on the right entrances and exits is tough. But how do you tell a fresh acorn from one that's been on the ground for a while? You don't. Instead, says Byford, you let the deer tell you.

"Deer are like most livestock," he explained. "When they get up from their beds, they usually defecate. And the beds won't be very far from the acorn patches they've been working over. Those areas with the most droppings should definitely be looked at first.

"But that's just the start," Byford added. "Lots of droppings could be misleading. There could be an accumulation from different times when the deer have been in and out of the area, so you have to be able to age the droppings. When you find several ages of droppings in a relatively small area, you can be assured that the deer have been frequenting that particular stand of oaks throughout the fall."

When Byford says that he's sniffing out new deer country, that's exactly what he means—only fresh droppings have a slight odor to them. Another way to age them is to take the pellets apart and examine them. Older ones are more fibrous and dry; fresher ones tend to be moist and pasty.

Once you determine that a particular stand of oaks is being visited regularly by deer, there are two ways to hunt it. One is to look for a primary scrape and figure out the best way to monitor it. Because acorns, more than any other phenomenon, tend to concentrate does, Byford feels that most, if not all, of a buck's favored scrapes in his home range will be on or very near oak knolls.

Many hunters have never seen a true primary scrape. According to Byford, one of the best places to find one is on the edge of an acorn-studded oak knoll. A hunter-wise buck may be reluctant to venture out into the oak stand, where the underbrush tends to be too thin for comfort. But as the rut approaches, overanxious bucks will be advertising their presence along the perimeter, and one just might make a foolish daylight excursion into the oaks.

The other method is a tree stand properly placed well back from major entrance and exit routes. But which ones? Generally, the top pick is going to be a bottleneck between the oaks and the beds. You can look for it at the head of a hollow, near a gap in the ridge, or along a natural travel lane with thick cover that acts as a funnel. But again, in years of mast abundance, you've got to be flexible and discerning; the deer will be following the acorns as they drop, and last week's hotspot could be worthless this week.

Byford has learned of a clever way to anticipate these changes and keep pace with the deer, rather

Fallen mast is not just a magnet for does; it can also be a hotspot for bucks as well.

than react to old patterns and forever be one step behind. From years of observation, he has noticed that oaks on the top of a ridge will usually be the first to drop their acorns. Next in line will be those trees that are a little farther down the slope. And so goes the progression. The deer, of course, know this and follow suit. So can you.

But what about years when acorns are scarce? That's the easiest hunting of all, because all you have to do is find that rare stand of oaks anointed with deer nuts and you'll have your hotspot. Not only will there be a concentration of deer present, but figuring out stand placements at strategic intersection points will also be far less perplexing. Locating these hidden treasures is a two-step process.

First, you need to find out where the huntable oak stands are in your region. If you hunt in a national forest, contact the headquarters and ask to talk to one of the foresters. Perhaps he'll have an inventory on file, with some maps to show you. State-forest bureaus, as well as counties that administer tax-forfeited lands, also keep such records. And don't forget aerial photographs. Because of their unique crowns, oaks are easy to distinguish from other vegetation types.

And second, you should know a little oak biology. There are two kinds of oaks: white oaks and red oaks. Within these two, there are many subspecies, but the main distinguishing feature is that it takes two years for the red oak to bear fruit; the white oak, on the other hand, is more like an apple tree, which flowers, sets and forms its fruit in one growing season. This is an important point, giving any deer hunter the luxury of scouting for red oak acorn production a year in advance. By the first summer, the fruit will be set and can be readily observed on the outer branches.

You should have little difficulty telling the two apart. White oaks have leaves with seven to nine rounded lobes. There are, however, seven to 11 lobes on a red oak leaf; they are sharp and typically three-pointed.

As mentioned earlier, deer seem to prefer white oaks over red oaks when given the choice. Also, it should be noted that white oaks dump their acorns first, as early as late August. Thus, it makes a lot of sense to know where both white and red oak stands are so that you can put together an early and late hunting strategy. Deer will eventually turn to the red oaks when they've exhausted their supply of white oak acorns.

Oaks prefer moist soils that are well drained. When doing your actual field work, take special note of the orientation of each oak grove you find. Mast failure can be the result of a number of factors, but chances are that you may be able to isolate them. Then, through a process of elimination, you just may find several areas with the potential to draw deer in like nothing you've ever seen or believed possible. As an example, if a drought was to blame for this year's mast failure, consider those stands that face north or northeast, where less moisture loss is likely to occur. Or if an early frost hit, consider those stands at higher elevations. Also, red oaks tend to be more susceptible than white oaks to crop fluctuations because they take two years to produce.

To boil it down, I'd look for potential acorn-bearing oaks in this manner. First, note where white oaks are in relation to red oaks. Then, check out north-facing stands, south-facing stands, higher elevations and lower ones to determine a pattern. Finally, repeat the successful pattern to find the next producing stand (or tree). For convenience' sake, I'd map this all out on a topographic map. It should prove to be a valuable aid in plotting future hunts, centering around acorn crops, for years to come.

Incidentally, recent research by Larry Marchington and Karl Miller at the University of Georgia has revealed that in years of mast-crop failure, bucks may make up to 60 percent fewer rubs than in years of normal acorn production. So, don't rush to the conclusion that there aren't many good bucks in an area where the mast crop is down from previous years. The bucks should still be present, but, according to the researchers, their rut intensity "may have been reduced in response to their [physical] condition."

Hunting acorn-related bucks when the rut approaches makes sense, but there is another time when it works on mature bucks. Myles Keller, nationally known trophy bowhunter, knows exactly when to do it.

"Apart from the rut, there aren't many percentage opportunities for bowhunters to score on a good buck, especially early in the season," he said. "Hunting around acorns right as they drop, though, is one of the few patterns that is worth a try. For a very limited time, even smart bucks in the 4½- to 5½-year-old range will load up on acorns. But you have to catch them coming out real early in the morning or you'll blow your chance there until the rut."

By "real early," Keller means being on your stand at least two hours before sunrise (be sure to check local game regulations). There is just no other way. And this pattern only lasts for a short time before the mating urge takes over, and hunger becomes nothing more than a minor nuisance for several months to come. To pull off this early season trick, you have to have a good mast crop that's dropping by the bow season opener. That usually means that white oaks will be involved because they tend to drop their acorns earlier than do most other species. This time, though, you'll be setting up on the edges, hoping to catch a buck coming off a late-night snack.

How significant is the acorn connection? Ask Bob Fratzke, a successful big-buck bowhunter from southern Minnesota.

"If you don't find the acorns," he stated in his book, Taking Trophy Whitetails, "you might as well hunt trophy bucks in your bathroom. Nothing else matters when acorns are good."

Deer by the Ear

By John Weiss

Under the right conditions, stationary deer offer hunters close shots. Bob Knopf photos.

There are two things that my friend Harvey Wilcourt loves more than anything else. One is ice-fishing, and the other is eating peanuts. It might not sound as though that bears any relation to whitetail deer hunting, but one time it actually helped me to collect a very big buck.

Harve and I had scheduled a day of winter fishing for walleyes, and the plan was to meet at a well-known parking area near the lake and then decide upon a particular frozen-over bay that might offer the best results. As it happened, however, car trouble delayed my arrival by more than an hour, so naturally, when I finally reached our meeting place, Harve had already headed out onto the ice-shrouded lake.

At first, I shrugged my shoulders, not knowing in which direction he might have headed. Then, I happened to look down at the ground near his parked vehicle, and guess what I spotted? Right, peanut shells! Right then, a wide smile came across my face because I instantly knew that tracking Harve would be easy.

In most places, the trail was relatively thin, but occasionally I'd come to an abandoned hole in the ice where shells littered the entire area. Then, the trail would lead off into the distance to another hole, and then still another. Eventually, I spied my partner in a distant channel, and we spent the remainder of the day fishing together. Without the discarded peanut shells showing the way, I might have never located Harve and might have ended up fishing solo that day.

The irony is that several years later, I duplicated the same type of feat, but this time the trail eventually led me to an eight-point buck. To the best of my knowledge, whitetails don't maintain any particular fetish for peanuts, but they do love corn. And after filling their paunches in a cornfield, it's quite common for them to carry off a cob in their mouths and continue eating from it as they travel to a nearby bedding site. Sometimes, they'll finish with the cob along the way and let it fall to the ground right there. Other times, they'll carry the cob all the way back to the actual bedding location, perhaps to snack upon later.

In any event, I had been hiking along the edge of a large cornfield near my home in southern Ohio, and in coming upon a threadbare trail exiting from the corn, I had found a partially eaten cob. Recalling my amusing experience with Harvey, I decided to follow the trail, and just inside the leading edge of a nearby beech forest I discovered another cob on the ground, and then still another. All of the cobs were in various stages of deterioration, so I knew that they had been dropped at different times over a period of weeks. Large, fresh deer tracks of uniform size and large droppings provided additional clues, and eventually, more than 300 yards into the timber, I came upon a lone bed. That confirmed I was in a buck's bailiwick, because had there been tracks of varied sizes and several beds, I could have inferred that the deer were only does.

After resting the area for two days, I snuck back into the spot and quietly fabricated a makeshift blind behind a convenient blowdown overlooking the trail. Later, when there was just enough light to make a shot, a gray shadow materialized in the distance, traveling right along the trail. My arrow caught the eight-pointer at the base of the neck, and after sprinting 50 yards, the buck collapsed in a heap.

It's no secret that bucks and corn go together like bacon and eggs, and we have plenty of all of those commodities, especially throughout the midwestern agricultural belt. In fact, after talking recently with my local extension agent, I learned that in 1986, in the nine major farming states stretching from Ohio to Minnesota, more than 46 million acres of land were planted to corn.

Moreover, acquiring hunting permission in agricultural regions is invariably easier than it is on other privately owned lands because of the extensive damage often inflicted by wild animals. In Wisconsin alone, it was estimated that during 1986, deer destroyed more than $22 million worth of corn, and this cost each farmer an average of $490. Add to this the combined losses of alfalfa, soybeans, truck-garden crops and other foods that whitetails regularly dine upon, and it should come as no surprise that though a majority of farmers certainly enjoy seeing deer on their land, they don't take kindly to whitetail populations reaching such levels that they severely cut into the farmers' annual incomes.

The exasperating problem that most hunters face is how to hunt those often mammoth and intimidating cornfields effectively.

The first task is to confirm that deer are indeed using the corn, and this is easily ascertained by merely hiking the perimeter of the field and looking for tracks entering and leaving the food plot. Obviously, the best time to do this is either after a rainy period, when the ground is soft, or after several days of light snowfall.

If the region has been experiencing several weeks of dry weather, however, and the terrain is like hardpan, tracks are not easily detected. It is in this case that other types of insight must be applied to the hunting situation. For example, one time I discovered a cornfield where many stalks had been knocked down and countless partially eaten ears were on the ground. Initially, I thought that I had found a mother lode of deer activity, but I was dead wrong.

As I learned later, several raccoons had been at work. The telltale giveaway—pointed out to me by a friend who is a serious naturalist—should have been the fact that the ears were only partially eaten. Raccoons rarely eat an entire ear of corn; instead, they knock down a cornstalk and bite off just the tender tip of the ear, then move on to the next stalk.

If the cornfield borders a climax forest, corn-hungry squirrels may also give the false impression that deer have been at work. But in this situation, the animals climb the stalks, nibble away at the ears, stuff their cheeks and then retreat to their dens, where the scavenged kernels are placed in storage. This leaves the ears still attached to the stalks but gives them a ragtag, moth-eaten appearance.

If deer are working the corn, however, the clues to look for in the absence of tracks are scattered cobs on the ground that have been cleaned of almost every kernel of corn. Also keep on the lookout for droppings.

Once it has been determined that deer are hitting a particular cornfield on a regular basis, the best mode of hunting must be decided upon. And contrary to what you might expect, the best method of hunting is not necessarily the tactic you might like to use most, but rather the one that most appropriately falls in line with the agricultural cropping practices in your region.

In many areas, conventional harvesting methods are engaged in sometime during October or November, when the corn is brown and cured. The picking operation leaves the cornfield in a stubble-like condition, yet there remains on the ground plenty of spillage residue to attract the interest of local deer. Under these conditions, with the previously standing cornstalks no longer present and the concealing cover therefore eliminated, midday hunting is virtually out of the question. The animals will predictably visit the corn *only* in the early morning hours or at dusk. If hunting pressure is intense in the region, the deer may even be strictly nocturnal in their feeding.

Conversely, in many other regions, it is becoming an increasingly popular agricultural practice to leave corn standing in the field for as long as possible. With grain-elevator storage costs escalating like never before, and future market prices always uncertain, many farmers nowadays are simply delaying their harvesting either until such time as they have a specific need for the corn for stock feed or until the price increases, which it often does in February or March. Consequently, the hunter now finds that he can effectively hunt the cornfields not only early and late in the day, but also during the midday hours.

Regardless of whether a solo hunter elects to use bowhunting equipment, a rifle, a slug-loaded shotgun, a muzzleloader, or a handgun, there are four options to choose from when hunting standing corn: sneak-hunting in and around the corn; sneak-hunting in and around nearby heavy-cover regions; taking a stand designed to intercept the animals coming to the corn; or taking a stand designed to intercept the animals as they leave the corn.

Hunting in cornfields can be highly productive. Set up far enough off a field edge so that you can hide, yet watch escape routes.

Still again, the right method to use may not necessarily be the hunter's favorite way to hunt, but it must be geared to existing conditions. The foremost determinant that I rely upon to make my decision is the presence or absence of *wind*—assuming there is standing corn, of course.

On a windy day, I do not want to be in a tree stand. Wind is the result of downdrafts of cold air meeting warm air. Therefore, no matter which direction the wind is coming from, it will have a tendency to force scents down toward the ground, and this will readily give away a hunter's location. Compounding the problem is the fact that deer do not like to move on windy days because the wind disallows the effective use of their sense of hearing. Calm days, on the other hand, or those during which the wind is only slightly and gently blowing from one specific direction are ideal for quietly waiting on stand for the deer to walk by.

Just the opposite is the case when hunting in and around the cornfield itself. Now is when a hunter wants the windiest conditions possible. This is because when whitetails bed during the midday hours, they feel most secure and safe by retreating into the heaviest, thickest cover they can find. In many agricultural regions, the terrain surrounding cornfields, such as gullies and forest lands, simply does not offer hiding cover that is as thick as that in the cornfields themselves. Consequently, the whitetails will commonly bed right in the cornfields in these areas.

Now it becomes obvious why the very time to hunt these cornfields is during periods of high winds. It is because under blowing conditions, a cornfield is a very noisy place. The leaves are dry and brittle later in the season, and the loud rustling and crackling noises that they make in the wind cover up so much human error in prowling around that a hunter can quite easily walk right up on deer without them suspecting his presence.

Moreover, a hunter doesn't have to worry about his scent when hunting in a cornfield. Wind in a cornfield is a tricky thing. It hits the stalks and broad leaves and bounces every which way. As a result, deer in a cornfield may catch a hunter's scent, but in most cases they will not be able to determine the direction from which it's coming. As a result, they lock up, or freeze, in position because they know that if they attempt to run, they may blunder right into trouble. And if the hunter then happens to step into the right row of corn, he may have an easy shot at a stationary buck.

In going back to calm days, during which patiently waiting in a tree stand or ground blind is the preferred method of hunting either standing corn or stubble fields, there are two tricks that I use to properly locate my stand. First, it's necessary to engage in enough scouting to know in advance where trails are located. It must be remembered however, that it's quite common for deer to leave a cornfield via a different trail than the one they used to enter the field, assuming, of course, that the deer are bedding somewhere other than in the corn itself. Therefore, a morning stand to intercept the deer leaving the corn will undoubtedly be in a different place than an evening stand that has been set up to ambush deer coming from their bedding areas to the corn.

Thus, what a hunter initially wants to do after locating trails is to ascertain what time of day they're being used. The direction in which tracks are pointing is a sure clue—if the tracks are pointing toward the corn, they were probably made in the evening; if they are directed away from the corn, they probably indicate an exit trail that the animals use in the morning. Also, the hunter should be on the lookout for corncobs. Because deer obviously do not carry cobs from their bedding region back to the corn-

field, but do carry cobs from the field to their bedding sites, the presence of intermittent cobs along the trail indicates in no uncertain terms that the travel route is a morning trail.

As a general rule, I do not like for either a morning stand or an evening stand to be too close to a cornfield where deer are feeding. If possible, depending upon his evaluation of the terrain, a hunter should try to situate his stands or blinds 100 to 200 yards from the cornfield so that he can overlook the exit and entrance trails that the deer are using to enter or leave the food plot.

There are several good reasons for this strategy. To begin with, the largest bucks in any given region do not like to expose themselves unnecessarily in broad daylight, especially in regions where hunting pressure is intense. They can pretty much be counted upon to leave the cornfield at the very hint of early morning's first light. Because it may still be too dark to shoot accurately, the hunter wants to be farther back down the trail that the deer are using so that by the time they reach the stand location, it will be fully light enough to see.

Conversely, in the evening hours, the very largest bucks seldom enter a cornfield when the sky is still brightly illuminated. They like to linger back in the shaded, heavy cover of their bedding areas, sometimes not actually entering the cornfield until after full dark. Naturally, therefore, if a stand or blind is positioned close to the cornfield, by the time the deer reach the location, it will be too dark to see.

In all of this, it should be kept in mind that though the hunter doesn't want to position his stand too close to the cornfield for either a morning or an evening watch, neither does he want his stand too close to the bedding area that the animals are using. This is simply too risky because the animals are very likely to detect the hunter as he tries to approach his stand site; and if they are spooked from the very region that they previously considered the safest place to be, they may not return for many days.

In fact, it's worth mentioning that during the course of scouting, I always move slowly but make plenty of noise. Sometimes, I even whistle to myself as though I'm engaged in some type of routine outdoor work such as that of a surveyor or forester. Whitetails are accustomed to this type of minor disturbance, and they will simply circle around the intruder. And because the deer have the opportunity to hide or sneak away undetected, they'll still have full confidence in the security of their chosen area, prompting them to return shortly after I've left.

Later, when I return to begin my hunting vigil, I stalk my stand. I actually sneak up on it just as though I were stillhunting through the woods. By doing this, the chances of any nearby deer recognizing my presence are much lower.

Pursuing whitetails when they're actually in the corn is one of deer hunting's most challenging and exciting endeavors. But the hunter should remember two things: If the terrain surrounding the cornfield is devoid of thick security cover, meaning that the corn itself is the very best place to hide and bed, the deer will probably cling to the corn all day and every day. This is especially the case if water is readily available in rain-filled puddles or tractor ruts. The second thing to remember—again—is that the windiest days are the best days to hunt.

Simply sneak-hunting around the perimeter of the cornfield can put venison on the meat pole, particularly during the early and late hours of the day, when the deer are feeding and have a tendency to work along "edges." I've most often found this to be the case when the cornfield is bordered on one or more sides by lush hay meadows planted to some legume such as alfalfa, red or white clover or lespedeza. This is because it's rather uncustomary for whitetails to gorge themselves on a single food type, as they are opportunists in their feeding habits and like variety in their diets. Therefore, if you know of a cornfield bordered by some equally preferred food, you've hit paydirt!

In sneak-hunting around the perimeter of a cornfield, a hunter shouldn't expose himself in the open by remaining along the outside edge. Instead, he should stay one or two rows inside the edge of the cornfield—just far enough in so that he's concealed yet can still see along the outside edge and into the adjacent, secondary food plot. The only exception to this rule is when the cornfield butts up directly against a brushy thicket or other bordering cover. In this case, the hunter can remain along the outermost edge of the corn and move slowly along with minimal chance of detection.

If the entire outside perimeter of the cornfield has been worked and no deer have been seen, it's now time to assume that the whitetails are deeper within the confines of the corn, where they are most probably either feeding or bedding.

If the hunter is familiar with the terrain from previous scouting missions—before the corn was planted—he should try to recall the locations in the field where there were rock piles, soupy swales, sand pockets and the like. These exist in many fields, and farmers simply plow and plant around them. Once the surrounding corn has grown high, however, such places are hidden from view, and they are the very types of locations where deer commonly like to bed. The hunter should sneak up on these places during windy conditions, and he might very well shoot an unsuspecting deer right in its bed.

If firearms are being used and several hunting partners are working together, staging drives is an excellent way to push deer through the corn to the opposite end of the field, where standers are likely to have shots. But there are a few important points to bear in mind when using this method. If the cornfield is large, it is imperative that a large number of drivers—spaced no more than eight to 10 rows apart—be employed, because otherwise the deer, reluctant to leave the security of the cover, will tirelessly circle and sneak back between the drivers.

Consequently, if there are only a few hunters participating in the drive, only smaller cornfields where the animals can be moved effectively in a predetermined direction should be hunted.

Also, in the interest of safety, drives in cornfields should ideally include stand hunters placed in tree stands, or at least on some other elevated vantage points such as hillsides or knolls. This way, they will be able to look down and through the rows of corn to see both the escaping deer and their approaching partners. Likewise, when they shoot from such higher locations, the angles of their shots will be acutely downward, rather than horizontal.

Bowhunters can also enact drives in cornfields, but instead of hunting parallel with the rows in an attempt to push deer to standers in the distance, they should hunt perpendicular to the rows. In this type of situation, no hunters need be placed on stand.

Along the edge of the cornfield, the bowhunters should be spaced about 100 yards apart. The team leader at one end of this drive line should then use his arm to signal the first hunter on the far end to enter the field. As this hunter enters the first row, he should look right and left, then move on to the second row, and so on. After about 30 seconds, the drive master should then motion the next hunter to enter the cornfield in the same manner. What results is that instead of a straight and even drive line moving through the field, there is a diagonal shift across the field. Therefore if a hunter enters a row and sees a deer he wants to shoot at, he can do so to either his right or left with complete confidence in safety, knowing that his partners to either side are far ahead of or behind him. If he does not wish to shoot, the deer will usually run parallel to the rows and eventually offer a shot to one of the next hunters in line.

Finally, one of the shrewdest ways I know to evaluate potential cornfield hunting situations, especially in unfamiliar regions, is to go to a local airport and hire a small plane to fly over the terrain. Most pilots charge an average of $30 per hour, and if two hunters split the expense, the cost per person is not prohibitive. But most important, in one hour of flying about 500 feet above the ground, a hunter can learn more about an area than he can in two weeks of driving back roads and scouting on foot. A topographic map should be brought along and the location and configuration of every cornfield in the region should be marked. Adjacent terrain and cover should be carefully examined, and it then should be easy to determine with a high level of accuracy how deer are living, moving and feeding in each specific region.

Believe me, if there are cornfields in the region you plan to hunt, you can be sure that there are bucks in the corn—if not continuously, then at least intermittently. In either case, you should make the effort to be on hand, too, and when you leave, the chances are excellent that you'll be dragging your deer behind you.

Back of Beyond Bucks

By Greg Miller

He was close. I hadn't heard or seen any-thing, yet I knew he was there. Every nerve in my body was tingling with anticipation. Slowly easing my .270 to the ready position, I waited. I didn't want to get caught off guard, but that's exactly what happened. The unmistakable sound of antlers rattling against branches told me that the deer that had just spooked was definitely a buck. Silently cursing myself, I remained as still as a statue, hoping for the best.

The buck had run only a short distance before stopping. There was no way he could have winded me, and I felt confident that he'd try to continue on his route by making a slight detour. I was right. A small twig snapped off to my left in the direction in which the deer had run, and seconds later a big-bodied buck stepped into a small clearing about 75 yards away. I hurriedly brought my gun to my shoulder, lined up the crosshairs and touched off a shot. The solid "thwack" of a bullet hitting home drifted back to me on the heels of the rifle's roar. The buck had vanished, but I could hear him crashing through the brush for a few seconds. Then all was silent.

I immediately climbed down from my tree stand and made my way to where the buck had been when I shot. There was a fair amount of hair but no blood. A little farther on, however, I found the start of a good blood trail. My hunting partners and I recovered the eight-pointer later that night with the aid of a lantern. I was extremely proud of this partic-ular animal, even though I have taken larger bucks.

I had taken him on, one on one, in his own environ-ment and I came out the victor.

I first located this buck just a few days before the start of the nine-day gun season in Wisconsin. I was scouting an area that had produced for me in the past when I came across the big deer's hoof prints in the fresh snow. The size of his track was enough to take my breath away! There was no doubt that this was a mature whitetail buck. There was also no doubt where I'd be concentrating my hunting ef-forts come opening day. There was one drawback, however, and I was fully aware of it. The tract of land the big buck called home was one of the big-gest, roadless pieces of real estate in the vicinity. A true wilderness area. Yet, I went into the season with complete confidence that I could eventually figure out the buck's travel pattern and get a chance at him. As indicated at the beginning of this article, I did, indeed, get my chance on the third day of the season, and I made the most of it.

Hunting for wilderness whitetails holds a special mystique for more than just a few deer hunters. Most hunts don't have as happy an ending as mine did. Still, for some unknown reason, wilderness hunting seems to cast a spell on almost everyone who tries it. Even unsuccessful hunters understand the special fascination of trekking through huge, roadless tracts of land for whitetail bucks. Although they fully understand that their chances of connect-ing on a big buck are slim at best, they return year after year to give it their best shot.

Part of the reason why wilderness deer hunters

Wilderness deer are difficult to hunt but the challenge is well worth the extra effort. Judd Cooney photo.

are attracted to the big country is the lack of hunting pressure, which makes for a quality hunt as far as I'm concerned. I may not see a lot of deer, but I can also go days without seeing another hunter. And if I do, it is usually a member of my own hunting group.

In 1984, seven hunters in my hunting group took six bucks during the gun deer season. In 1985, we went nine for nine. In 1986, we ended up with four bucks. We only had five hunters in camp that year. In 1987, we filled up on bucks—five for five. These are not all spikes and forkhorns, either. A lot of bucks are deer that most hunters would be proud to put their tag on. Our success rate during the bow season for deer is impressive as well.

Our system for success is not particularly complicated, nor is it a secret. It simply entails really knowing the country we hunt and paying strict attention to some very obvious details pertinent to whitetail deer and deer behavior.

Just what do I consider a wilderness area? Well, to be truthful, my definition contrasts sharply with Mr. Webster's. According to the dictionary, wilderness means "an absence of humans." Let's face it, there are few if any places left on earth where there is a complete absence of human presence. But it's as close as you can get.

Northern Minnesota, northern Wisconsin, northern Michigan and parts of Maine are all well-known as wilderness areas. Parts of the Adirondack Mountains in the East, the Ozarks in the South and the Rocky Mountains in the West could also be considered wilderness areas. Of course, much of the area where whitetails are found in Manitoba, Saskatchewan and Alberta is also wilderness. The tricks I've learned during 24 years of hunting wilderness bucks will work anywhere you have big woods.

I once had a long conversation with a fellow deer hunter who was at wit's end after trying for weeks to connect on a big wilderness buck.

"There's just too much country for that big buck to hide in," he complained. "I spend as much time as I can trying to get to know his stomping grounds a little better, but it seems fruitless. There's fresh sign throughout a 2-mile radius. How am I supposed to pick the one tree the buck will walk by when I'm there waiting?"

This is probably the number-one complaint I hear from hunters who have had their fill of attempting to figure out a wilderness buck. I have to admit that it is a complex problem, but it's one that definitely can be solved. Of the utmost importance is getting to know the exact lay of the land in the areas you plan on hunting. First of all, purchase some topographic maps of the areas you are going to hunt. These little beauties are as valuable as any other piece of your hunting equipment. Then get out and do some legwork. Carry the maps with you while you're walking in the woods. You'd be surprised at how fast you'll be able to familiarize yourself with a big block of land by walking and studying your map. Normally, we'll locate a likely looking spot on our map and then walk in to that spot. Nine times out of ten, we find something worthwhile.

Hunting a particular buck in a 20-square-mile roadless tract of land really can be very special. The previously mentioned hunter asked me, "How am I supposed to pick that one certain tree out of the thousands out there?" It can be done, believe me.

First of all, even though there may be fresh deer sign throughout the entire 4 or 5 miles of the buck's range, there will be one core area in which the buck will spend the most time. How do you find it? Here's where the legwork begins. Hopefully, you can do most of the scouting you need to do in the spring. There are two very important reasons for this. First, you don't want to be messing around scouting for sign during the open season. *Never* take a chance on alerting a big buck that you're fooling around in his home town while you're trying to hunt him. Secondly, sign is much easier to read in the spring. Rubs, scrapes and an occasional shed antler can tell you a lot about a certain buck or bucks. These things are much easier to find in the spring immediately after the snow melts. Plus, if you run a big wilderness buck out of his bedding area in the spring, he'll eventually return and forget about the whole incident by the time hunting season opens in the fall.

Though you may find rubs and scrapes scattered all throughout the buck's home range, you will usually find a real concentration in his core area. Concentrate your scouting efforts there. Hopefully, you'll find the buck's prime bedding area. Most times, this bedding area will be found in the thickest, most impenetrable part of the core area. If the terrain is swampy, look for the bucks to bed on small "islands" or high spots where they can evade hunters but stay dry while bedded down. Again, you might be able to use your topo maps to locate these high spots.

If you plan on hunting in or near a bedding area, remember that you must take every precaution to keep the buck from detecting your presence. I'll not argue that this is the best spot to try and waylay a big buck. However, most bowhunters don't realize just how careful you have to be when hunting near a buck's bedroom. Keep wind direction in mind at all times when selecting stand sites.

I prefer to hunt rub lines during the pre-rut for big bucks. A whitetail buck of any size just cannot resist rubbing his antlers on something every single day once the velvet has been shed. Because bucks are spending most of their time in the core area then, you'll find a lot more antler rubs there. Once the real rut begins, the bucks will start ranging out more, hence the reason for finding rubs made by a particular buck for miles in all directions away from the core area.

Hunting during the pre-rut is the best time to try and kill a big wilderness buck. At this time of the year, they are still using the travel patterns and runways that they've felt secure using during the late summer and early fall months. Consequently, this is where you'll find most of the rub lines established by a buck. Usually, the rub line will originate in or very near the buck's preferred bedding area. It will probably end up at a food or water source. If you can get away with it, try to locate your stand as close to the bedding area as possible. That way, the buck may show himself while there is still plenty of good shooting light left.

Just last year, I watched a huge buck as he nosed through an area. The big deer was well out of my effective bow range, so I was subjected to being a spectator. I learned a lot from the buck. First of all, he would never take more than three or four steps at any one time without stopping, looking and sniffing for danger. He would sometimes stand motionless for up to 20 minutes. Eventually, he'd flick his tail and take a few more steps, only to repeat the whole ritual again. The real rut was still a couple of weeks away, so although he was probably feeling the first stirrings of the breeding season, he wasn't showing the devil-may-care attitude oftentimes displayed by a buck caught up in the throes of an estrous-induced stupor. The buck was the epitome of caution and alertness. It took him more than an hour to go 100 yards.

Food plays a major role in dictating deer movement. Out of the 365 days of the year, the rut is a very short-lived thing. It may last only three weeks, give or take a few days. On the other hand, a whitetail deer has got to try to get something in its belly every single day. It's the survival of the fittest, and the fittest animals are those that are able to eat something on a daily basis. And if you don't think that a whitetail is keen on knowing where the best food sources are located in his range, guess again. That's why it's imperative to know the whereabouts of such things as stands of oak, fresh cuttings, regrowth after a fire, *any* type of agriculture and so on. Within a huge block of land, this may be just a small piece of the overall picture, but believe me, it will be a real magnet to almost all of the deer in the vicinity.

During a recent bow season for deer in Wisconsin, I located an alfalfa field in the northern part of the state. Now let me tell you, this type of thing is usually very rare in wilderness areas. You can just about imagine the sort of deer activity around that hay field. The great thing about this is the fact that I was the only person hunting the area. To make a long story short, on the very first night I stood near the alfalfa, I shot a 10-point buck with my bow. He was the fifth buck to walk by me at a range of 12 yards in less than five minutes. After loading the buck into my vehicle, I happened to look out into the field. It was full of deer! At least six of them were bucks!

A year later, my brother Jeff and I hunted an area that had been logged off the previous spring. We never saw fewer than 10 deer between us. During another bow season, I shot a hog of a buck in a preferred feeding area. This 214-pound eight-pointer teased me for three straight days before I finally got the exact shot I wanted.

Once the frenzy of the true rut begins, it becomes really tough to kill a big wilderness buck. There is absolutely no rhyme or reason for the behavior or travel patterns of bucks at this time. When they get with a hot doe, you can throw all of the information and data you've collected on deer right out the window. I have seen areas go from red hot to ice cold in a matter of 12 hours. A big buck may herd an estrous doe away from all of the other deer in an effort to get her alone. That may mean going to some isolated patch of brush or grass that only the buck knows about. Consequently, a lot of other, smaller bucks will follow at a safe distance, hoping to get in on the action. If you don't know where these breeding areas are, you can be out of the ball game during the peak of the rut. It's happened to me more times than I care to remember. In a really huge piece of real estate, finding one of these breeding areas can be quite a task.

Because wilderness deer are in contact with humans much less than their farmland relatives, it is imperative that a hunter be much more careful about such things as noise and human odor. Though you may be able to get away with just a little more when hunting deer in agricultural areas, you'll find just the opposite to be true in the wilderness. It only takes one mistake to send a big-woods buck into a nocturnal pattern. He then becomes virtually impossible to kill.

I'm very careful about washing all of my hunting clothes in baking soda and then storing them in plastic bags. I wear knee-high rubber boots on all of my hunting excursions. And, I use no scent of any kind. That's right, I said that I use no scent of any kind. No cover scents, no sex scents and no food scents. For some reason, a lot of hunters think that using a cover or attractant-type scent is the

Whitetail buck bedded down. Leonard Lee Rue III photo.

cure-all for hunting whitetails. My train of thought would suggest that maybe a commercially made scent might alarm a big buck more than it will relax him or pique his curiosity. As a rule of thumb, I try to remain odor free.

When entering and departing my hunting sites, I'm very careful not to make any unnecessary noise. The clang of a tree stand or, worse yet, the sound of a human voice can have disastrous results. Breaking a few small branches or twigs is sometimes unavoidable. But this is a sound that deer are used to hearing, so don't get shook up if it happens. Be more concerned with unnatural noises, such as the sound that a nylon backpack makes as it zips through the brush, for example.

Wisconsin's gun deer season usually opens after the peak of the rut. Hunting for wilderness whitetails at this time can be challenging, to say the least. The biggest mistake most gun hunters make is that they hunt breeding or rut areas for bucks when, for the most part, the breeding is over.

A guy who hunts out of our gun-hunting camp shot a tremendous whitetail buck during the 1983 gun season. The season opened very near November 15 that year, and the bucks were still actively pursuing does. He shot his buck as it came charging into view, obviously absorbed by the feeling of peak rut. From 1984–86, this fellow hunted that same stand and never saw as much as a fawn, let alone a deer with antlers. The reason? My buddy was hunting a breeding area in years when the rut was over. As I said, the bucks were still pretty sexually active during the opening weekend of gun season in 1983. In the next three years, Wisconsin's firearms deer season opened a full week later, on a date closer to November 23. By then, the rut is about over and the bucks are back using the haunts they frequent during the pre-rut. Hunting travel routes going to and from known food sources would be much more productive than hunting breeding areas. Rub lines once again become a very good place to set up an ambush, as these are the routes that the bucks feel secure and comfortable using.

Gang-driving deer effectively is just about a lost cause in the big country. But getting deer, especially bucks, to move in a direction you want them to is not impossible. Once again, this entails knowing the exact lay of the land and, more importantly, how the deer in a specific area will react to human intrusion. Our hunting group and a couple of others I know have become proficient at pushing bucks past waiting hunters. Ideally, we like to have no more than six hunters involved in this type of a hunt. We have even made these pushes with as few as two people. Remember, the more hunters you have, the more human scent and noise you have.

First of all, we like to know where a certain buck or bucks may be bedding. We then send our standers into certain prearranged ambush points. At a designated time, one or two drivers start into the bedding area. Moving slowly and letting the wind blow directly from them to the deer, the pushers attempt to get the bucks to sneak out of the bedding area and past one of the standers. We like to make the bucks think that we're not trying to drive or herd them in any way. If they suspect a setup, they're more likely to remain hidden.

A few years back, five of us made two different pushes on the sixth day of the gun season. We killed three deer on those two pushes. Big deal, you might say. To us, it certainly was. You see, those three deer were taken in a block of land that was 18 miles square and without a through road. One of my hunting partners on that day, Paul Gumness, knows that piece of land as well or better than I do. Putting our heads together the night before we made those pushes, we came up with an effective plan of attack. It worked to perfection. On the second push, I shot a big, thick-necked eight-point buck with an 18½-inch spread. He was sneaking out the side of the push and heading for an alder-choked creek bottom when I ambushed him. Paul and I figured out exactly what that buck would do even before he did it.

We don't always win. During the 1987 gun season, three of us played hide-and-seek with a monster buck for five days. It seemed that the buck always managed to do the right thing at the right time. On two separate occasions, I heard him walk by me on one of these pushes. Both times, he was in brush too thick to attempt a shot. I strongly suspect that the buck somehow knew exactly where I was positioned each time. Even though I was walking almost a mile out of my way to get into the area without being detected, that big fella knew the game plan. He was a perfect 10-pointer about 18 or 19 inches wide, with extremely long tines and good mass. I originally found this buck during the bow season and watched him tend a doe in a open beaver marsh on an early November evening. I was perched in a tree stand only 50 yards away, so you might say I got a real good look at him. He'll be there again next year.

If we get a fresh snowfall, we can do much better at figuring out where a big buck may be holding. Although tracking down a big wilderness buck is tough business, it can be done. Once again, you must know the country intimately, if for no other reason than to just keep from getting hopelessly lost. (It's no real pleasure to spend a night in the woods.) The bucks we've tracked definitely like to make a circle to get back to where we started them, but that circle may be 5 or 6 miles around. Attempting to get your standers ahead of the buck can be difficult at best. I'd say that you're much better off tracking the deer alone or with one other person walking off to one side and slightly behind you. Sneak along and try to pick the buck off if and when he relaxes his guard.

Tracking a wilderness buck is not a method of deer hunting I would recommend to everyone. More times than not, the buck wins. And unless you actually see the deer that made the track you're following, you could be taking an awful chance. I've seen very few deer hunters who could tell a buck track from a big doe track just by looking at them. There's nothing more frustrating than tracking a big deer all day and then finding out that your "buck" is really a big, slick-headed doe. I've heard of it happening almost every year.

I have to admit, though, that we have taken up a rack simply by looking at it. But we hunt these same bucks all during the bow season. You might say that we get to know our deer intimately. And some of the bucks are so large that there's no doubt when you see their hoofprint in the snow. Even if I run a buck such as this through a herd of other deer, I can still keep on his track at a trot. These bucks often have a track almost as large as a calf elk, so I can separate their print from another deer's simply by glancing at it.

Wilderness whitetail hunting may not be even close to a sure thing, but that's the way it is. It isn't easy. The wilderness deer hunters I know who are consistently successful have gotten that way because of a lot of hard work and dedication. There's no other explanation. Luck plays such a small role that it's not even worth mentioning.

Next Year's Deer

By John O. Cartier

Most whitetail hunters have heard and read too many times that it's best to hunt from a stand (blind), and that the blind should be built long before the hunting season begins. The veteran hunter knows that this apparently logical statement is 50 percent dead wrong. I'll never forget the first time I learned that the worst period to build a blind can be long before the hunting season begins.

I'd heard several stories from landowners and hunters about sightings of a particularly large trophy buck in a specific area only a few miles from my rural home in northern Michigan. The men who had seen this buck claimed that it was an unusually wide-racked 12-pointer, and that its antlers were so light-colored that they looked almost like ivory. No hunter had ever seen the buck during the fall hunting seasons, but he had been sighted several times during the spring and summer over a period of three years.

The mystery and intrigue in these stories prompted me to make a try for this whitetail. I knew a farmer who owned 320 acres in the area that the buck frequented, and he gave me permission to hunt a small woodlot on his spread.

I began scouting it in June. There were deer tracks all over in those hills of hardwoods. I picked a stand site that seemed ideal. It was on the side of a ridge that overlooked three ravines that all funneled down to a major runway 50 yards below me. I reasoned that deer working down any of the ravines or traveling that well-used runway would be almost bound to present perfect shots.

I built a small blind with used lumber that almost matched the color of numerous blowdowns in the area. Several months earlier, we'd had a tremendous windstorm that had bordered on the ferocity of a tornado. Wind gusts had ripped mature beech and cherry trees right out of the ground. The roots of many hemlocks couldn't hold against the smashing force of the wind. In woodlots, the trees that had toppled had gone down in a line that ran from northwest to southeast. It was that way in the woodlot where I built my blind in July. The weathered lumber seemed to blend right in with the windfalls that ran in a line across still another ravine behind my blind. The foliage was so thick in that ravine that I couldn't see how many windfalls were there, but it didn't seem to matter because the deer apparently were going to show in front of my position.

I was in that blind long before dawn on the first day of rifle deer season. I hadn't been back to the woodlot since before the leaves had fallen, and the coming of daylight brought some new revelations. There were a lot more windfalls in the area than I had expected to see, and the entire woodlot was far more open than I had assumed it would be. Within moments, I was into the worse case of buck fever I've ever had.

Though the odds must have been about a million to one, the first deer I saw was the huge ivory-racked buck. He was unaware of my presence, only about 70 yards away, but in a location where I couldn't get a shot. I was lucky I spotted him at all because he was in the ravine behind my blind where I hadn't expected to see any deer. I have no idea why I turned and looked back there—maybe it was a sixth sense of some kind.

Even as I turned my head, I didn't see the buck, just a flicker of movement, probably a switch of his tail. Then, I spotted the light-colored antlers. Suddenly, the whole deer was in focus. For maybe three seconds, I was looking at a wide-open, dream-shot

45

opportunity. During that flash of time, there wasn't a twig between us. I bent low, grabbed my .243 Winchester from its rest against a beech trunk, whirled around on the box I was sitting on and whipped the rifle to my shoulder, staring toward the spot where I'd seen the deer.

He had moved only a few feet, but he was now partially hidden in a tangle of blowdowns. My heart began pounding furiously as I realized that I shouldn't yet even try a shot. The buck's neck and chest were hidden behind massive limbs. "Wait him out," I told myself. "He doesn't know you're here, and he's barely moving. You'll get your chance. Don't do anything dumb."

I'll never really know whether I did anything dumb or not. Maybe I should have tried getting one of my 100-grain bullets through those tangles.

The buck kept moving and grazing while I kept watching him through my scope and waiting for him to step somewhere in that maze of blowdowns where I could touch off a reasonable shot. The pressure of being that close to such a fine trophy and not being able to shoot was just too much for my nervous system. I was aware that the palms of my hands were sweating and that my arms were beginning to twitch and shake. The longer I waited, the worse the buck fever became.

Although the entire episode lasted no more than three or four minutes, it seemed like hours. Every move the buck made put him behind ever-thicker cover. It was almost as though he had planned it that way. I'll always wonder whether maybe he really did, but it still seems impossible. Suddenly, he was gone. I just didn't see him anymore, though I kept staring and staring. Then, I realized that he had walked behind a knoll that I hadn't noticed. The dream buck was gone. I never saw him again—ever. I don't think any hunter ever got a shot at him. News of a rack like that would travel fast in my area. Two years later, there were still reports of a few people seeing the buck in the late summer, then nothing. It was as though the whole thing had been some kind of a dream.

Anyway, after the buck had eluded me, I was so worked up and shaking so much that I had to get out of the blind and walk around awhile to try to calm down. I walked over to the ravine and immediately spotted a well-used runway showing a great many fresh deer tracks. I was greatly surprised because I couldn't recall having seen any amount of deer sign back in there during my midsummer scouting. The situation so intrigued me that I walked down to the bottom of the ravines in front of my blind where I had previously seen signs of so much deer travel. Now, there was practically none. It was immediately obvious that the area's whitetails had drastically changed their travel routes since the last time I had been there.

I mentally kicked myself when it dawned on me what my discovery meant. If I had done my preseason scouting a few days, instead of a few months, before the season opened, I would have been aware

of that runway where the buck had been and I would have been watching that precise area. And if I had been watching in that direction, I most likely would have seen the buck much sooner, probably soon enough to have had a wide-open shot. The thought replaced my lingering buck fever with an enormous feeling of disgust.

Although that incident happened many years ago, it focused my ever-growing fascination on the subject of off-season scouting. In recent years, it has become increasingly clear to me that preseason scouting isn't nearly as beneficial as post-season scouting. Whitetails in heavily hunted country often change their habits dramatically from the day before rifle and shotgun seasons begin to the day after.

I sincerely believe that the only reason why I saw that trophy buck at all was because the time was daybreak of the first day of rifle season. I would bet that soon afterward, when the buck began hearing lots of shooting, he immediately vacated the area and traveled to some secret spot where he knew from previous years' experience that there wouldn't be any hunters. I believe that's why hunters never spotted that buck during hunting seasons. He simply wasn't around.

All whitetails do that to some extent. They change their routines when the gunfire begins. They vacate given areas for others that offer more safety. This in itself promotes the necessity for using travel routes far different than those used before the hunting season opens.

Another very important factor is the availability of food. Deer that feed in crop fields have to look elsewhere after the crops are harvested. After one natural crop—say, beechnuts—is consumed, the animals have to look for another natural crop on which to feed. All of this points out that when you select a stand site, you want to select a place where the deer will be when you're hunting them, not where they were prior to the season.

A further factor to keep in mind is that you're not going to learn much about deer movement patterns while you're actually hunting on a stand. You're sitting constantly in one spot, waiting for a buck to come to you. You have almost no contact with what the animals are doing outside your immediate area.

The best way to lick all of these disadvantages is to do most of your scouting the week after your hunting season ends. This is the time when you'll find whitetails in the places they go as soon as the shooting starts. The behavior of the deer is still the same as it was when the hunting season was open. The animals are feeding in the same places, traveling the same runways, and are still on the lookout for hunters because they have no inkling that the gunners have all gone home to stay. Also, and of great importance, the terrain looks the same as it did during deer season. When you have this last ad-

Post-season is the best time to search out a buck's bedding area. Backtrack right to him. Denver Bryan photo.

Whitetail buck rubbing antlers. Irene Vandermolen photo.

vantage, you'll almost never build a blind in the wrong place, as I did when trying for the ivory-racked buck.

Many unsuccessful hunters, disgusted with having to face another winter without venison, decide to hunt a new area next deer season. If you're in this group, decide first to hunt a place that has the optimum number of whitetails per square mile. It's relatively easy to do this.

Studies by deer biologists in several midwestern states have shown that forest growth consisting of seedlings, saplings or brush of less than 5 inches in diameter can support about 40 deer per square mile during the winter. By contrast, a square mile of forest harboring trees with trunk diameters of five to 11 inches will hold only 10 deer. Surprisingly, another square mile showing saw timber (trees of more than 12 inches in diameter) will support about 20 white-tails. A good rule of thumb is the thicker the brush, the more deer you'll find, particularly in edge-cover brush.

In the upper Midwest and other states where winter can be severe, the early spring is the ideal time to home in on general whitetail hotspot areas. Snow cover always melts first in open fields, where sunshine may hit all day. Deer are always attracted to the edges of these fields, where they find first bare ground and the resultant first edible weeds and grasses.

Scouting at this time consists of no more than driving back roads in terrain consisting of crop fields, abandoned farmland, and mixed woodlots showing the ideal types of edge-cover brush. Drive through this type of country shortly after dawn or at dusk, and you may be amazed at the high number of whitetails you'll see. In my area of Michigan, it's not unusual to see 50 or more deer in a single

field during spring breakup—but certainly not in all fields showing apparently similar terrain. I've seen 100 deer in a field a mile away from another field that held no deer, even though the latter field seemed to offer even better adjacent edge cover. Suffice it to say that for reasons I can only guess at, whitetails definitely prefer certain areas over others. Find a field showing lots of deer, and you won't be too far from a hunting hotspot.

The next step is to find where that hotspot is likely to be. The best bet may be to look for buck rubs in ideal edge cover. When you find a fair number of rubs in a given area, you can be sure that the area is favored by bucks, or at least it was last fall. Check around for scars of rubs made in previous years. They may be weathered and old, but you can spot them if you look closely. When you find them, you can be assured that bucks have been using the area for several years, a good indication that several bucks will probably be in that area next hunting season.

An excellent bet in the early spring, while there's still some snow in edge-cover thickets, is to follow large sets of deer tracks that probably were made by bucks. Don't follow tracks in the direction that the animal was traveling. Turn around and backtrack him to find out where he has been. You'll find his feeding and bedding areas, and the travel routes he uses while moving to and from these areas. This is an extremely useful technique when the first snow cover develops immediately after deer season closes. Now, you can pinpoint how deer are using travel routes while they still think that they are being hunted.

At this time in the late fall or early winter, you'll almost always find bedding areas that are not visible from buildings, roads, or other sites of human activity. They'll be in gullies, behind knolls, in thick brush behind broken terrain, in river bottoms, and in other places where normal human activities can't be seen or heard. Hunted deer want to bed in places where they can be immediately alerted to the oncoming sounds of human activity where such activity isn't supposed to be.

I had another dramatic example of this trait last fall during Michigan's late Canada goose season. With firearms deer season over, I was scouting for geese in a secluded cornfield where I'd had great shooting the year before. I had to walk a half-mile to get to the field, which was in a lowland area surrounded by hardwoods.

When I approached the 80-acre field from the north, I had to cross a 50-yard-wide gully that was laced with thick brush. The first time that I walked over the ridge and started down the bank, that gully seemed to explode with deer. White flags seemed to be flying almost everywhere. I spotted at least three bucks with fine racks, and a dozen or so other deer.

That experience was so fascinating that I returned to the gully the next morning, even though I had found no geese. There were a bunch of deer in the

Tree rubbed by rutting buck. Leonard Lee Rue III photo.

gully again, including several easy-to-spot bucks. Later in the year, I asked the landowner whether I could hunt deer there but was turned down.

Anyway, backtracking deer during the off-season can easily turn up bedding bonanzas, and if you find them right after the hunting season closes, you can almost bet that the deer will return to the same place as soon as firearms deer hunting begins next fall. This fact emphasizes the importance of "structure." Any seasoned fisherman is well aware of how important a lake's bottom structure is to fishing success, but most deer hunters don't even consider the fact that terrain structure dictates how whitetails will behave and where they'll travel.

The key to selecting good structure is to look for edge cover that has dips and depressions. Deer hate to use level areas because they know that they can be seen from many adjacent places. Conversely, a deer in most any type of ravine, gully or other depression feels relatively secure because it knows that it is hidden.

Many years ago, I used to hunt an area of sand dunes harboring pockets of scrub pine. I loved to hunt there because I'd often see deer up to a half-mile away. It was like hunting in the relatively open foothills of the western states. It would often amaze me how frequently I would suddenly see a deer standing in clear view on the edge of a sand dune where seconds before there had been nothing. I'm sure that in all of those cases, the animals had simply been using dips and depressions in the dunes to stay out of sight until their travel route suddenly forced them over some sort of ridge. I shot a lot of deer in those dunes that would suddenly appear in full sight less than 100 yards away. They had probably been close to me for a long time, though I'd had no inkling of their presence.

Similar incidents through the years convinced me of the importance of the structure concept. Whitetails want to be in places that are down, hidden under lips of land or behind thick edge cover. You'll almost never find runways, or whitetails, on elevated structure such as ridges or the tops of hills and knolls. Remember also that deer generally feel threatened by danger from above, not below. They want to be in places where the only possible danger can come from above. In most whitetail country, the best time to find these places is after all foliage is down. Now, say the week after deer season, you can easily see the dips, depressions and so forth that were invisible to the hunter who scouted during the summer. Look for the thickest and most uneven cover in the area. That's where the deer are going to be when they're being hunted.

I do most of my off-season scouting in full daylight on sunny days because I'm looking for sign more than I'm looking for deer. Such things as old rubs, scrapes, structure and runaways are much easier to spot and study in good light. I haven't elaborated on scrapes in this article because a whole book could be written on this single subject, but I want to point out one fact. You won't find scrapes in many places, but mentally note those spots where you do. Many studies, particularly one in the Ozarks, have concluded that more than 95 percent of the scrapes made in a given area will be used again the following year if the bucks that made them are still alive. Scrapes will still show up distinctly right after deer season closes.

Sometimes, you may be able to get your buck just by paying attention to what's happening around you, even if you're not actively scouting during the off-season. This happened to me last fall. There's a certain spot on the shoreline of an inland lake near my home where I sometimes stop to clean fish. The time was late October, just a few weeks before our November deer season. While I was filleting a nice catch of crappies, I became aware of some out-of-place noises.

Suddenly, I realized that I was listening to falling acorns. There were acorns bouncing off limbs, plopping onto the ground and even splashing into the lake under overhanging oak limbs. I'd heard acorns fall many times in years past, but I'd never heard so many falling in so short a time period. This made a great impression on me for two weeks.

I was aware that peak acorn crops come in three or four-year cycles, and I had recently read in the *Detroit Free Press* that the statewide crop was way down. So, the area I was in was a major exception to most areas in Michigan. I reasoned that the local whitetails knew that, too. Some very basic scouting confirmed that suspicion. There were signs of herds of deer pawing through the leaves while getting at the mast crop. The four-pointer I bagged a few weeks later was one of the easiest bucks I ever got. He dropped within 100 yards of where I had cleaned those crappies.

How to Avoid Bowhunting's Blunders

by Thomas L. Torget

Mistakes. Blunders. Miscues. Every bow-hunter makes them. That's how we learn. But though even the most successful bowhunter fouls up occasionally, he rarely repeats his mistakes. That's why his success rate increases over time. He realizes that in bowhunting, doing *most* things right is never enough. The margin for error is too small. When you're only 15 yards from a whitetail buck, the tiniest goof involving noise, scent, movement or equipment will leave you with a "white salute."

So, what does this say to the novice? Must he hunt for five years before he can anticipate success? Not at all. The careful, conscientious novice bowhunter *can be successful almost immediately.* To do so, however, he must avoid the critical mistake nearly every bowhunter makes during his first few years in the sport. By getting these important errors out of his hunting pattern immediately, the novice will enjoy success much sooner than he would otherwise.

The mistakes I'm talking about are ones that the novice may not even recognize. His newness to the sport causes him to overlook critical details. But details are the difference between harvesting a buck and merely enjoying a day in the woods. After a few seasons of missed opportunities, most bowhunters will have made and eliminated these seven mistakes. Eliminate them before making them, and you're several seasons closer to consistent success.

Mediocre stand placement: Finding a good stand location is never easy. Most hunters know that the task begins by locating a primary trail connecting bedding and feeding areas. The next step is finding the intersection of two or three secondary trails crossing the primary trail. Interpretation of deer tracks, droppings, rubs and scrapes tells the hunter which trails are most promising. Based on this information, he selects his stand site.

Once a well-traveled trail loaded with deer sign is found, many bowhunters think that their job is over. They shimmy up the nearest oak or pine, hang their tree stand and begin wondering whether the Pope and Young Club buck they're about to bag would look better on the right or left side of the family room's fireplace.

If they aren't careful about *exactly* where they place their stand, however, these bowhunters will end up with nothing but house dust on that family-room wall. Locating your stand along a well-used game trail ensures only one thing: You will *see* deer. To harvest a good buck, stand placement must be much more than simply okay—it must be *outstanding.* And it's easy to understand why when you consider what you're attempting to do. You're trying to stage a complex event in which all of the following occur: Deer will pass within 15 to 20 yards of your stand on a daily basis; at no time will these deer smell, see or hear you; and the deer will move in a direction that allows you to draw and shoot your bow without detection and without obstruction of arrow flight.

The first part—getting close to where deer pass—is what most bowhunters concentrate on, and it's obviously the most important. But unless you enjoy seeing deer come close, detect your presence and race away, you must recognize that getting close to deer is never enough when you bowhunt. When success depends on your ability to remain undetected while only 20 yards from an undisturbed deer, there can be no mistakes. You must do more than simply place your stand downwind from the game trail.

A common example of mediocre stand placement is placing yourself directly above rather than adjacent to a game trail. Shooting straight down at deer is almost always a bad idea. It's an awkward angle, few bowhunters practice it, and effective arrow placement is difficult. Far better shots are afforded the bowhunter on stand 10 to 20 yards adjacent to the game trail. And deer are much more likely to spot you if you're in a tree directly along a game trail than if you're off to one side.

Proper placement of stands requires plenty of background cover, whether you're in a tree stand or ground blind. When setting up a stand, I always assume that every deer passing by will look directly at me. So, I avoid silhouetting myself against the sky and place my tree stands at least 15 feet above the ground. A well-camouflaged hunter who remains motionless is rarely detected by deer. This is true even if the deer looks directly at him, as long as there is adequate background cover and the hunter does not move. But a single glance at a human torso swaying in the trees will send any deer scurrying.

It's critical that you anticipate the direction from which deer are most likely to approach. You won't be right every time, but by positioning yourself on stand according to the expected direction of travel, you minimize movement and thus bolster your chances of having a shot at undisturbed game.

Anticipating direction of travel is also a key to identifying shooting lanes. Many a trophy buck owes his survival to a tiny twig or leaf. That's all it takes to deflect an arrow and turn a "can't miss" opportunity into a bitter lesson. My first-ever shot at a whitetail buck was missed because I failed to notice a quarter-inch tree branch above my head while in a ground blind in south Texas. My 15-yard shot buried itself into the dirt at the buck's feet when my upper bow limb struck the branch upon release. Don't repeat my mistake. Identify several shooting lanes and clear them of branches that could interfere with a clear shot.

Insufficient attention to wind and scent: It's impossible to overstate the importance of wind and scent to a bowhunter's success. Just consider the enormous difference between a rifle hunter controlling his scent at 100 yards and a bowhunter controlling his at 15 yards.

Tim Whiteford, a well-known Houston bowhunter and bowhunting-equipment dealer, believes that most bowhunters consistently underestimate a deer's ability to detect human scent.

"Most bowhunters think that being 'pretty careful' about scent is enough," Whiteford explained. "But I believe that to be consistently successful, you must be a fanatic about scent. Most guys think that if they wear clean clothes, avoid aftershave and don't smoke on stand, they're 'scentless.' They're not. For example, they never even consider how much human scent is on the bow and arrows' they've been perspiring on all summer!"

Minimizing human scent takes effort. It means washing hunting clothes (including your hat) in scentless soap or baking soda, storing them in airtight containers such as plastic trash bags, bathing at least once daily with scentless soap and avoiding smelly places (two of the worst are gasoline stations

Though a bit thin on background cover, the overhead branches of this tree should effectively screen this bowhunter and help him avoid being detected by deer. Tom Huggler photo.

and roadside restaurants). Don't smoke, don't eat spicy foods, and don't use aftershave or scented deodorant. All of this can seem a big bother, and it's tempting to compromise a bit on details. But each compromise reduces your chances for success.

But even following these rituals won't leave you scentless. So, you must do what a buck does: constantly monitor wind direction and use it to your advantage. Deer always prefer to travel into the wind; so should you. A buck will move in a crosswind and, on occasion, in a tailwind under certain conditions (such as to avoid crossing an open area

Too low and too much in the open—this bowhunter has already been spotted by tattletale does. Proper stand placement is critical for hunting success. Richard P. Smith photo.

offering little cover). I keep track of wind direction by taping a 4-inch piece of sewing thread to my upper bow limb. The slightest whiff of wind will move it. It tells me how to approach my stand and helps me anticipate the most likely direction of game movement.

Throughout the season, winds shift due to weather changes. I do most of my hunting in Texas. During the early part of the October bow season, the wind usually blows out of the southeast. As cold fronts move in, the wind shifts to the north. The early fronts are mild, and the wind soon swings back to the southeast. The change can take a day or a week. A tree stand that's perfect in a southeast wind can be disastrous in a north wind. So, I usually place two tree stands at a promising game crossing. I'll use one in a southeast or east wind and the other in a north wind.

Careless approach to and from stands: I used to think that the hunt began when I climbed into my tree stand and ended when I climbed down. Travel to and from my stand, though always cautious in manner, was never "part of the hunt." That all changed the day I spooked six whitetails—including a beautiful eight-pointer—that were feeding 20 yards from my stand. I was headed to the stand for an afternoon hunt and was paying little attention to my approach. The deer spotted me as I moved through a relatively open area 60 yards from them. They snorted and disappeared in an instant.

A common mistake is shooting too soon. Unless a deer has detected you, there's no reason to expect him to race away. Be patient. The worst thing you can do is alert him to your presence by quickly swinging your bow into position and drawing for a quick shot. He's almost sure to see the movement and bolt away. And if he doesn't present a broadside or quartering away shot, let him pass. Chances are good that he'll be back tomorrow or next week. Shoot and miss, however, and the odds are high that you've seen the last of that buck for the season.

But don't be so patient that you pass up good shots to wait for perfect ones. I learned that lesson the day an eight-point Texas whitetail fed to within 18 yards of my tree stand. Standing broadside, head down and feeding, he offered me an excellent shot. Because I was convinced that he'd come closer, however, I elected to wait. Thirty seconds later, he caught my scent and exploded away.

Invariably, some of the deer passing your stand will look directly at you. When they do, don't assume that you must shoot instantly. I've had several shots at deer minutes after they'd given me the once-over. By remaining motionless, I convinced the deer that I was part of the landscape. If I make the tiniest move, however, I'll always be rewarded with a snort and a white salute. I've learned the hard way to be patient and take the first good shot.

Failure to take notes: For all of their cunning, deer are creatures of habit. This can be their undoing if you're wise enough to learn these habits. Not just general deer habits, but the habits of the individual bucks in the specific area you hunt.

Exactly when do they arrive at and leave their bedding areas? Do they travel on the right or left side of the creek? Where do they cross the creek? How does the moon phase affect their daily schedule? How do their travel patterns differ as the season progresses?

Careful observance throughout the season will provide you with answers to these key questions. Such answers offer critical clues to the habits of specific bucks. If you're like me and lack a photographic memory, it's best to keep thorough notes. I record everything of significance, including all weather conditions, moon phases, my time of arrival and departure from my stand, and all game sightings (including such details as direction of travel, time of sighting, behavior of the animal and so on). I also record any information about my hunting partners' game sightings.

Race At Morning

By William Faulkner

Charcoal drawing of William Faulkner by Soss Melik, courtesy National Portrait Gallery, Smithsonian Institution

I was in the boat when I seen him. It was jest dust-dark; I had jest fed the horses and clumb back down the bank to the boat and shoved off to cross back to camp when I seen him, about half a quarter up the river, swimming; jest his head above the water, and it no more than a dot in that light. But I could see that rocking chair he toted on it and I knowed it was him, going right back to that canebrake in the fork of the bayou where he lived all year until the day before the season opened, like the game wardens had give him a calendar, when he would clear out and disappear, nobody knowed where, until the day after the season closed. But here he was, coming back a day ahead of time, like maybe he had got mixed up and was using last year's calendar by mistake. Which was jest too bad for him, because me and Mister Ernest would be setting on the horse right over him when the sun rose tomorrow morning.

So I told Mister Ernest and we et supper and fed the dogs, and then I holp Mister Ernest in the poker game, standing behind his chair until about ten o'clock, when Roth Edmonds said, "Why don't you go to bed, boy?"

"Or if you're going to set up," Willy Legate said, "why don't you take a spelling book to set up over? He knows every cuss word in the dictionary, every poker hand in the deck and every whisky label in the distillery, but he can't even write his name. Can you?" he says to me.

"I don't need to write my name down," I said. "I can remember in my mind who I am."

"You're twelve years old," Walter Ewell said. "Man to man now, how many days in your life did you ever spend in school?"

"He ain't got time to go to school," Willy Legate said. "What's the use in going to school from September to middle of November, when he'll have to quit then to come in here and do Ernest's hearing for him? And what's the use in going back to school in January, when in jest eleven months it will be November fifteenth again and he'll have to start all over telling Ernest which way the dogs went?"

"Well, stop looking into my hand, anyway," Roth Edmonds said.

"What's that? What's that?" Mister Ernest said. He wore his listening button in his ear all the time, but he never brought the battery to camp with him because the cord would bound to get snagged ever time we run through a thicket.

"Willy says for me to go to bed!" I hollered.

"Don't you never call nobody 'mister'?" Willy said.

"I call Mister Ernest 'mister,' " I said.

"All right," Mister Ernest said. "Go to bed then. I don't need you."

"That ain't no lie," Willy said. "Deaf or no deaf, he can hear a fifty-dollar raise if you don't even move your lips."

So I went to bed, and after a while Mister Ernest come in and I wanted to tell him again how big them horns looked even half a quarter away in the river. Only I would 'a' had to holler, and the only time Mister Ernest agreed he couldn't hear was when we would be setting on Dan, waiting for me to point which way the dogs was going. So we jest laid down, and it wasn't no time Simon was beating the bottom of the dishpan with the spoon, hollering, "Raise up and get your four-o'clock coffee!" and I crossed the river in the dark this time, with the lantern, and fed Dan and Roth Edmondziz horse. It was going to be a fine day, cold and bright; even in the dark I could see the white frost on the leaves and bushes—jest exactly the kind of day that big old son of a gun laying up there in that brake would like to run.

Then we et, and set the stand-holder across for Uncle Ike McCaslin to put them on the stands where he thought they ought to be, because he was the oldest one in camp. He had been hunting deer in these woods for about a hundred years, I reckon, and if anybody would know where a buck would pass, it would be him. Maybe with a big old buck like this one, that had been running the woods for what would amount to a hundred years in a deer's life, too, him and Uncle Ike would sholy manage to be at the same place at the same time this morning—provided, of course, he managed to git away from me and Mister Ernest on the jump. Because me and Mister Ernest was going to git him.

Then me and Mister Ernest and Roth Edmonds sent the dogs over, with Simon holding Eagle and the other old dogs on leash because the young ones, the puppies, wasn't going nowhere until Eagle let them, nohow. Then me and Mister Ernest and Roth saddled up, and Mister Ernest got up and I handed him up his pump gun and let Dan's bridle go for him to git rid of the spell of bucking he had to git shut of every morning until Mister Ernest hit him between the ears with the gun barrel. Then Mister Ernest loaded the gun and give me the stirrup, and I got up behind him and we taken the fire road up toward the bayou, the four big dogs dragging Simon along in front with his single-barrel britch-loader slung on a piece of plow line across his back, and the puppies moiling along in ever'body's way. It was light now and it was going to be jest fine; the east already yellow for the sun and our breaths smoking in the cold still bright air until the sun would come up and warm it, and a little skim of ice in the ruts, and ever leaf and twig and switch and even the frozen clods frosted over, waiting to sparkle like a rainbow when the sun finally come up and hit them. Until all my insides felt light and strong as a balloon, full of that light cold strong air, so that it seemed to me like I couldn't even feel the horse's back I was straddle of—jest the hot strong muscles moving under the hot strong skin, setting up there without no weight atall, so that when old Eagle struck and jumped, me and Dan and Mister Ernest would go jest like a bird, not even touching the ground. It was jest fine. When that big old buck got killed today, I knowed that even if he had put it off another ten years, he couldn't 'a' picked a better one.

And sho enough, as soon as we come to the

bayou we seen his foot in the mud where he had come up out of the river last night, spread in the soft mud like a cow's foot, big as a cow's, big as a mule's, with Eagle and the other dogs laying into the leash rope now until Mister Ernest told me to jump down and help Simon hold them. Because me and Mister Ernest knowed exactly where he would be—a little canebrake island in the middle of the bayou, where he could lay up until whatever doe or little deer the dogs had happened to jump could go up or down the bayou in either direction and take the dogs on away, so he could steal out and creep back down the bayou to the river and swim it, and leave the country like he always done the day the season opened.

Drawing by Edward Shenton

Which is jest what we never aimed for him to do this time. So we left Roth on his horse to cut him off and turn him over Uncle Ike's standers if he tried to slip back down the bayou, and me and Simon, with the leashed dogs, walked on up the bayou until Mister Ernest on the horse said it was fur enough; then turned up into the woods about half a quarter above the brake because the wind was going to be south this morning when it riz, and turned down toward the brake, and Mister Ernest give the word to cast them, and we slipped the leash and Mister Ernest give me the stirrup again and I got up.

Old Eagle had done already took off because he knowed where that old son of a gun would be laying as good as we did, not making no racket atall yet, but jest boring on through the buck vines with the other dogs trailing along behind him, and even Dan seemed to know about that buck, too, beginning to souple up and jump a little through the vines, so that I taken my holt on Mister Ernest's belt already before the time had come for Mister Ernest to touch him. Because when we got strung out, going fast behind a deer, I wasn't on Dan's back much of the time nohow, but mostly jest strung out from my holt on Mister Ernest's belt, so that Willy Legate said that when we was going through the woods fast, it looked like Mister Ernest had a boy-size pair of empty overalls blowing out of his hind pocket.

So it wasn't even a strike, it was a jump. Eagle must 'a' walked right up behind him or maybe even stepped on him while he was laying there still thinking it was day after tomorrow. Eagle jest throwed his head back and up and said, "There he goes," and we even heard the buck crashing through the first of the cane. Then all the other dogs was hollering behind him, and Dan give a squat to jump, but it was against the curb this time, not jest the snaffle, and Mister Ernest let him down into the bayou and swung him around the brake and up the other bank. Only he never had to say, "Which way?" because I was already pointing past his shoulder, freshening my holt on the belt jest as Mister Ernest touched Dan with that big old rusty spur on his nigh heel, because when Dan felt it he would go off jest like a stick of dynamite, straight through whatever he could bust and over or under what he couldn't, over it like a bird or under it crawling on his knees like a mole or a big coon, with Mister Ernest still on him because he had the saddle to hold on to, and me still there because I had Mister Ernest to hold on to; me and Mister Ernest not riding him, but jest going along with him, provided we held on. Because when the jump come, Dan never cared who else was there neither; I believe to my soul he could 'a' cast and run them dogs by hisself, without me or Mister Ernest or Simon or nobody.

That's what he done. He had to; the dogs was already almost out of hearing. Eagle must 'a' been looking right up that big son of a gun's tail until he finally decided he better git on out of there. And now they must 'a' been getting pretty close to Uncle Ike's standers, and Mister Ernest reined Dan back and held him, squatting and bouncing and trembling like a mule having his tailed roached, while we listened for the shots. But never none come, and I hollered to Mister Ernest we better go on while I could still hear the dogs, and let Dan off, but still there wasn't no shots, and now we knowed the race had done already passed the standers, like that old son of a gun actually was a hant, like Simon and the other field hands said he was, and we busted out of a thicket, and sho enough there was Uncle Ike and Willy standing beside his foot in a soft patch.

"He got through us all," Uncle Ike said. "I don't know how he done it. I just had a glimpse of him. He looked big as a elephant, with a rack on his head you could cradle a yellin' calf in. He went right on down the ridge. You better get on, too; that Hog Bayou camp might not miss him."

So I freshened my holt and Mister Ernest touched Dan again. The ridge run due south; it was clear of vines and bushes so we could go fast, into the wind, too, because it had riz now, and now the sun was up, too; though I hadn't had time to notice it, bright and strong and level through the woods, shining and sparking like a rainbow on the frosted leaves. So we would hear the dogs again any time now as the wind got up; we could make time now, but still holding Dan back to a canter, because it was either going to be quick, when he got down to the standers from that Hog Bayou camp eight miles below ourn, or a long time, in case he got by them, too.

And sho enough, after a while we heard the dogs; we was walking Dan now to let him blow a while, and we heard them, the sound coming faint up the wind, not running now, but trailing because the big son of a gun had decided a good piece back, probably, to put a end to this foolishness, and picked hisself up and souled out and put about a mile between hisself and the dogs—until he run up on them other standers from that camp below. I could almost see him stopped behind a bush, peeping out and saying, "What's this? What's this? Is this whole durn country full of folks this morning?" Then looking back over his shoulder at where old Eagle and the others was hollering along after him while he decided how much time he had to decide what to do next.

Except he almost shaved it too fine. We heard the shots; it sounded like a war. Old Eagle must 'a' been looking right up his tail again and he had to bust on through the best way he could. "Pow, pow, pow, pow" and then "Pow, pow, pow, pow," like it must 'a' been three or four ganged right up on him before he had time even to swerve, and me hollering, "No! No! No! No!" because he was ourn. It was our beans and oats he et and our brake he laid in; we had been watching him every year, and it was like we had raised him, to be killed at last on our jump, in front of our dogs, by some strangers that would probably try to beat the dogs off and drag him away before we could even git a piece of the meat.

"Shut up and listen," Mister Ernest said. So I done it and we could hear the dogs; not just the others, but Eagle, too, not trailing no scent now and not baying no downed meat neither, but running hot on sight long after the shooting was over. I jest had time to freshen my holt. Yes, sir, they was running on sight. Like Willy Legate would say, if Eagle jest had a drink of whisky he would ketch that deer; going on, done already gone when we broke out of the thicket and seen the fellers that had done the shooting, five or six of them, squatting and crawling around, looking at the ground and the bushes, like maybe if they looked hard enough, spots of blood would bloom out on the stalks and leaves like frogstools or hawberries, with old Eagle still in hearing and still telling them that what blood they found wasn't coming out of nothing in front of him.

"Have any luck, boys?" Mister Ernest said.

"I think I hit him," one of them said. "I know I did. We're hunting blood now."

"Well, when you find him, blow your horn and I'll come back and tote him in to camp for you," Mister Ernest said.

So we went on, going fast now because the race was almost out of hearing again, going fast, too, like not jest the buck, but the dogs, too, had took a new leash on life from all the excitement and shooting.

We was in strange country now because we never had to run this fur before, we had always killed before now; now we had come to Hog Bayou that runs into the river a good fifteen miles below our camp. It had water in it, not to mention a mess of down trees and logs and such, and Mister Ernest checked Dan again, saying, "Which way?" I could just barely hear them, off to the east a little, like the old son of a gun had give up the idea of Vicksburg or New Orleans, like he first seemed to have, and had decided to have a look at Alabama, maybe, since he was already up and moving; so I pointed and we turned up the bayou hunting for a crossing, and maybe we could 'a' found one, except that I reckon Mister Ernest decided we never had time to wait.

We come to a place where the bayou had narrowed down to about twelve or fifteen feet, and Mister Ernest said, "Look out, I'm going to touch him" and done it; I didn't even have time to freshen my holt when we was already in the air, and then I seen the vine—it was a loop of grapevine nigh as big as my wrist, looping down right across the middle of the bayou—and I thought he seen it, too, and was jest waiting to grab it and fling it up over our heads to go under it, and I know Dan seen it because he even ducked his head to jump under it. But Mister Ernest never seen it atall until it skun back along Dan's neck and hooked under the head of the saddle horn, us flying on through the air, the loop of the vine gitting tighter and tighter until something somewhere was going to have to give. It was the saddle girth. It broke, and Dan going on and scrabbling up the other bank bare nekkid except for the bridle, and me and Mister Ernest and the saddle, Mister Ernest still setting in the saddle holding the gun, and me still holding onto Mister Ernest's belt, hanging in the air over the bayou in the tightened loop of that vine like in the drawed-back loop of a big rubber-banded slingshot, until it snapped back and shot us back across the bayou and flang us clear, me still holding onto Mister Ernest's belt and on the bottom now, so that when we lit I would 'a' had Mister Ernest and the saddle both on top of me if I hadn't clumb fast around the saddle and up Mister Ernest's side, so that when we landed, it was the saddle first, then Mister Ernest, and me on top, until I jumped up, and Mister Ernest still laying there with jest the white rim of his eyes showing.

"Mister Ernest!" I hollered, and then clumb down to the bayou and scooped my cap full of water and clumb back and throwed it in his face, and he opened his eyes and laid there on the saddle cussing me.

"God dawg it," he said, "why didn't you stay behind where you started out?"

"You was the biggest!" I said. "You would 'a' mashed me flat!"

"What do you think you done to me?" Mister Ernest said. "Next time, if you can't stay where you start out, jump clear. Don't climb up on top of me no more. You hear?"

"Yes, sir," I said.

So he got up then, still cussing and holding his back, and clumb down to the water and dipped some in his hand onto his face and neck and dipped some more up and drunk it, and I drunk some, too,

and clumb back and got the saddle and the gun, and we crossed the bayou on the down logs. If we could jest ketch Dan; not that he would have went them fifteen miles back to camp, because, if anything, he would have went on by hisself to try to help Eagle ketch that buck. But he was about fifty yards away, eating buck vines, so I brought him back, and we taken Mister Ernest's galluses and my belt and the whang leather loop off Mister Ernest's horn and tied the saddle back on Dan. It didn't look like much, but maybe it would hold.

"Provided you don't let me jump him through no more grapevines without hollering first," Mister Ernest said.

"Yes, sir," I said. "I'll holler first next time—provided you'll holler a little quicker when you touch him next time, too." But it was all right; we jest had to be a little easy getting up. "Now which-a-way?" I said. Because we couldn't hear nothing now, after wasting all this time. And this was new country, sho enough. It had been cut over and growed up in thickets we couldn't 'a' seen over even standing up on Dan.

But Mister Ernest never even answered. He jest turned Dan along the bank of the bayou where it was a little more open and we could move faster again, soon as Dan and us got used to that homemade cinch strop and got a little confidence in it. Which jest happened to be east, or so I thought then, because I never paid no particular attention to east then because the sun—I don't know where the morning had went, but it was gone, the morning and the frost, too—was up high now, even if my insides had told me it was past dinnertime.

And then we heard him. No, that's wrong; what we heard was shots. And that was when we realized how fur we had come, because the only camp we knowed about in that direction was the Hollyknowe camp, and Hollyknowe was exactly twenty-eight miles from Van Dorn, where me and Mister Ernest lived—jest the shots, no dogs nor nothing. If old Eagle was still behind him and the buck was still alive, he was too wore out now to even say, "Here he comes."

"Don't touch him!" I hollered. But Mister Ernest remembered that cinch strop, too, and he jest let Dan off the snaffle. And Dan heard them shots, too, picking his way through the thickets, hopping the vines and logs when he could and going under them when he couldn't. And sho enough, it was jest like before—two or three men squatting and creeping among the bushes, looking for blood that Eagle had done already told them wasn't there. But we never stopped this time, jest trotting on by with Dan hopping and dodging among the brush and vines dainty as a dancer. Then Mister Ernest swung Dan until we was going due north.

"Wait!" I hollered. "Not this way."

But Mister Ernest jest turned his face back over his shoulder. It looked tired, too, and there was a smear of mud on it where that ere grapevine had snatched him off the horse.

"Don't you know where he's heading?" he said. "He's done done his part, give everybody a fair open shot at him, and now he's going home, back to that brake in our bayou. He ought to make it exactly at dark."

And that's what he was doing. We went on. It didn't matter to hurry now. There wasn't no sound nowhere; it was that time in the early afternoon in November when don't nothing move or cry, not even birds, the peckerwoods and yellowhammers and jays, and it seemed to me like I could see all three of us—me and Mister Ernest and Dan—and Eagle, and the other dogs, and that big old buck, moving through the quiet woods in the same direction, headed for the same place, not running now but walking, that had all run the fine race the best we knowed how, and all three of us now turned like on a agreement to walk back home, not together in a bunch because we didn't want to worry or tempt one another, because what we had all three spent this morning doing was no play-acting jest for fun, but was serious, and all three of us was still what we was—that old buck that had to run, not because he was skeered, but because running was what he done the best and was proudest at; and Eagle and the dogs that chased him, not because they hated or feared him, but because that was the thing they done the best and was proudest at; and me and Mister Ernest and Dan, that run him not because we wanted his meat, which would be too tough to eat anyhow, or his head to hang on a wall, but because now we could go back and work hard for eleven months making a crop, so we would have the right to come back here next November—all three of us going back home now, peaceful and separate, but still side by side, until next year, next time.

Then we seen him for the first time. We was out of the cut-over now; we could even 'a' cantered, except that all three of us was long past that, and now you could tell where west was because the sun was already halfway down it. So we was walking, too, when we come on the dogs—the puppies and one of the old ones—played out, laying in a little wet swag, panting, jest looking up at us when we passed, but not moving when we went on. Then we

come to a long open glade, you could see about half a quarter, and we seen the three other old dogs and about a hundred yards ahead of them Eagle, all walking, not making no sound; and then suddenly, at the fur end of the glade, the buck hisself getting up from where he had been resting for the dogs to come up, getting up without no hurry, big, big as a mule, tall as a mule, and turned without no hurry still, and the white underside of his tail for a second or two more before the thicket taken him.

It might 'a' been a signal, a good-bye, a farewell. Still walking, we passed the other three old dogs in the middle of the glade, laying down, too, now jest where they was when the buck vanished, and not trying to get up neither when we passed; and still that hundred yards ahead of them, Eagle, too, not laying down, because he was still on his feet, but his legs was spraddled and his head was down; maybe jest waiting until we was out of sight of his shame, his eyes saying plain as talk when we passed, "I'm sorry, boys, but this here is all."

Mister Ernest stopped Dan. "Jump down and look at his feet," he said.

"Ain't nothing wrong with his feet," I said. "It's his wind has done give out."

"Jump down and look at his feet," Mister Ernest said.

So I done it, and while I was stooping over Eagle I could hear the pump gun go, "Snick-cluck. Snick-cluck. Snick-cluck" three times, except that I never thought nothing then. Maybe he was jest running the shells through to be sho it would work when we seen him again or maybe to make sho they was all buckshot. Then I got up again, and we went on, still walking; a little west of north now, because when we seen his white flag that second or two before the thicket hid it, it was on a beeline for that notch in the bayou. And it was evening, too, now. The wind had done dropped and there was a edge to the air and the sun jest touched the tops of the trees now, except jest now and then, when it found a hole to come almost level through onto the ground. And he was taking the easiest way, too, now, going straight as he could. When we seen his foot in the soft places he was running for a while at first after his rest. But soon he was walking, too, like he knowed, too, where Eagle and the dogs was.

And then we seen him again. It was the last time—a thicket, with the sun coming through a hole onto it like a searchlight. He crashed jest once; then he was standing there broadside to us, not twenty yards away, big as a statue and red as gold in the sun, and the sun sparking on the tips of his horns—they was twelve of them—so that he looked like he had twelve lighted candles branched around his head, standing there looking at us while Mister Ernest raised the gun and aimed at his neck, and the gun went, "Click. Snickcluck. Click. Snick-cluck. Click. Snick-cluck" three times, and Mister Ernest still holding the gun aimed while the buck turned and give one long bound, the white underside of his tail like a blaze of fire, too, until the thicket and the shadows put it out; and Mister Ernest laid the gun slow and gentle back across the saddle in front of him, saying quiet and peaceful, and not much louder than jest breathing, "God dawg. God dawg."

Then he jogged me with his elbow and we got down, easy and careful because of that ere cinch strop, and he reached into his vest and taken out one of the cigars. It was busted where I had fell on it, I reckon, when we hit the ground. He threwed it away and taken out the other one. It was busted, too, so he bit off a hunk of it to chew and throwed the rest away. And now the sun was gone even from the tops of the trees and there wasn't nothing left but a big red glare in the west.

"Don't worry," I said. "I ain't going to tell them you forgot to load your gun. For that matter, they don't need to know we ever seed him."

"Much oblige," Mister Ernest said. There wasn't going to be no moon tonight neither, so he taken the compass off the whang leather loop in his buttonhole and handed me the gun and set the compass on a stump and stepped back and looked at it. "Jest about the way we're headed now," he said, and taken the gun from me and opened it and put one shell in the britch and taken up the compass, and I taken Dan's reins and we started, with him in front with the compass in his hand.

And after a while it was full dark; Mister Ernest would have to strike a match ever now and then to read the compass, until the stars come out good and we could pick out one to follow, because I said, "How fur do you reckon it is?" and he said, "A little more than one box of matches." So we used a star when we could, only we couldn't see it all the time because the woods was too dense and we would git a little off until he would have to spend another match. And now it was good and late, and he stopped and said, "Get on the horse,"

"I ain't tired," I said.

"Get on the horse," he said. "We don't want to spoil him."

Because he had been a good feller ever since I had knowed him, which was even before that day two years ago when maw went off with the Vicksburg roadhouse feller and the next day pap didn't come home neither, and on the third one Mister Ernest rid Dan up to the door of the cabin on the river he let us live in, so pap could work his piece of land and run his fish line, too, and said, "Put that gun down and come on here and climb up behind."

So I got in the saddle even if I couldn't reach the stirrups, and Mister Ernest taken the reins and I must 'a' went to sleep, because the next thing I knowed a buttonhole of my lumberjack was tied to the saddle horn with that ere whang cord off the compass, and it was good and late now and we wasn't fur, because Dan was already smelling water, the river. Or maybe it was the feed lot itself he smelled, because we struck the fire road not a quarter below it, and soon I could see the river, too, with the white mist laying on it soft and still as cotton.

Then the lot, home; and up yonder in the dark, not no piece akchully, close enough to hear us unsaddling and shucking corn prob'ly, and sholy close enough to hear Mister Ernest blowing his horn at the dark camp for Simon to come in the boat and git us, that old buck in his brake in the bayou; home, too, resting, too, after the hard run, waking hisself now and then, dreaming of dogs behind him or maybe it was the racket we was making would wake him, but not neither of them for more than jest a little while before sleeping again.

Then Mister Ernest stood on the bank blowing until Simon's lantern went bobbing down into the mist; then we clumb down to the landing and Mister Ernest blowed again now and then to guide Simon, until we seen the lantern in the mist, and then Simon and the boat; only it looked like ever time I set down and got still, I went back to sleep, because Mister Ernest was shaking me again to git out and climb the bank into the dark camp, until I felt a bed against my knees and tumbled into it.

Then it was morning, tomorrow; it was all over now until next November, next year, and we could come back. Uncle Ike and Willy and Walter and Roth and the rest of them had come in yestiddy, soon as Eagle taken the buck out of hearing and they knowed that deer was gone, to pack up and be ready to leave this morning for Yoknapatawpha, where they lived, until it would be November again and they could come back again.

So, as soon as we et breakfast, Simon run them back up the river in the big boat to where they left their cars and pickups, and now it wasn't nobody but jest me and Mister Ernest setting on the bench against the kitchen wall in the sun; Mister Ernest smoking a cigar—a whole one this time that Dan hadn't had no chance to jump him through a grapevine and bust. He hadn't washed his face neither where that vine had throwed him into the mud. But that was all right, too; his face usually did have a smudge of mud or tractor grease or beard stubble on it, because he wasn't jest a planter; he was a farmer, he worked as hard as ara one of his hands and tenants—which is why I knowed from the very first that we would git along, that I wouldn't have no trouble with him and he wouldn't have no trouble with me, from that very first day when I woke up and maw had done gone off with that Vicksburg roadhouse feller without even waiting to cook breakfast, and the next morning pap was gone, too, it was almost night the next day when I heard a horse coming up and I taken the gun that I had already throwed a shell into the britch when pap never come home last night, and stood in the door while Mister Ernest rid up and said, "Come on. Your paw ain't coming back neither."

"You mean he give me to you?" I said.

"Who cares?" he said. "Come on. I brought a lock for the door. We'll send the pickup back tomorrow for what ever you want."

So I come home with him and it was all right, it was jest fine—his wife had died about three years ago—without no women to worry us or take off in the middle of the night with a durn Vicksburg roadhouse jake without even waiting to cook breakfast. And we would go home this afternoon, too, but not jest yet; we always stayed one more day after the others left because Uncle Ike always left what grub they hadn't et, and the rest of the homemade corn whisky he drunk and that town whisky of Roth Edmondziz he called Scotch that smelled like it come out of a old bucket of roof paint; setting in the sun for one more day before we went back home to git ready to put in next year's crop of cotton and oats and beans and hay; and across the river yonder, behind the wall of trees where the big woods started, that old buck laying up today in the sun, too—resting today, too, without nobody to bother him until next November.

So at least one of us was glad it would be eleven months and two weeks before he would have to run that fur that fast again. So he was glad of the very same thing we was sorry of, and so all of a sudden I thought about how maybe planting and working and then harvesting oats and cotton and beans and hay wasn't jest something me and Mister Ernest done three hundred and fifty-one days to fill in the time until we could come back hunting again, but it was something we had to do, and do honest and good during the three hundred and fifty-one days, to have the right to come back into the big woods and hunt for the other fourteen; and the fourteen days that old buck ran in front of dogs wasn't jest something to fill his time until the three hundred and fifty-one when he didn't have to, but the running and the risking in front of guns and dogs was something he had to do for fourteen days to have the right not to be bothered for the other three hundred and fifty-one. And so the hunting and the farming wasn't two different things atall—they was jest the other side of each other.

"Yes," I said. "All we got to do now is put in that next year's crop. Then November won't be no time away atall."

"You ain't going to put in the crop next year," Mister Ernest said. "You're going to school."

So at first I didn't even believe I had heard him. "What?" I said. "Me? Go to school?"

"Yes," Mister Ernest said. "You must make something out of yourself."

"I am," I said. "I'm doing it now. I'm going to be a hunter and a farmer like you."

"No," Mister Ernest said. "That ain't enough any more. Time was when all a man had to do was just farm eleven and a half months, and hunt the other half. But not now. Now just to belong to the farming business and the hunting business ain't enough. You got to belong to the business of mankind."

"Mankind?" I said.

"Yes," Mister Ernest said. "So you're going to school. Because you got to know why. You can belong to the farming and hunting business and you can learn the difference between what's right and what's wrong, and do right. And that used to be enough—just to do right. But not now. You got to know why it's right and why it's wrong, and be able to tell the folks that never had no chance to learn it; teach them how to do what's right, not just because they know it's right, but because they know now why it's right because you just showed them, told them, taught them why. So you're going to school."

"It's because you been listening to that durn Will Legate and Walter Ewell!" I said.

"No," Mister Ernest said.

"Yes!" I said. "No wonder you missed that buck yestiddy, taking ideas from the very fellers that let him git away, after me and you had run Dan and the dogs durn night clean to death! Because you never even missed him! You never forgot to load that gun! You had done already unloaded it a purpose! I heard you!"

"All right, all right," Mister Ernest said. "Which would you rather have? His bloody head and hide on the kitchen floor yonder and half his meat in a pickup truck on the way to Yoknapatawpha County, or him with his head and hide and meat still together over yonder in that brake, waiting for next November for us to run him again?"

"And git him, too," I said. "We won't even fool with no Willy Legate and Walter Ewell next time."

"Maybe," Mister Ernest said.

"Yes," I said.

"Maybe," Mister Ernest said. "The best word in our language, the best of all. That's what mankind keeps going on: Maybe. The best days of his life ain't the ones when he said 'Yes' beforehand: they're the ones when all he knew to say was 'Maybe.' He can't say 'Yes' until afterward because he not only don't know it until then, he don't want to know 'Yes' until then. . . . Step in the kitchen and make me a toddy. Then we'll see about dinner."

"All right," I said. I got up. "You want some of Uncle Ike's corn or that town whisky of Roth Edmondziz?"

"Can't you say Mister Roth or Mister Edmonds?" Mister Ernest said.

"Yes, sir," I said. "Well, which do you want? Uncle Ike's corn or that ere stuff of Roth Edmondziz?"

Are Gadgets Good?

By Eldon Thomas

Here are three deer hunting scenarios involving the use of sex lures for bucks:

In Pennsylvania, a rifle hunter has carefully chosen a natural blind near the junction of two deer trails. Fresh droppings and hoof prints indicate that the trails are being heavily used. With the aid of a stick, the hunter makes a mock scrape at the point of intersection and dribbles a little doe-in-heat scent into the depression. Then, he climbs into his nearby blind, a clump of birches with a natural cavity in the middle. Thirty minutes later, a fine six-point buck moves along the trail. When he stops to check out the phony scrape, the hunter delivers a shot through the buck's lungs. The next day, the hunter writes a letter to the lure manufacturer, extolling the virtues of its superior product.

In northern Wisconsin, a bowhunter has made a scent trail with the help of a drip-tube applicator. The trail begins on the far side of a clearing, passes across the opening and ends in edge cover on the near side, where the hunter has a tree stand. He figures that deer crossing the opening or moving along either edge will intercept his trail. The hunter has carefully chosen his stand in the crotch of a lightning-split oak with plenty of conifer-tree canopy to avoid skylighting. He hunts every day for a week without seeing a buck, although on two occasions he spots does crossing the clearing and several times hears deer snort behind him. Frustrated, he returns home, throws out what is left of his bottle of lure and ponders writing a nasty letter to the manufacturer.

In Alabama, another bowhunter has tied a drag rag soaked with hot doe urine to his left boot. Well before daylight, he walks to make a scent trail from the edge of a peanut field to deep-woods security cover. Leaving the scent rag tied to his boot, he climbs into his tree stand. He reasons that deer feeding in the peanut field will seek the safety of deep woods soon after daylight. And he is right. At 7:30, an aroused buck with hat-rack headgear pogo-sticks along the mock trail. The hunter has nocked his arrow but has yet to draw. He never gets the chance because the deer quickly looks up, his passion suddenly changed to red alert. He and the hunter stare each other down for a tense moment. Finally, the buck swaps ends and disappears. The hunter debates whether or not to spend the afternoon brooding over his misfortune at the neighborhood bar.

Three hunters from three different states. Each had the chance to score on a dandy buck, but why did only one succeed? All three appear to be knowledgeable deer hunters, and the bucks were certainly suckered into killing range, thanks to the use of lure. Right?

Those two assumptions contain flaws. Let's look at each situation again. The Pennsylvania hunter chose the right spot—at the junction of two well-used trails—for his stand. Odds are good, however, that he would have shot the six-pointer regardless of the phony scrape because the deer was using the trail anyway. The Alabama hunter made a crucial mistake by leaving the drag rag, which contained the strong odor of hot doe, tied to his boot. Had he positioned the rag in a nearby bush, he might have been able to draw his bow unseen. The Wisconsin hunter made a poor choice of location for both his scent trail and stand. The favorable wind that allowed him to watch the clearing and be undiscovered by deer using it also sent his odor cone behind him. Obviously, that was where most of the deer were.

Although they have been around for a few years now, lures and scents—both the sex attractants and the masking odors—are among the hottest-selling items of what I call the "deer gadgets" on today's market. At the Shooting, Hunting, Outdoor Trades (SHOT) Show held in Las Vegas last winter, I counted 47 companies making these products. And there is a host of new deer gadgetry either on sporting-goods shelves now or soon on the way. Synthetic rattling antlers that can carry the sound of fighting bucks a distance of a half-mile or more are big sellers. So are grunt calls that imitate the piglike sounds of sexually aroused bucks. Today, you can buy sophisticated listening devices that will allow you to hear a deer walking through leaves on the other side of the woods that you are posting. Simple trail timers, which employ a stopwatch and thread,

can tell you to the minute when a deer passed by.

Binoculars that never need focusing, sophisticated scopes with bullet-drop compensators, superquiet clothing, and new camouflage patterns that are computer-coordinated are also part of the high technology that has invaded the deep woods. This is not a debate of the ethical merits of such sophisticated gear—I test and use some of the products myself—nor is it a defense of their existence. There is no question that the deer hunting gadgets work—and that they can make a good hunter better. Each hunter must decide their merits and values for himself. There are three practical problems, however, that I see associated with their use.

One problem is that many hunters rely on gadgetry to do the grunt work of learning deer behavior and developing woodsmanship skills. In other words, they want shortcuts to experience. In some respects, America is rearing a whole generation of such deer hunters who have grown up watching too

Gadgets do not ensure a hunter success, but they can help tilt the odds in his favor.

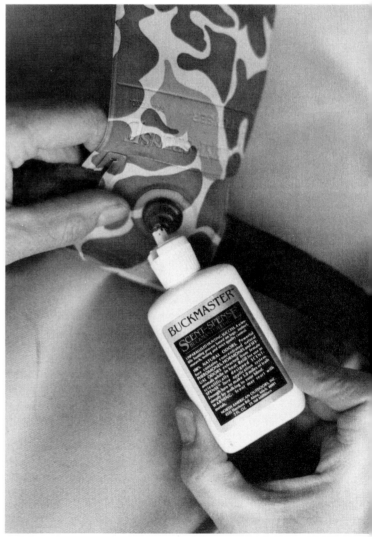

Scents for masking and attracting are among the hottest items on the gadget market.

many four-color videos and reading too many slick advertisements that dramatize products and don't emphasize the importance of learning basic hunting skills.

Instant gratification is a syndrome of modern living that is directly linked to the mass media. "Got a headache? Take this pain reliever," is not far removed, as an advertising slogan, from, "*Pssst.* Didn't get your buck? Try this hot new buck lure." "Sandwich hunters" is what a game-biologist friend of mine calls those who expect to arrive in deer camp on the eve of the opener, step into the woods the following morning and tag a monster buck.

On the one hand, it's an unfair moniker because some hunters use the gadgetry to learn more about deer behavior. Trail timers and scent trails can teach a hunter key facts about deer movements and behavior before, during and after the rut, as well as changes attributed to hunting pressure and weather patterns. Good camouflage, noiseless clothing and human-masking odors, such as fox or skunk urine, help bring deer close enough for killing shots. Therefore, they can help a good hunter become a better hunter.

On the other hand, some hunters, mostly older, experienced sportsmen, have no use at all for high technology.

"I don't believe in any of it," said Leo Perlick, who is 78 years old and has been hunting Michigan whitetails for 64 years. Perlick has shot 49 bucks in the last 54 seasons while hunting in the eastern Upper Peninsula, a notoriously deer-poor area when compared with the rest of the state. "Knowing your hunting area is the most important part of success," said Perlick, who is a stillhunter. "Being able to see deer by first identifying the flick of an ear or a leg in the underbrush is second in importance. All of the fancy gadgets you can buy won't help you to do that. There is no substitute for effort or experience."

"When I started deer hunting 50 years ago," said expert deer hunter Ken Peterson of Davidson, Michigan, "we didn't have any of that stuff. I learned to hunt deer by studying deer and by learning what they do, where they travel, when they eat and what they eat." Peterson, who used to be the outdoor editor for the *Flint Journal* and who has written articles for *Outdoor Life*, began stillhunting in 1962 because "waylaying a buck on a runway ceased to be a challenge." He said he has tried some of the gadgetry but has discarded it. Why? "It didn't add to my abilities to take a buck."

A second problem with deer gadgetry is that its successful use nearly always relies on theory. Reduced to a real hunting situation, though, theory may hold less water than a sieve. For example, theory may dictate that a buck's will to survive caves in to his instinctive desire to breed during the rut. That is why some bucks "throw caution to the winds." In areas of heavy hunting pressure, however, many of these stud bucks grow unbelievably cagey, even during the distracting period of the rut. They hole up in areas that are impenetrable, such as dry islands in a swamp, or that are unlikely, such as expressway medians or boulder piles in the middle of a farm field. Other factors that can punch theory in the nose are the variables of wind, weather, terrain, time of rut, scarcity or abundance of deer, and food availability.

I used to hunt deer on heavily hunted public land in northern Michigan where most of the bucks are culled as yearlings. The cover was second-growth jack pines and oaks with few openings that afforded much visibility. Many times, deer passed behind my back. Some spooked when they caught my scent or saw me move; others I never saw but noticed their tracks on my way back to camp. I theorized that if I attached a couple of pickup truck mirrors to trees on either side of my blind. I would see these deer before they saw me. It didn't work. On the first day, the mirrors caught the sun's reflection, and I never saw so much as a flag. The second day was overcast, but the deer continued to spot me or smell me long before they came into view of the mirrors. So much for my theory and contribution to high technology.

The third problem is that hunters either expect the deer gadgetry to correct a basic flaw of their own making, or they make common-sense mistakes when they apply the advanced technology. As an example of the first, I should have set up my blind and the mirrors in a crosswind rather than having the breeze in my face. Playing the wind game is also critical if you want to use grunt calls, sex scents and rattling antlers. Whitetail expert Noel Feather, who has bow-killed several huge bucks in Illinois, markets his own line of the above-mentioned products. "At least 60 percent of the key to scoring is to be a good hunter," Feather said. "The hunter who thoroughly scouts his area and chooses a good blind or stand with an eye to the prevailing wind is going to up his odds. The other 40 percent lies in correct use of the product itself."

Feather said that hunters make a big mistake when they use a masking scent that is not native to an area. An example is relying on the scent of apples in Northern wilderness where there are no apples. Another flaw is applying sex lures to the hunter's body; this can rivet a buck's attention and even provoke an attack. Hunters who apply scent to their boots actually make a trail that grows weaker as they approach their stand. And some hunters overdo it when rattling or calling. "Too little is better than too much," Feather said. "In my seminars, I advise hunters to use a grunt call instead of rattling first thing in the morning. Rattling requires movement on the part of the hunter. You might not see a close-in buck, which, when alerted, could be watching you. Using the grunt call first offers insurance."

So, do you need gadgetry this fall? If you intend to use it to cover up your lack of hunting skills, the answer is no. But there is no question that it can improve your luck while helping you to become a more knowledgeable hunter.

Biggest Deer of the East

By Jeff Murray

Do you ever dream about herculean bucks that look more like Clydesdale horses than whitetail deer? Would you like to down a trophy so heavy that a tag team of pro wrestlers couldn't haul it out of the woods? I've taken a few that dressed out far in excess of the 200-pound mark, but someday I'm going to nail one that's at least a third bigger. I know that they're out there because I once saw one, and I can't stop thinking about it.

It happened one fall day while I was playing hooky from a much-despised geometry class during my freshman year of college. I was driving the back roads on the outskirts of town when I saw it. The huge animal literally glided over the hood of my Rambler wagon as it leaped from one side of the little dirt road to the other. Though this all took place in the blur of a millisecond, my mind replays the episode like a VCR—freeze-frame pushed when the animal is at the crest of its bound. I can just see that 3-foot flag waving in the air as the deer completes a 20-foot leap.

But the story doesn't quite end there. The deer disappeared as it slipped around a little knoll that bordered the shoulder of the road. Despite the fact that this took place during Minnesota's firearms season—and I had my rifle cased in the trunk—I tore after the overstuffed deer unarmed. I *had* to get another glimpse of its massive body. Besides, everyone knows that no deer, after jumping over a car, would ever stop for long enough to let a hunter come crashing through the bush.

But guess what? As I rounded the edge of the knoll, what do you think was standing broadside, no farther than 15 paces away? You guessed it. We stared at each other for a long minute before the huge deer turned and lumbered through a maze of breast-high balsams. I would estimate its live weight to have been in the neighborhood of 375 pounds.

How big was the rack? Well, here's the juicy part, and the main reason for bringing up the story. The deer didn't have one. That's right, the biggest whitetail I ever saw in the woods was a doe! And I'm not stretching the details one iota. I don't have to. My home state of Minnesota, where I do most of my hunting, is also home to the nation's biggest-bodied deer, and I see a lot of animals that would boggle the minds of many hunters from other regions. But Minnesota isn't the only place to find big deer. In fact, they're scattered in pockets throughout the nation. You just have to know where to look and ask the right questions.

What exactly is a "big" buck? What might qualify for a state record? What's the body-weight world record for a whitetail?

Answers to these and other questions aren't easy to come by. What's big to you may not be so big to a hunter from another locale, even though your buck might be among the largest from your area. Unfortunately, there isn't a uniform method of scoring big-bodied deer similar to the Boone and Crockett Club system for judging antler size. Furthermore, the records of whitetail body weights in many states

63

are often sketchy and therefore misleading. As a result, many huge deer are tagged each year but their weights are not documented. Yet, the story often leaks out to local hunters. A fascinating account of a number of heavy-bodied animals is contained within the pages of Leonard Lee Rue III's book, *The Deer of North America*. But first, some basic big-buck biology.

There are about 30 subspecies of whitetail deer in North and Central America, of which half are present in huntable populations in the Lower 48 states. Mammalogists have broken the genus *Odocoileus* into these groupings to take into account regional differences routinely observed in deer. There are long-legged deer and short-legged deer. Some have darker coats, some have lighter ones, and though some do not grow very large, others attain considerable size.

According to contributors to the book *White-Tailed Deer Ecology And Management*, the *borealis* subspecies seems to outgrow the others. It is native to portions of the provinces of Ontario and Quebec, and parts of the states of Minnesota, Michigan, Wisconsin, Illinois, Indiana, Ohio, Pennsylvania, New York, Vermont, New Hampshire, Rhode Island, New Jersey and Massachusetts. The *dakotensis* subspecies is also a large-bodied deer; it is indigenous to parts of British Columbia, Alberta and Saskatchewan, and the states of Montana, Wyoming, Colorado, both Dakotas and western Minnesota.

These two subspecies are genetically different from all of the others in many respects, but they will generally allow for a higher upper limit of a deer's weight. This doesn't guarantee, however, that a monster buck can be taken as easily in Massachusetts as in Minnesota. Obviously, there are other conditions necessary for growing a big buck that must be factored in. Age is one. If a buck can reach the magical 4½-year mark, it can begin to reach its full growth potential. Deer continue to grow until their eighth year, but their skeletal maturity is reached as they enter their fifth year of life.

Another factor is nutrition. Because dominant breeding bucks lose weight during the fall—close to 25 percent of their summer body weight, according to most studies—they must be able to build up good fat reserves going into October. Plentiful mast crops help because they have a concentration of essential nutrients as well as a high caloric content. But certain areas of the country that are blessed with an abundance of calcium in their soils tend to produce large deer; calcium is a bare-bones requirement (no pun intended) for good skeletal development.

Finally, latitude seems to have a bearing on how large whitetails get. Bergmann's Rule states that individuals of a species tend to be smaller in warmer climates. A basic explanation for this observation is that a large-bodied animal conserves heat more efficiently than a smaller one; thus, northern Wisconsin—or Michigan or Minnesota—deer tend to grow larger than do their cousins in the more southern reaches of their respective state.

The main problem with northern whitetails is that the nutritional scene is not nearly as rich as it is farther south. A shorter growing season, followed by a woody browsing period with a lower food value, often negates the positive effects of genetics. But what would happen if you could transplant northern *borealis* into a nutrient-rich environment with a longer growing season? Would the deer barely survive, or would they thrive?

Well, that's exactly what the old Georgia Game and Fish Commission did from 1944 until the late '60s. At least 24 Georgia counties were stocked with 439 whitetails from Wisconsin; private sportsmen's groups added hundreds more.

The results of these transplants have been encouraging, to say the least. The depleted Georgia herd was restored and beefed up with a strain of whitetails that not only grows bigger bodies than its Dixie counterparts, but also grows trophy racks. Boone and Crockett listings reveal an intriguing correlation between the Peach State and the state of Wisconsin; Georgia leads the South with 24 typical and six non-typical entries, and Wisconsin is second in the nation to Minnesota with 73 typicals and 52 non-typicals.

Another interesting footnote to the Georgia story is a monster buck taken from Worth County by a Florida hunter, Boyd Jones, in 1972. It weighed 355 pounds, dressed. The question in my mind that begs an answer is, "Could this be a Wisconsin-strain whitetail?" Heyward Brown, former president of the Worth County Wildlife Club, has no doubts about the answer.

"We started our restocking program from scratch," said the 82-year-old hunter. "We didn't have a single deer in the county before we brought in 10 does and six bucks from a guy from Babcock, Wisconsin. Today, we have trophy deer, and they're larger and healthier than most others in Georgia."

Jimmy McDaniel, a biologist with the Florida Game and Fresh Water Fish Commission, witnessed the scaling of Jones' mammoth buck. Besides tallying the buck's dressed weight and estimating its live weight (426 pounds), McDaniel also measured the animal's height at the shoulder, and its girth. Both turned out to be 45 inches. The buck's teeth were then aged. The result? Only 3½ years old!

Another monster buck, also weighing 355 pounds field-dressed, was shot by Horace Hinkley in 1955 near Bingham, Maine. This state continues to produce behemoth bucks to hunters who know wilderness tactics and can match wits with older and wiser deer. But it still takes as much luck as skill to down a 300-pound-plus animal these days. The narrative in Rue's book, alluded to earlier, suggests that Hinkley had a little of both going for him.

It was a rainy November day; Hinkley's wife, Olive, had taken a stand on a ridge opposite her

Horace Hinkley and his buck that dressed out at 355 pounds.

The state of Michigan is no slouch when it comes to producing large-bodied whitetails. The largest Michigan buck was taken on the last day of the 1919 deer season by a Flint resident, Albert Tippett. According to Richard P. Smith's book, *Michigan Big Game Records*, it was midday, and Tippett was hunting during the tail end of a prolonged snowstorm. While wading through waist-high drifts in the woods, Tippett jumped the monster buck from beneath a snow-laden spruce. The buck paused after bolting 70 feet, giving Tippett the only shot that he would need to down the trophy animal. It dressed out at 354 pounds, and was estimated to have weighed 425 pounds on the hoof.

Smith lists the state's second and third heaviest Michigan deer in his book. Both were taken from the Upper Peninsula. L. E. Valley, Sr. nailed a Chippewa County buck that dressed out at 345 pounds on railroad scales. It was traveling with two other bucks and four does when a domestic dog chased them all past Valley's deer stand. The non-typical rack scored 203⅝ Boone and Crockett points.

In 1967, Leo Furaitor tagged a 13-point buck (204 non-typical Boone and Crockett points) from the U.P.; it dressed out at 324 pounds. Two years later, in the fall of 1969, Mark Ritchie accomplished quite a feat on his first deer hunt. The Dexter, Michigan, native shot a doe that dressed out at 240 pounds and was later estimated to have been 14 years old. But Ritchie didn't rest on these laurels. In 1984, he shot a whitetail that is Michigan's state-record typical buck.

For many years, the "unofficial official" world-record heavyweight whitetail was Tippett's 354-pound 1919 buck. But many bigger bucks have reportedly been taken. According to the author of *A Century Of Wisconsin Deer*, a 386-pound whitetail was shot in 1924 in Sawyer County. A 378-pounder from Iron County was reportedly taken in 1941. Both of these represent dressed, not live, weights. These and other extraordinary bucks never made it into the archives of officialdom because they were not officially witnessed (more on this below).

There are many reports of outsize bucks coming from states in the Midwest. An Iowa buck was scaled in 1962 with a verified live weight of 440 pounds; an Illinois bowhunter took a 370-pounder (live weight) in 1970 from Carroll County; a 400-pound, car-killed *doe* was the talk of much of Ohio a half-dozen years ago; a 1986 rifle-shot Ohio buck dressed out at 344 pounds. Jim Schoby of the Ohio Division of Wildlife witnessed the scaling of a road-killed whitetail in 1976 that had a field-dressed weight of 316 pounds. It was just a six-pointer.

According to a news item carried in *Outdoor Life*, Del Solholt shot a 341-pound buck (dressed) near Carrington, North Dakota, in 1959. And 14-year-old Scott Rexroth from Oskaloosa, Iowa, nailed a beautiful buck that dressed out at 316 pounds. The story behind this trophy proves that it can happen to anyone—again, with a little luck.

husband. Around midmorning, Hinkley fired at a buck and missed. Moments later, Olive's rifle rang out, and after a short pause she shouted that she had downed a big buck. What to do? Rush over to help out, sneak over to her stand, or sit tight? Hinkley acted on a hunch. There must be more deer in the scrub beech thicket, he thought. Better sit tight.

It was a good thing that he didn't respond. Right after he made his decision to stay, the huge buck appeared, and he was able to down it with a single shot. It was far too big to move alone, so he had to get help. And he didn't weigh the buck for three days, but the dried-out monster still tipped the 355 mark—dressed. Officials of the Maine Department of Inland Fisheries and Wildlife estimated that the deer's live weight would have been close to an astonishing 475 pounds.

Albert Tippett's huge whitetail buck was taken in Michigan in 1919. Richard P. Smith photo.

Rexroth was told by his father to find a comfortable spot on top of a little hill. Eleven other hunters would be putting on a drive headed in his direction. Scott momentarily debated the merits of yet another drive—the third of the day—and perhaps a ride on his three-wheeler would be just as fruitful—but he eventually opted to follow Pop's plan.

Scott bumped a deer on his way up the hill but kept on for the top, where a perfect stump was waiting to be sat upon. Ten minutes hadn't elapsed before a crashing noise preceded the monster buck, seen bolting a fence. It was heading directly toward the first-year deer hunter.

"At the top of his jump, the buck looked right at me," Scott told me. "I guess he didn't like what he saw because he changed directions upon landing

and veered away from me and down the hill."

A steady swing from Scott's Model 1100 Remington pump allowed him to place the slug at just the right spot: on the spine and through the lungs. The buck fell in a heap at the shot.

This is one buck that was literally holed up. One of the drivers came upon a big brush pile and, after walking around it, decided to climb on top of it—just in case. That's when the trophy sprang from the deadfall and headed in young Rexroth's direction. You have to wonder how many big bucks elude hunters every year by seeking similar hideouts.

Though most hunters are happy to add 50 to 75 pounds of venison to their freezer in the fall, Scott Rexroth's family had to be tickled with the 156 pounds of deer meat that his 316-pound buck yielded. That's a lot of venisonburger.

In 1981, however, a Duluth Chippewa man, George Himango, reportedly shot a buck on the Fond du Lac Indian Reservation that produced even more meat. How much more? Would you believe 196 pounds of boneless venison?

What's more, Himango's whitetail reportedly dressed out at 402 pounds, tying the "unofficial" all-time record set in 1926 by fellow Minnesotan Carl J. Lenander (see below). According to a 1982 report in the *St. Paul Pioneer Press*, the huge animal was bagged just prior to the 1981 Minnesota deer season, during the Indian reservation's season, which had been set a week earlier by tribal law.

"It was about 3 o'clock in the afternoon," Himango told outdoor writer Dennis Anderson. "My brother, my cousin and I were on separate stands when I heard the animal coming through the woods behind me. I turned around and could see it walking through the brush. But the cover was heavy, so I didn't realize that it was a buck, and I couldn't see how big it was. I couldn't risk a shot.

"I waited and waited. The deer disappeared into the bush. That's when I said to myself, 'You should have taken the shot.' But the animal stopped in the brush and just stayed there. About six minutes elapsed before I heard it move again. By this time, I was positive that it was a buck, so I picked an opening and waited for the deer to come out."

But instead of crossing the opening, the deer turned and walked right toward Himango. Then, it snorted, lowered its head and pawed the ground. "I had put buck scent and deer urine near my stand," he told Anderson. "My brother had taken a six-pointer that morning, and I had taken the urine and spread it all over my stand."

Anderson further quoted Himango as saying that it took the three men three hours to drag the buck one-eighth of a mile. But that was the easiest part. They had a rougher time getting the animal into a canoe so that they could get it across the lake from where they were hunting.

Like many of the behemoth-bodied bucks that we've chronicled, this one had a large rack, but not quite large enough for the Boone and Crockett record

Carl Lenander's monster Minnesota buck had a field-dressed weight of 402 pounds.

books. It scored 154 Boone and Crockett points.

Rounding out the Himango buck story is an incredible twist of irony. Himango told the newspaper that his deer was weighed at a Duluth butcher shop, where it tipped the scales at precisely 402 pounds—the same weight as Lenander's record buck. But the story doesn't end there. When I asked LeRoy Rutske, the Minnesota Department of Natural Resources' big-game specialist, which one of the two 402-pound bucks the state recognized as its official record, he said, "Neither."

"It's impossible to officially recognize [a deer-weight record] in Minnesota," he told me. "Not even the governor could do it. We just don't keep such records. It keeps us out of trouble, and besides, we don't have the manpower to go out and check the weights of whitetails across the state."

This raises an obvious question. If Minnesota doesn't ascribe any "official" status to the Lenander buck, how can it be considered the all-time world record? The answer to this bureaucratic idiosyncrasy is a simple one. Other states *do* maintain deer-body-weight records. And whatever tops their lists pales when compared with the Lenander buck. By an unusual twist of fate, Lenander's buck gained national notoriety in an official capacity when Minnesota officials unwittingly "recognized" the buck in a 1961 conservation department publication, *Technical Bulletin No. 5*. A picture of Lenander and his buck appeared on page 19 with a caption that flatly stated that the dressed weight of the deer was 402 pounds.

Meanwhile, Himango's buck will probably remain in statistical limbo.

Which leads to the question of the day: What should you do if you are fortunate enough to shoot a potential record-weight buck? Three things. First, make sure that you comply with all of your state's regulations, including properly tagging and registering the animal. Second, have the deer weighed on accurate, certified scales. And third, make sure that your trophy is officially witnessed by at least one state conservation official.

PART 2

HUNTING MULE DEER

Biggest Deer of the West

By Jim Zumbo

The buck seemed to appear out of nowhere. He walked briskly along a trail in the canyon bottom below me, and it took me a moment to collect my senses and hoist the rifle to my shoulder.

I aimed across the questionable sights of the old .30/40 Krag and squeezed the trigger. To my surprise and delight, the buck bounded up a sagebrush slope and collapsed. He was mine—the first muley of my life. I was 21 years old, using a rifle borrowed from a college classmate.

I approached the deer and noted the heavy antlers, but I was also impressed with his size. I had no idea how big he really was because I'd never seen another mule deer in the flesh, but I knew that he was far bigger than any whitetail I'd ever seen in the East, where I was raised.

Later, we hoisted the buck onto accurate grain scales and learned that he weighed 232 pounds. I wasn't as overwhelmed as I might have been due to my inexperience, but to this day I have not killed a heavier buck, and I can say that I've hunted muleys in practically every western state and Canadian province.

Many hunters, and outdoor writers, believe mule deer to be much larger than whitetails. These people have not spent much time in the North, where whitetails dress out at more than 300 pounds. Although it's true that the average muley probably weighs more than the average whitetail, it's only because whitetails are overcrowded in many regions and never attain large sizes.

Game managers have authentic, official weights of mule deer. Most deer are weighed at check stations along highways, but some are also weighed in the field during surveys.

Some amazing weights have turned up in areas where one wouldn't expect muleys to grow abnormally large. According to the highly respected book *The Deer Of North America* by John Taylor, "There are authentic records of bucks from Modoc County, California, weighing 380 pounds field-dressed and of British Columbia specimens weighing about the same."

Being suspicious, I checked with the California authorities to try to confirm these incredibly heavy bucks. Wildlife officers were aware of the statement in the book, but were unable to locate documented records of the super-bucks. That's not to say that Taylor's research was inaccurate, but simply that the claim can't be supported with available evidence.

The idea that California produces huge bucks at all is contrary to widespread opinion about the state's deer, but Modoc County is in the extreme northeastern part of California. The region is inhabited by the Rocky Mountain mule deer subspecies, which is considered to be the largest antlered and the heaviest of the seven mule deer subspecies.

Interestingly, California has made an attempt to officially document heavy deer. Between 1969 and 1985, the California Fish and Game Commission's Records Award Program accounted for large numbers of validated deer weights. The rules required the deer to be field-dressed, which meant completely gutted, but with head, legs, and skin attached. (This is the generally accepted interpretation of "field-dressing.") Besides the weight information, the deer had to be weighed on official scales, and witnesses were required to sign the validation form.

The heaviest buck was a 282-pound animal taken by Emett L. Burrough of Redding in 1969. The deer was killed in Modoc County in the state's northeast corner.

My next step was to investigate Taylor's claims about British Columbia's heavyweight bucks. Wildlife officials in the province had no documented records of exceptionally heavy deer, and said that meat-processing plants were a source of information. However, locker plants record "hanging weight," which means the carcass minus the head, hide and legs.

One B.C. official said that it wasn't uncommon for very large muleys to have a hanging weight of 220 pounds or so, and indicated he'd heard of one that went 250 pounds. He admitted, however, that the weighing had not been witnessed, and he couldn't be positive that the weight was accurate.

There's a vast difference between hanging weight and field-dressed weight. Dr. Ray Field of the University of Wyoming is an authority on livestock and big-game weights, and offered his formula to convert hanging weight to field-dressed weight. Simply divide the hanging weight by .84. By doing so, the 250-pound B.C. buck comes out to 298 pounds. Field cautioned that the formula works best for average deer. A buck with a massive rack could have an extra 10 pounds or so of antlers.

For the purposes of comparing deer weights,

The author approaches a muley buck that dressed at 225 pounds.

Most of these Colorado bucks topped the 200-pound mark. Two (third from left, second from right) dressed at 230.

field-dressed weight is always used for obvious reasons. A deer must be quickly gutted as soon as it's killed or the meat will spoil.

There are often inconsistencies in field-dressed weights as well. Some hunters routinely cut off the lower legs, and some slit the animal from brisket to throat and remove the windpipe. Consequently, the true weight can be off by several pounds.

According to the Boone and Crockett Club record book, Colorado is by far the top state for trophy bucks. Dick Hopper of the Colorado Division of Wildlife said that the state's heaviest confirmed buck weight was 248 pounds dressed. However, the *Outdoor Life* archives list two other Colorado muley bucks that, by all indications, are the heaviest ever killed by modern-day hunters.

According to the July 1957 issue of *Outdoor Life*, O. I. Ranck of Long Beach, California, shot a huge muley near Meeker, Colorado, that had a verified field-dressed weight of 360 pounds. State game manager Gilbert Hunter estimated the deer's live weight at 522 pounds.

Ironically, it was Hunter who also weighed in what many believe to be the largest deer ever shot in North America—whitetail or muley. Lawrence Rowe was hunting near Allen's Park, Colorado, in 1938 when he toppled a huge muley buck that hog-dressed at 410 pounds. Alive, that deer would have weighed a little less than 600 pounds.

It's important to understand that many huge bucks aren't weighed, and those that are may not be officially recorded.

Murry Burnham, well-known predator caller and big-game hunter who manufacturers Burnham

Brothers calls, has hunted in Colorado extensively over the years. He says he witnessed the weighing of a buck that went 245 pounds. Burnham said it was the biggest buck he'd ever seen.

Don Anderegg, one of the owners of Old World Meats in Grand Junction, Colorado, has been in business for more than 25 years. The heaviest deer he ever weighed on his scales went 225 pounds, hanging weight. According to Field's formula, the buck would have field-dressed at 268 pounds.

Neighboring Utah produces very large deer. According to Rudy Drobnick of the Utah Division of Wildlife Resources, a confirmed 307-pound field-dressed buck was killed near Logan about four years ago. Drobnick said that the buck's weighing was witnessed and notarized.

Drobnick reported that another Utah buck, also officially recorded, weighed 305 pounds dressed. That deer, taken in the Oquirrh Mountains, was believed to be a whitetail/mule deer hybrid. Although whitetails are commonly considered to be absent from Utah, there is a small herd in the Oquirrhs.

Drobnick worked at the Daniel's Canyon deer check station on Route 40 east of Salt Lake City for about 25 years. The station is open 24 hours a day throughout the hunting season, and all deer are checked. The biggest buck Drobnick ever weighed was 244 pounds. It was taken from the southern slope of the Uinta Mountains about 15 years ago.

According to Drobnick, an Idaho buck weighed 307 pounds dressed. It was weighed on official Idaho Fish and Game Department scales.

The Deseret Ranch in Utah produces some of the best bucks in the state. Game manager Shane Davis said that each buck taken is weighed on accurate scales. It's not uncommon for bucks to weigh 220 pounds dressed, and the very biggest will top out at 235 pounds.

Arizona is well-known for producing trophy bucks, most of them in the famous Kaibab region. Ray Lee of the Arizona Game and Fish Department noted that the biggest officially recorded buck weighed 276 pounds and was taken four years ago.

Few people realize that Nevada is an excellent mule deer state, producing more mature bucks in proportion to the total harvest than any other state. George Tsukamoto of the Nevada Department of Wildlife said that there are no confirmed records of giant bucks, and stated that deer in the 240-pound dressed-weight range are about the largest reported.

Wyoming had no huge bucks to report, but Dr. Harry Harju of the Wyoming Game and Fish Department said that it's difficult to obtain accurate measurements, and few hunters take the trouble to weigh their bucks.

"My wife killed a huge buck recently," Harju said. "It took three men to load it into the truck, and four men to hang it. I don't know how big that buck was because I didn't weigh it. Some hunters no doubt would have estimated it to be a 250- or even a 300-pounder."

My research for this article took an interesting twist as I was talking to my neighbor, Marv Allerheiligen. We were filling the water trough in my horse pasture, and the conversation turned to big bucks.

"What's the biggest buck you've ever killed? I asked.

"You wouldn't believe me," Marv said. Upon my insistence, he told me the story.

"I was hunting with my buddy up the South Fork of the Shoshone River," Marv said. "It was 1958, and I was 17 years old. In those days, the season started on September 10, and it was about 80°. We had decided that my pal would have the first shot, and we spotted a herd of big bucks. One of the bucks was a giant, completely dwarfing the others—all of which were big in their own right.

"My buddy shot and missed," Marv continued. "His gun jammed, and he hollered at me to take the big buck. I got him, and we weighed him on official scales."

"How big was he?" I asked.

"310," Marv answered.

I looked for a twinkle in Marv's eyes, but I didn't see any. I believe that my neighbor was telling the truth.

Montana probably gets the top price for consistently producing the biggest bucks. According to Harley Yeager of the Montana Department of Fish, Wildlife and Parks, a 340-pound deer leads the list.

"This buck is the biggest in Montana's Big Game Trophy Book," he said. "No one knows who shot it or where it was taken, but the deer was documented by Ken Greer of our Bozeman office. Ken is

Murry Burnham poses with big-racked, big-bodied muley that dressed at 225.

now retired, but was meticulous when it came to official weights and measurements. I know that buck dressed out at 340."

Another huge Montana deer weighed in at 300 pounds even. It was taken in 1954 by Buster Dodson near Sidney. The deer had superb antlers as well, scoring in the top 100 in the non-typical category of the Boone and Crockett record book with 264⅝ points. It had an antler spread of 41 inches.

Jack Atcheson, Sr., an outfitter and booking agent in Butte, Montana, had an interesting story to tell.

"I was hunting with Hank Aldrich from California in the Madison Range," he said. "We were up the West Fork of the Madison River, hunting in sparse timber at about 7,000 feet. Hank shot a giant buck, and we dressed it and laid it over a log to cool. It was too late to get it out that night. The next morning, we approached the buck and scared off a badger that had eaten about 8 to 10 pounds of meat from the hindquarters. When we got the deer to town, we weighed it on accurate grain scales. The buck weighed 298 pounds. Hank was cheated out of the magic 300-pound figure by the badger."

Does a 400-pound (field-dressed) muley exist? I haven't found one yet, but I'm still looking.

I'll also be looking when I'm climbing the mountains with a deer tag in my pocket and a rifle slung over my shoulder. But I'll be most grateful for anything decent that comes along. Maybe, though, someday I'll get really lucky and beat my ol' neighbor Marv.

Mega-Muleys

By Kathy Etling

The wind coming off the sagebrush flat was hot. Sand stung our faces as my husband, Bob, and I worked our way around the stark, silent canyon. We were hunting for trophy muleys on the Bolten Ranch in southern Wyoming. It was October but felt more like summertime.

From a distance, the canyon looked like a sheer rock face. But as we got closer, we could see into shadows—that meant a rend in a cliff here, a small shelf there. Once in the canyon, we worked around rubble that had fallen from the mesa above.

Bob eased along 25 yards ahead of me and 30 yards below me. He'd already passed a huge boulder on its down-slope side when I started to ease by on the other side. That's when I heard the clatter of hooves on stone. "Buck," Bob shouted.

It's a muley's nature to follow a canyon rim; once jumped, most bucks will lope around the canyon edge, giving you ample opportunity for a shot. Only the really big ones scramble straight up and over or swap ends and dash out of sight before you know what's happening.

This particular buck had a rack about 24 inches wide and fairly high. But he didn't have the mass that's built into a mega-muley's headset. He darted past Bob and, true to form, around the canyon rim. I swung with him as he bounded across the rimrock on the canyon's other side. He stopped and looked at us for a long minute before he put it into high gear and disappeared into the next drainage.

I let him go because we were after a real mega-muley, a 30-inch buck. And although we've taken some fine bucks in the years we've hunted out West, that magic 30-inch trophy has always eluded us.

Hunting trophy mule deer can be the most challenging hunting there is. The mountains are high and rugged. The deserts are vast and arid. By its sheer immensity, the terrain is enough to do in many

hunters. Shoot a deer in many areas, and you might spend a couple of days getting it out. Especially if you're hunting on your own off the beaten path.

The buck jumped wasn't a real trophy—just a little bit above average. But he had hidden himself under the edge of a boulder in a desolate canyon and stayed hidden until first Bob and then I walked to within 5 yards of his hiding place. Even from a few feet away, it was impossible to detect its presence.

Over the years, mule deer seem to have learned that protection from both the elements and hunters can be found in the strangest places. This past season we discovered that: mule deer will crawl under overhanging boulders; they will hide in crevices and caves; they will hole up under earthen banks; and they will hold tight no matter how close you get to them. Trophy muleys are probably a match for any whitetail. But knowing their tricks can help a hunter hang a mega-muley on his wall.

Mule deer live in some of the most Godforsaken land there is. To look at the barren wastelands where we hunted would be to deny that any deer existed there at all. But in these canyons, deer tracks and droppings were everywhere. We found large racks, too, remnants of a killer winter.

We also found a spot on a ledge where a deer had bedded. The impression of his body was obvious in the sand on the shelf. Too cramped to stand, the buck had to crouch like a cougar to get out of that shelf. We could tell from the tracks that he had seen us coming, backed off the ledge, and then fled up a nearly vertical rock chimney.

But many mule deer do have chinks in their defensive armor, especially younger bucks such as the one we jumped. First, he ran where we could see him even when other, safer escape paths were available. Second, he stopped and looked back. A trophy wouldn't have waited.

One reason why a trophy muley's weaknesses are

Bob's buck was headed up a rock face when Bob fired. Bob Etling photo.

more apparent than those of whitetails is because of the vastness of the muley's range. Once spotted or jumped, a muley will often have to run a tremendous distance to get out of the hunter's sight. High-powered rifles and optics make the difference to a trophy mule deer hunter where they often might not count as much to a trophy whitetail hunter.

When muleys decide to hide, they can hide almost anywhere. We decided that the dense sagebrush along one particular creek just might be prime muley cover. The creek bed was about 50 yards wide, but the creek itself was tiny—only about 3 feet wide—and it meandered back and forth across the bed as it slowly flowed downstream.

Bob stayed in the creek bed while I walked along the waterway's rim in case a buck dashed up the side. We hadn't walked far when a buck scrambled out of the creek and bounded across the desert. We let the small four-pointer go.

Later, Bob told me that the creek bed was full of deer beds hollowed out under the huge sagebrush. Piles of droppings provided evidence that mule deer spend lots of time in locations such as these.

Many of the muley hiding spots we discovered were depressions made by the deer themselves. Some beds were between rocks, some completely under rocks; almost all were full of old deer droppings. Deer prefer spots such as these to avoid sun, snow, rain, wind and hunters.

Not all muleys will let you walk right up on them. One day, Bob and I were walking out of a gully when we noticed a group of does bedded up on the side of a steep slope. When we started walking again, Bob noticed movement far ahead—a buck and a couple of does. The deer had seen us and decided to clear out. There was no time for a shot even if the buck had been a trophy.

After more than a week of looking for big-racked bucks on this portion of the ranch, we decided to head for public ground on the other side of Route 71. We had hunted an area called the Atlantic Rim once before and knew that the hunters on top forced big bucks over the steep edge. So, we decided to climb up the Rim's rugged south face and work our way parallel to the Bridger Pass Road.

The climb was nearly vertical, but we saw enough does and small bucks on the way up to keep it interesting. Soon, our newly discovered hunting tactics began to pay off.

We eased forward with the wind in our faces. This time, I went first and Bob followed. We hadn't gone far when we scared another buck out from under a rock. He jumped up within 10 yards of me.

On the next drainage, Bob went first. He eased across a steep shelf, about 50 yards long, where a few tattered aspens clung precariously. As Bob disappeared from view, a nice muley popped out from almost the same place where Bob had entered the aspens. The buck looked back and then snuck along the ledge, popping out over the top as I watched in astonishment.

Later that same morning, we watched from above as six does and fawns bedded in a shallow ditch. Any hunters on the same level as the deer would never have seen them. All of them were lying on the shady side of a ditch that couldn't have been more than 18 inches deep. If six does can disappear that thoroughly, think what a wary old buck could do.

We passed up at least 25 bucks in the 20- to 24-inch range since we'd started hunting. Larger bucks were pretty scarce because almost an entire age-class of deer was lost in the winter of 1983–84. We had thought that trophy deer would have been more numerous, but it was obvious that we'd miscalculated.

Luckily, we still had another hunt planned, this one a guided hunt at the Bolten Ranch Club, which is located on the western side of Route 71. Because hunter numbers are limited, we felt that our chances of finding a trophy might be better.

Jon Anderson, manager of the operation, was waiting for us when we pulled in that evening. But the story was the same there: lots of bucks were being spotted but no real trophies.

The first day, we saw at least 20 bucks. One drive pushed a group of five bucks—two of them with 25-inch racks—to within 300 yards of me. They were bigger than any I'd seen, but 300 yards is a little farther than I like to shoot. Still, I was feeling pretty optimistic because it was our first day there.

During the drive, I learned even more about muleys. I saw bucks that leaped up on rocks to watch the drivers walk right under them. These mule deer should have scurried out of there. But once the driv-

ers had passed, the bucks began feeding again, confident of their ability to go unnoticed.

That evening, Ken Auer, another trophy mule deer hunter from Houston, Texas, told us about a good buck he'd spotted a mile behind the ranch house. Auer's standards were even higher than ours, but because he was leaving the next day, he told us where he'd last seen the big buck.

The next evening, Bob was on his own so I headed up to the basin that Auer had pointed out. That night, Bob told us that he jumped the big buck and even got a shot as the animal dove over a high earthen bank. But after checking for blood and coming up empty-handed, he decided to wait until morning to resume his search.

In the morning, I went out with Jon after three big sagebrush bucks were spotted by a sheepherder. Bob went back to look for his buck. When he found the spot where he'd jumped the buck, he discovered that the deer had holed up under an earthen bank behind some mountain mahogany bushes. Tall grass grew down from above, further obscuring the deer's hiding spot.

Although he checked the area for several hours, he found no blood. So, he decided to stillhunt through a nearby stand of aspen. As soon as he entered the thicket, he jumped a deer. By dogging its tracks, Bob jumped the deer twice more. But the tactic brought no results. He decided to hunt the edge of the aspens, where a high sagebrush hill melted into the aspen pocket.

By quietly walking along the side of the hill, Bob was able to sneak even closer to the deer in the aspens. The fourth time the deer bounded off, Bob could tell that the animal was really making tracks.

"All of a sudden, I could hear a difference in the sound of the hooves," Bob said. "They weren't beating into fallen leaves and striking blowdowns. Instead, they were definitely clattering on rocks.

"I knew that the animal was going higher, probably right over the sheer shale face of the mountain on the other side of the aspen pocket. My only chance was to position myself where I could see the rock face, so I ran up the side of the sagebrush hill.

"I'd no sooner gotten into position when I saw this huge buck burst into view above the aspens, making a beeline for the top as fast as he could. I no sooner got the scope on him than I fired.

"The deer veered downhill and was immediately out of sight. I heard some crashing in the aspens and then nothing but silence."

The one shot from Bob's .30/06 Weatherby Fiberguard had done the trick. The 150-grain Nosler solid-base spitzer bullet powered by 59 grains of H4831 went right through the big buck's heart at 200 yards.

Did we get our mega-muley? Well, I wound up with nothing, and the sight of those nice bucks on the drive will probably haunt me for the next year. But Bob's buck had antlers 28 inches wide and 20 inches high. And though the rack could have been a little heavier for mega-muley status, Bob was still plenty happy.

Hunting Arctic Mule Deer

By Ron Spomer

Even though mule deer don't live in the Arctic, you can hunt them as though they did. On their primary range in the Rocky Mountain West, the Arctic comes to them by blasting down from the north in the fall. If you know where and how to hunt under arctic conditions, you can catch the big bucks cold.

Deep snow and bitter cold aren't everyone's idea of an optimal hunting environment, but that's okay. Most hunters don't want to be out under those conditions, but you do if you want to get the drop on a real trophy buck.

Winter doesn't make Ol' Mossyhorn stupid, but it does force him and his peers into narrower behavior patterns, and that makes it a lot easier for you to locate him. In trophy-buck hunting, as in real-estate sales, location is everything. You can't kill a big buck until you find him.

Muleys have many places in which to hide under normal climatic conditions. They often prefer gently sloping basins knee-deep in mountain shrubs, with a gentle stream bubbling through scattered aspen woods bordered by a wide, dense stand of conifers. There are too many such places for a hunter to cover in one season. Besides, when man-scent wafts through such a paradise, experienced bucks are more than eager to move to isolated canyons, sage flats, impenetrable alder thickets and endless dog-hair stands of fir. There's so much available habitat early in the fall that you can walk your legs down to stumps and never see a big buck.

That's why I say we should thank the heavens for snow and cold. Fierce weather and a thick blanket of white eliminate thousands of mule deer hiding and feeding places, and force deer that don't want to freeze or starve into narrower, more specific habitats. Find these places, and you're halfway to a buck.

One predictable result of the first big snow is the downhill migration. Snow falls faster and piles up higher in the mountains, and that pushes muleys to lower elevations. Research has shown that muleys can't feed through much more than one foot of crusted snow or two feet of soft snow, though mature bucks can tough it out longer than does and fawns. Some really big bucks can survive belly-deep snow in the high country by resorting to special microhabitats. We'll discuss these later.

Generally, you can expect muleys to start showing up in the foothills a few hours to two days after a big snowstorm hits the high country. To take full advantage of the situation during and immediately after a storm, hunt traditional migration corridors leading down from the peaks. These often include long ridges or the bottoms of drainages where tall timber protects deer from strong winds, snowfall and extreme cold. Junctions where two ridges or drainages meet, as well as low saddles between drainages, are excellent places to hunt.

After an early big blow, don't expect hundreds of deer to be standing around in the bottomland alfalfa fields. That's late-winter behavior. If hunting season is open, they'll stop their descent as soon as they find suitable browse and escape cover at elevations below the 2-foot snow depth. To locate them, hunt uphill until your knees are buried in snow and then look for fresh sign where escape cover and good browsing areas meet. Pockets of dense timber near windblown hilltops and open slopes are good.

Don't get caught in the middle of a card game when a storm stops. If it's been nasty for two or more days, the deer will be hungry and eager to feed as soon as the weather clears. That's the time to catch them sneaking out of seclusion a bit earlier than normal and staying out a bit later. Check the edges of bedding areas in the evening and routes back from feeding areas at dawn.

I once got caught with seven other hunters in an opening day blizzard out on the plains. By the second day, several guys got nervous and plowed their way home. On the third day, two more left. By the evening of day five, I was quite lonesome, but the sky finally cleared. Without leaving camp, I glassed more than 30 mule deer. They were popping out of the snow everywhere. The next morning, I stalked and killed an above-average 4 × 4 buck in brilliant sunshine.

If you find lots of does but no mature bucks after a storm, you have to hunt with what I call the "exceptions" in mind. These are places and behavior patterns that are favored by deer that have been burdened by excessive antler growth over two or more hunting seasons. They know that it isn't safe to hang out where the snow is shallow and hunters thick.

The first exception is old-growth timber. It's one of those microhabitats I mentioned earlier, and few hunters know about it. Those who do often have the resident big bucks all to themselves.

In those rare pockets where the Forest Service has allowed mature trees to escape the chain saws, an unusual ecosystem provides remarkable, storm-proof habitat for deer. While blizzard winds outside the old-growth woods exceed 60 mph, inside it's almost as calm as the inside of a cathedral. The old trees creak and groan as their towering crowns are beaten by the howling gusts, but the violence is tempered down at ground level.

The thick canopy catches most of the snow, too. Research indicates that snow depth in old-growth woods is only half of what it is in adjacent clearcuts. And, contrary to common misconception, browse is available in old-growth timber. The natural mixed stand of trees provides diversity, openings and miniature environments where shrubs and forbs grow. In addition, mule deer feed heavily on storm-dropped branches of Douglas fir and Western red cedar.

Obviously, it's worth locating these patches of ancient trees in your hunting grounds. The easiest way to find them is to ask regional foresters. Have them mark the stands on your topographic map, and mark any that you find yourself.

Another way to locate old-growth timber is to use binoculars. The next time you're glassing a big vista, look for islands of tall trees rising above the surrounding forest. Study them, and you'll probably see that they're a different shade of green, too. These patches are often located on north-facing slopes where wildfires missed the trees because of the dampness.

Don't mistake old second-growth timber for true old-growth woods. Most hunters have never seen old-growth because most of it has been cut or burned in accessible Western forests. What many mistake for old-growth are even-age stands of second-growth lodgepole pine, ponderosa pine and Douglas fir that sprouted or were planted after fire or clear-cutting. These second-growth areas look barren at ground level because they are. There is little or no diversity, and the canopy is closed. The tree trunks are uniform in size, closely packed and generally small enough so that you can wrap your arms around one. That's not good deer habitat.

In old-growth timber, there is a variety of truly huge trees, and they are interspersed with saplings and a variety of shrubs and forbs of varying sizes on which the deer feed.

Once you've found an old-growth stand in muley country, you have an ace in the hole. Stillhunt it immediately after a storm or, if you can reach it, during a big blow. You'll enjoy the shelter as much as the big deer you'll find there.

The second exception may surprise you—barren hillsides. Just below the downwind crests of hilltops and ridges, arctic winds swirl and die. The bulk of them are funneled up and over the top. Like cattle on the plains, muleys often sit tight on the downwind side of these heights, where they are relatively safe from bitter winds.

It seems odd to us shivering humans that any creature would opt for open heights instead of protected woods or brush, but mule deer are remarkably thermo-efficient. As long as they have plenty of quality browse, they can withstand temperatures way below freezing. By lying out of the wind just below a ridgeline, a deer has merely to step over the top to reach the windscoured slope where grasses, forbs and short brush have been freed of snow. After feeding, they go right back to the downwind side.

On lower ground east of the Rockies, this is a standard ploy, but there are similar places in the high country. These are exposed subalpine ridges that provide big bucks with places in which to withstand storms that send most deer packing.

The third exception is really a behavior pattern rather than a habitat. Where big bucks don't have high-country microhabitats to exploit, snow does force them lower, but at their first opportunity they climb right back up again. If an early snow is followed by balmy weather, big bucks move higher as soon as possible, especially if hunting pressure encourages them to do so.

There is an exception to the exceptions. When the rut comes, every buck, even the wariest, abandons his bachelor digs to reach the does. This is the time to forget the buck hideouts and concentrate on find-

Trophy bucks like this one do not customarily linger where access and hunting are easy. Michael Francis photo.

ing does. Whither they goeth, the bucks goeth, and so should you. But when the rut winds down, climb again.

Scientists have discovered that muley bucks usually winter apart from and above the does and fawns. This provides the females and the young with maximum forage. At the end of the rut, mature bucks in mountainous terrain climb higher again.

They slip right back into their hideouts if they can.

To sum up: Snow deeper than 2 feet forces big bucks down to lower elevations. Old-growth timber lets bucks stay much higher than normal. Wind-blown ridges scoured clean of snow also allow bucks to remain at higher elevations. Mature bucks return to higher elevations as soon as the snow allows them to do so. All bucks drop down to the does during the rut, but after the rut, the bucks again climb higher.

There are, of course, exceptions to these generalizations. Wise old bucks will frequently hide out in very odd places where they feel safe from hunters. But when you're hunting in arctic conditions, always keep the general effects of snow and cold in mind.

In addition to reducing the living space available to bucks, arctic weather does some other nice things for hunters. Snow, for instance, makes deer easier to spot. The dark, blotchy form of a mule deer against a snowy hillside sticks out like a cherry atop an ice cream sundae. But don't let this lull you into neglecting your glassing. Despite their increased visibility against snow, or maybe because of it, muleys hide with remarkable skill. They magically disappear behind the smallest young conifer or the skimpiest patch of deciduous brush. Scour each slope and pick it apart piece by piece. Watch for flickers of motion and for horizontal and vertical lines that are out of place.

The biggest favor snow grants us is tracks. It's almost like having a network of spies to tell us, "Two came by here not long ago. See where they browsed on these branch tips? See where they bedded under that fir? They went thataway."

In Colorado, my party had good tracking snow, but the bucks were slipping around us in thick oak brush and pinyon pines. On the second-to-last evening of the season, our guide and outfitter, Greg Pink of Montrose, scratched his head and then took two of us to a long, grassy meadow where he had found encouraging marks in the snow. Deer had stuck their noses down for a bite and left antler prints on each side. We took stands at the edge of the meadow and killed a three-pointer and a four-pointer when they eased out of the dense forest to feed.

Regardless of how much you know about mule deer under arctic conditions, you can't hunt them successfully unless you can survive, and being comfortable ups your confidence. It isn't just a matter of wearing long johns.

As everyone is saying these days, to stay warm and dry, dress in layers. But make sure that each layer is coordinated with the next. The innermost layer should consist of one of the new hydrophobic materials. Polypropylene and Thermax are excellent because they both insulate and wick away moisture. You can get socks in this material, too, though I've found that thick polypro socks slide around too much. I prefer two layers of wool.

The next layer should provide substantial insulation. Heavy wool pants are traditional, and wool is a good choice, though it is slower to dry than Lake Superior if it gets wet. The new Polar Fleece or bunting-pile pants are warmer than wool, quieter and amazingly hydrophobic. They're also much lighter, but wind goes through them as easily as it does through a screen door.

To stop the wind, a garment must have a tight weave, and tightly woven fabrics make a rasping noise against brush. Wear windproof nylon pants or other hard fabrics over wool or fleece, and you might as well blow a trumpet while you stalk. Wear the nylon under the insulation, and the wind will blow the warm air right out of all of those microfibers. The best option may be to wear fleece pants with a Gore-Tex core. The waterproof Gore-Tex will rustle slightly when you move, but it won't be exposed to rasp against twigs, and the inner half of the fleece will do its insulating job unhindered by bitter breezes.

Cover your torso with a shirt(s), vest, jacket or windbreaker. Light wool is the standard in shirts. Vests and jackets should be of the same material as the pants, or of a soft outer material with an insulating layer of Thinsulate, down, or Hollofil. I like to wear down vest over my wool shirt and cover it with a Polar Fleece jacket. It's a light, quiet combination, and the vest stuffs into a small space if I need to remove something.

Over the jacket, I wear an insulated parka or windbreaker with high collar and hood. Again, it's important to keep the outer material soft and quiet for stillhunting. If it's particularly cold or I'm planning to take a stand, I pull insulated coveralls over my wool or fleece pants.

I wear felt-lined boots for stand hunting, but I use Thinsulate-insulated, Gore-Tex-lined leather hiking boots for stillhunting. For maximum warmth in a head covering, I like a Gore-Tex, down-filled, Trooper-style hat with furry earflaps. I also use one or two stocking caps. A balaclava—a stocking cap that pulls down to cover your face and neck, leaving only the eyes uncovered—is excellent. Against biting winds, a face mask or muffler is essential.

An adept gun hand is critical to any hunter's success. I keep my hands unfrozen by poking them first into those wonderful, thin polypropylene gloves, and then into heavy, Gore-Tex/Thinsulate hunting gloves or mitts. I've never been comfortable shooting with a heavy glove to hamper my squeeze. When I expect action, I remove the right glove. The polypropylene glove stays in place, and I put my right hand into a pocket until I get the shot. My fully gloved left hand carries the rifle.

The only other equipment you'll need will be a dependable rifle and sight, a calorie-rich lunch, a good compass, weatherproof matches, firestarters, and similar gear. Three space blankets can be a lightweight lifesaver. I like a quiet fleece pack in which to carry these essentials plus any clothing I remove during the course of the hunt.

Thus outfitted, anyone should be able to hunt all day and keep his attention focused on deer, not his shivering carcass. Hunt in the snow, climb to the secret hideouts of the bucks and shoot a wallhanger. It will warm your heart. 🦌

Just Plains Muleys

By Ron Spomer

Mule deer are a product of the Rocky Mountains. You don't find them in the Appalachian Mountains, the Olympic Mountains, the Alaska Range or a dozen other ranges. So why was the biggest muley buck I ever shot standing on the flats of western South Dakota?

South Dakota. That's one of those boring states like Nebraska and Kansas and Oklahoma—the kind you yawn through on your way "out West." It would be interesting to know how many eastern hunters cross the dull "plains" states every autumn en route to a Rocky Mountain mule deer rendezvous. It would be even more interesting to know how many mule deer watch the hunters drive by.

Truth is, the high plains between the Rockies and the 100th meridian—the north-and-south line cutting from the middle of North Dakota down through Texas—are a mule deer hunter's delight. There probably aren't any world-record muleys there, but right now plenty of plains bucks are lugging around antlers that would make most Rocky Mountain muley fans blither. And those big bucks are a lot easier to wrap a tag around than the average mountain muley.

Muleys live in the plains states for one reason: habitat. Look closely at this flat, barren land, and you'll see that it isn't. There are countless places for deer to eat, sleep and thrive in. Dry washes, coulees, badlands, juniper ridges, hardwood stream bottoms, and riverside brush patches give them everything the mountains do, except high-elevation nose bleeds. Scattered grainfields provide them with something more: abundant protein on which to grow fat. The deer are there; all you have to do is find them.

But finding can be tough for newcomers, who are usually confused by the vastness of the plains. Stand on your tiptoes, and you can see for miles. Where in all of that nothing do you find a deer? In the blemishes, of course.

It doesn't take a forest to hide a mule deer. Give a muley a patch of grass or a wrinkle in the land, and it'll disappear as effectively as any whitetail. I once watched a mature, heavy four-pointer walk across a bare grassland. One second he was a brown beacon in a sea of yellow; the next second he was gone. There were no trees, no brush patches, no canyons. He had just disappeared.

I had walked out to solve this mystery and had about given up when I flushed him from a small, natural ditch that I could jump across. There was no concealing brush in it, just grass up to my ankles. In effect, that buck had been hiding *inside the earth.*

Once you learn this about plains muleys, your attitude will change from "Where could they possibly be?" to "How can I possibly hunt all of the potential hiding places?" And that's the key to success. You must recognize your need to narrow all of that terrain down to the most productive spots. Otherwise, you could hike an area all season and kill nothing but a good pair of boots.

The quickest route to the heart of an area's mule deer herd is through its farm fields. On the dry, high plains, wheat and alfalfa crops are deer magnets. I've seen does and fawns camp in alfalfa for days. When they finished feeding, they plopped down in that soft, green vegetation and chewed cud until it was time to stand up and browse again. This, of course, was before hunting season, but even during the season, antlerless muleys are often in hay and grain early in the evening and long into the morning. Bucks aren't often that stupid, and

similar to hunted game everywhere, they lay low until dark. But cast headlights across the fields two hours after sunset, and you'll probably see a few sets of antlers.

Because of this, farm fields are good starting points. If you hunt a private ranch, just ask the rancher which fields the deer are using. He'll be more than happy to direct you. Otherwise, scout field edges for trails leading to and from. Generally, crop fields lie in valleys near streams or "on top," meaning the relatively flat uplands between drainages.

Valley deer usually have plenty of brush, tall grass, junipers or deciduous woods in which to bed near their food. Sometimes, this riparian habitat looks more like whitetail country than muley cover, but you'll find big-eared deer here just the same—deer that are often acting more like whitetails than muleys.

I've kicked hefty bucks from dense willows that I'd have sworn would have strangled them. Last December, while pheasant hunting in western Kansas, a friend and I flushed a half-dozen muleys from an isolated patch of head-high weeds in a drainage surrounded by short pasture grass. We were within 10 yards of the deer and shooting at ringnecks before the muleys bolted.

A similar thing happened when I was hunting sharptail grouse in a Montana hay field that lay right next to the ranch house. A stream, its route marked by frequent outbursts of willows and cottonwoods, looped through the field. While breaking through a strip of this cover to reach the other side, I disturbed six muley bucks that bounced out in single file—a massive non-typical in the lead was followed by two prime four-pointers, then two three-pointers and a forkhorn. They probably hadn't left that field all summer.

If you find yourself near such stream habitat, scout the stream bottom itself for large tracks, as the bottom will frequently be just a dirt or mud runway by early autumn. If you find tracks, sit on a high bluff bordering the valley and glass bottomland fields early and late in the day. Thrash dense cover later if you have to.

Muleys feeding in upland fields usually bed in nearby drainages, which can vary from shallow, short, grassy swales to deep, wooded draws stretching for miles toward a river. Generally, such long draws (so named because they draw runoff water from the uplands), or coulees, branch again and again as they near the uplands, creating an incredible web of deep sidedraws filled with oaks, hackberries, junipers, elms, plums, snowberries, and similar brush capable of hiding countless deer. You can work out one draw to its end, stride a dozen yards to either side, and find another that is just as secluded and paralleling the first.

This big muley buck could soon disappear into a grass patch or landscape wrinkle.

Such a setup is paradise for bucks. By following these narrow coulees, the bucks travel to feed fields with minimum exposure. When disturbed in the fields, they quickly bounce into the nearest draw to escape. Follow, and they'll readily leapfrog one or two channels to give you the slip.

Despite this abundant escape terrain, muleys usually select a few favorite draws and stick to them until repeatedly disturbed or urged to move by rut or changed food supplies. During one October in South Dakota, I watched the same band of bachelor bucks in the same draw for weeks. They were always within a one-quarter-mile core area, even though dozens of similar habitats led off in every direction. At sunset, they'd browse their way up to an old wheat field. Dawn pushed them back into their loafing quarters. When I looked for them in November during the rifle season, they were scattered far and wide, rutting.

Hunting upland grainfields and their bordering coulees becomes a game of sign scouting, glassing and hiking. I prefer to watch field edges at dusk and dawn. If that doesn't pay, I'll watch for tracks as I walk those edges in a convoluted course winding around all of the finger draws. Major trails don't usually start until well down a draw, after various side-draws have joined to concentrate deer travel. This could be as far as a mile from a feed field. Deer feel secure there, and they move earlier and later in the day along these trails deep in the coulees. These are perfect locations for a bowhunter's stand.

Predictably, such main trails soon dwindle as animals traveling them wander off to find bedding sites on side-slopes, up side-draws, in brush patches, beneath trees and atop small knolls within the coulee bottom. There seem to be no preferred bedding sites within these draw systems. I've seen deer in all of the above locations, but I find most—probably because they're more visible—lying on open, short-grass side-hills.

The most productive way to hunt coulee bedding areas is slowly and by glassing intensely. I routinely drop into a draw from a feed field at midmorning and move quickly for the first one-quarter mile or so. Then I slow to a standard whitetail-woods pace: walk one step, pause two. This is essential to visually sweep the new terrain that appears around bends in the stream, over knolls and ridges, at the mouths of side-draws and so on. Move impatiently, and the big ears and eyes of a bedded muley will spot you the instant your head pops into view. The object is to see them first because once you do, it's a simple matter to get behind them with the wind in your favor, and ease up for an easy shot.

Many hunters who can't force themselves to still-hunt at the proper pace opt for deer drives. They place stand hunters at strategic points near heads of draws and at crossing points between draws, then send walkers up the system from the bottom. It isn't unusual for standers to see one or two dozen muleys scatter like quail. Shots are sometimes long, but deer frequently stop in the open after they've

By glassing from a point with a view, you might encounter such a lovely sight as this.

climbed out of a draw and put a ridge between themselves and drivers.

Where crop fields aren't common, such as on national grasslands and Bureau of Land Management grazing lands that are open to public hunting, finding muleys becomes a little more difficult. Still, it is certainly easier than trying to sift one from a Rocky Mountain Douglas fir forest.

The best way to locate muleys is with binoculars. Select an outpost that has a commanding view of a major draw or river bottom, prop your elbows on your knees, and start glassing as soon as it's bright enough. Resist the desire to move if you don't immediately see something. For every hillside and brush patch you see, there will be two you don't. A buck feeding in a narrow draw could step in and out of view in an instant.

When you're confident that an area is empty, hike to the next overlook and start scouring new terrain. Deer will stop moving soon after the sun hits them early in the season, so watch the shadows. During the rut, expect the unexpected anytime; but normally, two hours after sunrise, concentrate on finding bedded deer.

When rifle seasons begin, normal plains deer patterns are drastically disrupted. Hunters crisscrossing the land send deer running back and forth looking for undisturbed cover. This is a good time to sit on a promontory and glass until you see a buck slip into a patch of cover and hold. Then it's time to hurry over and take him.

Another useful tactic is to hunt rugged landscapes where few other hunters dare to go. Badlands are ideal. The convoluted spires, ridges, ditches and channels of eroded plains soils are ideal for hiding. Muleys don't normally prefer these places, but they will seek sanctuary in these spots when pressed. You can wait at the edge of badlands to intercept deer heading toward them on opening

day, or you can stillhunt through these areas after the first day. There's no easy way to hunt these rugged places. You scramble and poke through the maze, and if you get a shot, it's usually a quick, close one at a surprised deer.

In some areas, muleys act similarly to pronghorns in that they use distance as a protective moat. In eastern Montana. muleys often lie in the middle of huge flats hundreds of yards from the nearest cover and race away when anyone tries to close to a reasonable shooting distance. The best way to outwit these deer is to slip in during darkness.

Open spaces are what makes plains hunting such a pleasure. Game is readily visible to anyone with sharp eyes, binoculars and spotting scopes, yet there are sufficient bumps, gullies, and forms of ground vegetation to provide stalking cover. Because of this, hunter success runs in the 50 to 85 percent range. That's good news for anyone simply wanting to kill a deer, but it does create problems for trophy hunters.

Plains bucks are usually taken when they are young, and this leaves few to grow old and heavily racked. In order to find mature males, a hunter has to identify restricted harvest areas. These could be isolated units that few hunters penetrate, limited-permit-entry units, newly opening units that have been closed for several years or, most commonly, private land with limited hunting pressure.

When applying for permits in any plains state, ask local biologists which units provide the best opportunities for trophy bucks, if that's what you're interested in. If you just want meat for the table and you have the legal option, shoot a doe and let the little forkhorns grow up. Forkhorns are usually still young and dumb, and they're frequently easier to outwit than older does.

Private land hunts for big bucks are becoming more common in eastern Montana, Wyoming, Colorado, New Mexico and western Texas as ranchers begin to manage their herds for fee hunting. Prices vary widely from $100 to $2,000, but well-managed ranches offer an excellent opportunity to kill a big buck. Other ranchers, particularly in western North Dakota, South Dakota, Nebraska, Kansas and Oklahoma, may charge smaller trespass fees without regulating hunting to favor big-buck production. Surprisingly, many private lands are still open at no charge to ethical, polite hunters who ask permission and get to know ranch owners.

Vast sections of public lands in most plains states provide lots of hunting ground, but you have to search diligently for scarce big bucks. Smaller bucks and does are usually easy to find.

Plains states game departments can provide you with "where and when to go" information, as well as maps identifying public lands.

Yes, mule deer are a product of the Rockies, but they discovered the dry plains long ago. The next time you're looking for a great Rocky Mountain mule deer hunt, why not skip the mountains and enjoy a "just plains" delightful hunt?

Pick Pocket Muleys

By Dwight Schuh

We were sitting on a hillside in northern Utah at sunrise, watching nine bucks. They fed along the top of a sagebrush ridge, heading toward a patch of serviceberry where they would undoubtedly bed for the day.

"What do you think of this western hunting?" I said softly to Glenn Helgeland, a native of Wisconsin.

"It's great. Just look at all those bucks. But it takes some adjustment," Glenn whispered. Formerly an editor of an archery magazine, Glenn now operates his own publishing and promotion business that specializes in deer hunting books, videos and sports shows. He's hunted all over the United States under a variety of conditions. "Back East, you're hunting as soon as you walk out the door or out of camp because the whitetails live wherever there's any timber or cover.

"Out here you might hike four or five miles just to find a pocket of deer. It's a tremendous adjustment to realize that deer live in pockets, and that you have to find them before you can hunt them."

Even from a Midwesterner's perspective, Glenn had seen something that even many native Westerners ignore. With those words, he had very well summarized the essence and most important principle of all good mule deer hunting, what I call the "pocket principle."

In a nutshell, that means that all deer country is not created equal. It may all look similar, even to a trained eye. But for various reasons, deer prefer small parts of their range and they congregate in those pockets. In any good mule deer range, more than 90 percent of the bucks, I believe, will occupy less than 10 percent of their range—the 90/10 rule—even if it all looks good. You can hunt for days in the best mule deer country and see few if any good bucks if you ignore that fact.

Before specifics about pockets can be discussed, a couple of overriding principles about bucks must be recognized. One is that bucks generally live by themselves or in bachelor groups, not with does. Sure, there are exceptions, but that's true in most cases (except during the rut).

A corollary is that most bucks live on the margins, on the periphery of the richest deer country. Does and fawns select the lush spots, the alder bottoms, meadows, aspen groves and other places where lots of food, easy terrain, plentiful water and good cover make for easy living. Nature apparently has relegated these prime areas to the animals that need them most and has pushed the bucks to the edges, either low, inhospitable desert country, or, more commonly, high-elevation rims and isolated alpine reaches. I suppose that bucks live there for biological reasons, such as reducing competition with does and fawns, but sometimes I wonder if the big old bucks, like many of us hunters, don't just like to be alone in high and wild places. That may be a fanciful notion, but it can be a good guiding rule for finding big bucks.

That provides a framework for identifying buck territory, or "buck pastures," as many hunters call them. Now the question is: Where within that terri-

83

Mule deer bucks typically live in bachelor groups or by themselves. Judd Cooney photo.

tory will the bucks be found?

And that brings us back to the pocket principle. Just being in good buck country doesn't guarantee you'll see many bucks. Even within their preferred ranges, bucks live in these small pockets, and it's these select, isolated spots that you must find for great hunting.

To a large extent, these pockets are defined seasonally by the acronym FESS—food, escape, sex, solitude. During early seasons, *food* ranks foremost. All western states have bow seasons opening from mid-August into early September, and several have high-country rifle hunts in September. Bow hunts normally attract relatively few hunters, and most early rifle hunts are limited entry, so overall hunting pressure is light and deer carry on in normal routines.

At the same time, bucks are growing antlers—antler growth continues into early September—and putting on fat for the winter, so they have a high energy demand. As a result, they don't necessarily seek good escape cover; rather, they concentrate around the best feed.

In the West, prevailing storm winds blow from the southwest, so snow piles up in cornices on the lee northern and eastern slopes just below the tops of ridges, and this accumulated snow provides water well into the summer. Shrubs and grass flourish there, and that's where bucks congregate to eat. Even from a long distance you can look at a desert or alpine mountain range and judge those spots by the color and pattern of vegetation, by the green strips and patches among more arid surroundings.

That gets you into potentially good buck country, but you can't rely on that alone because the bucks may use only some of the prime pockets and ignore the rest. That's where the 90/10 rule applies. Besides, bucks may also shift from one pocket to another, and you might miss them if you go strictly on looks of the country. In Nevada, I once kept tabs on a herd of more than 80 bucks. One day, they would congregate to feed at the head of a big open bowl. Then, they'd slowly sweep across the bowl like a moving tide and end up the next day a mile away in another basin. They completed this cycle every three days, nature's version of rest/rotation grazing, I suppose. If you went just by the looks of the country and checked one of the basins when the bucks weren't there, you'd swear that the entire area was deserted.

For that reason, I think it's important to operate by the old cliche, "Deer are where you find them." During early seasons, the most reliable way is to spot with high-power optics. As I've said, energy needs take priority over escape at this time of year, so bucks will feed in the open, often throughout the day, where they're very visible. Bucks are easier to see in the late summer than at any other time, so long-distance spotting is the logical way to find them.

Remember one point in locating pockets this way—don't stop looking just because you see a couple of bucks somewhere. They may represent only the tip of the iceberg. Move around and keep looking until you find the core buck pastures, the prime pockets. Those are the sources of great hunting.

By mid-September, bucks' antlers are fully grown and energy demand decreases. Rich food isn't as important. At the same time, general hunting seasons are getting under way. Timing varies among states, but most western rifle seasons open in October and, in my opinion, these seasons are the major influence on the lives of mule deer during the mid-fall period. Food becomes secondary, and *escape* takes precedence.

And that should guide your search. Now, as deer harassed by hunters seek the refuge of thick brush and timber, the big binoculars and long-distance spotting methods aren't as effective, and you may have to rely on intuition and reason to find the deer. By that, I mean that you ask yourself, "Where would those bucks go with an army of hunters after them?" The obvious answer is: Some place where there aren't any hunters.

Without question, maps have led me to some of my best hunting, because they reveal hard-to-reach places. I look for four things that represent security for deer.

One is distance. A three- or four-mile hike will eliminate most hunters, so I look for spots where I can hike that far away from any roads. Deer will congregate just beyond walking range of the average foot hunter, and that's the distance at which I want to start hunting.

Two is terrain. Cliffs and slides that make for tough hiking mean good hunting. Any "Hell-Hole Canyon" or other ominous sounding place gets my attention. But not all good spots are so labeled. One excellent timbered bench I know overlooks a major highway. The bench actually is easy to hunt—once you get there. But to do that you have to wade a river and climb one-half mile straight up through big red cliffs. Few hunters ever do, so during the season bucks really accumulate on that bench.

The third thing I look for is private land. In the West, private and public lands are intermixed in checkerboard fashion, and that can make getting to some public lands very tough. On a plateau in northwestern Colorado, locked gates block roads across private land, which blocks road access to large sections of national forest. Yet, public lands are continuous across the plateau; you simply have to walk to reach them. I found this to be a virtual wilderness area, because most people stopped at the locked gates. To reach the remote pockets of public land, I walked out the fencelines, always careful to stay on the public side, and I had excellent hunting.

Vegetation is the fourth type of security cover I look for. Thick stuff such as oak brush or black spruce timber will hold lots of good bucks when the shooting starts. You can't always locate these on maps, because even topographic maps don't distinguish between kinds of vegetation, but you can locate likely aspects—northern slopes and moist basins where thick brush might grow—and then check them out on the ground.

You won't spot many deer in the open at this time, so you have to rely on sign to confirm the presence of deer. When you've selected a few likely escape pockets, hike from one to the other to evaluate sign there. Bucks will be very concentrated in the best escape pockets, so fresh tracks and deeply cut trails should be obvious.

That approach worked for Rex Thomas and me during Utah's general rifle season. We started hunting the ridgetops where many roads made the hunting easy, but it didn't take us long to see that was a mistake. Everyone else was doing the same and the deer had left.

We sat in the shade of an aspen tree and pored over a map. Despite all of the roads on top, the bottoms of several big canyons were shown as roadless. So, we loaded our backpacks with three days' provisions and headed to the bottom of the deepest canyon. Down there, dense timber covered the north-facing slopes and oak brush the south. Our chances for spotting deer were slim, so we spent the first day just looking for sign. In one timbered draw we found the ground plowed to dust by deer hooves, the first concentration of fresh sign we'd see the whole trip. The next morning, while still-hunting, I killed a fine old buck. He was feeding calmly at midmorning; no one had disturbed him there. The hunting was simple once we found where all of the deer had taken refuge. That's usually the way it is with October hunting.

In November, *sex* replaces escape as the overriding force in the lives of deer. Not all western states allow hunting at this time, but in several—Montana, Idaho, Colorado, Arizona—general rifle seasons hit the rut, and some states have bow and muzzleloader seasons during the rut. Obviously, now, you won't look for buck pastures because bucks and does have come together, but the pocket principle still very much applies. But rather than searching for bucks alone, you'll search for does, still congregated in their prime areas, and the bucks that have come out of the woodwork to service them.

In *Mule And Black-Tailed Deer Of North America*, Valerius Geist says: "As the period of breeding approaches during the rutting season, males have sorted themselves into groups of unequal bucks that stay continuously within the home range of a female group. Large bucks are dispersed over the female home ranges, distributed so that each finds a locality where it can defend itself against others."

Simply put, there will be one big, dominant buck in each doe area, and other smaller bucks of various sizes will be hanging around that core group. So, from mid to late November, you have to find these doe groups, which can be fairly easy with snow on the ground and the deer rut active.

Just remember an important point about this time of year. Because weather can vary greatly from year to year, concentration points for does may change drastically. In 1985, Idaho got severe snowstorms as early as October. By November, most mule deer had been pushed from high ranges onto sagebrush lowlands at the 5,000-foot elevation. During 1986–87, Idaho had a drought with very little snow, and during those years, deer remained in heavy timber as high as 9,000 feet right on through November and December seasons.

So, even though you're looking for key pockets—in this case, does with bucks in attendance—you can't predict their exact locations. You

may have to look far and wide to find them. As in the summer, use your binoculars and scope. If there's snow on the ground, deer are fairly visible against the white backdrop. They'll be concentrated, and they're on the move with rut, which makes them easy to see. You can also see trails in the snow, and that's probably the best way to locate late-season deer. With a scope under good light conditions, you can spot deer trails three or four miles away, which helps you locate prime pockets.

By late November, when the rut diminishes, older bucks start drifting away from does, and *solitude* becomes the guiding force. Again, quoting Geist: "Large bucks then (after peak of rut) enter a stage of protracted rest and hiding. Quite apathetically, they rest in thickets, and occasionally they temporarily join small males and even solicit listless sparring matches. Bucks begin to disappear from female ranges, and the apparent ratio of males to females drops. After the rut, large bucks go into seclusion and rest. They drift off, probably to peripheral patches of winter habitat, which results in the well-known phenomenon of bucks' wintering at higher elevations in deeper snow."

I've seen that clearly demonstrated a number of times. One year, Cliff Dewell and I hunted a late bow season in Idaho, just after Thanksgiving. We found hundreds of does in the sagebrush lowlands, and because we saw a few small bucks chasing does there, we assumed that the rut was still in full swing and we'd eventually find big bucks there.

But we never did. So we climbed the surrounding inhospitable ridges where fierce winds and deep snow prevailed. No animal in its right mind would be up there, we thought, let alone any sane hunter. But that's where we found the bucks—big ones. The western sides of the ridgetops were blown bare of snow, and the bucks were feeding on exposed grass and stunted shrubs there. Then they were moving back to the lee eastern sides to bed in snow three to four-feet deep.

Again, we found these deer by glassing at long range, looking for deer, or for trails that would lead to deer. At this time, following the rut, the buck-pasture concept very clearly applies. You may find general wintering areas by locating big herds of does, but you'll find the bucks by themselves around the edges of core areas, just as you do in the summer.

One final thought deserves emphasis. Never be satisfied with the status quo. It's easy to pick one spot and hunt there day after day, year after year. You're comfortable there because you feel at home. But if you hunt that way, you could be missing the very best. Look beyond the usual spots. Just over the next ridge or across the next canyon may be hunting twice as good as you've ever known. Scoring in hunting is like scoring in bowling because bucks live in pockets. Hit the pocket, and you get a strike; miss the pocket even a little, and it's just another open season.

Run and Hide Muleys

By Walter L. Prothero

Back in the early '70s, when I was conducting my research on elk behavior for a degree in wildlife biology, I ran into more than a few big mule deer bucks. Though my primary concern was with elk behavior, I couldn't help but become distracted by the huge bucks I'd sometimes see in the high Absarokas just north of Yellowstone, in Yellowstone itself, and in northern Utah. Before anything else, I was a deer hunter, so I started taking notes. After a few years of this, I began to realize that, behaviorally, there were basically two kinds of bucks. One would rely on running to escape, the other would rely on hiding. Often, there would be bucks of each type on the same mountain.

Since then, I've kept notes on the types of bucks taken by hunters. Whenever a big buck was killed, I'd try to find out exactly how it happened. What I've noticed is a new pattern in the behavior of big bucks. Most would rather hide to avoid detection than run to escape danger. This is even more true in heavily hunted areas, with some places inhabited almost exclusively by deer that are hiders. Only in remote country, such as the Beartooth-Absaroka Wilderness in Montana and various areas in central and northern British Columbia, will deer still run from what they perceive as potential danger. With today's flat-shooting rifles and superior scopes, the runners are the first to get killed off. The bucks that survive are deer that have been raised by does that tend to hide in response to human activity, or those that learned early in life that it's safest to hide when hunters are about. Back in the '60s, the golden age of mule deer hunting in Utah where I learned to hunt, it seemed that the big bucks I took were all runners.

I believe that the natural tendency for mule deer—ones that haven't been hunted extensively—is to run from approaching danger. Then they'll stop, if in the open, and watch their backtrail to make sure that the danger is far enough behind. If it continues to threaten them, they'll run some more. With their ground-eating bound, trot, flatout run and endurance, they were pretty safe from all predators from mountain lions to primitive man. Then came the rifle, and soon the methods of escape that evolved over millions of years were no longer effective. Before mule deer had time to adapt to this new threat, they'd gained the reputation of being the whitetail's retarded cousin. Now that they are adapting, they are finally being regarded as an intelligent and desirable trophy. There are still places where big bucks can be taken almost as they were more than 25 years ago when I began hunting in the now overpopulated country of Weber County. Mule deer still stand and gawk at hunters across a canyon in the wilderness of British Columbia, in the Sun River country and in the Beartooth-Absaroka Wilderness of Montana.

Hunting in such areas is mostly a matter of getting out early when bucks are feeding in the open, or again late in the afternoon or early evening. Brushing them out into the open where the hunter can get a shot is another good technique. It's a joy to hunt bucks like this. Little hunting pressure means lots of runners, and you can daydream about how all mule deer hunting used to be.

Hunting runners is simply an easier proposition than hunting the hiders, at least if you're somewhat of a marksman. The most common and easiest method to flush out runners is to simply sidehill up a canyon with the idea of flushing deer onto the opposite slope where you can get a shot. Back in the

'60s, this was about the only technique I used. I'd simply work up-canyon on one of the side slopes, preferably the one with more brush or timber, with the idea of spooking deer out of the brush below and up onto the relatively open south- or west-facing slope. The shots are often long, 200 or 300 yards, but if the slope is open you may have time for several shots if you muff the·first.

One of the runners I recently killed—which scored 201 Boone and Crockett Club points—was taken using this method. I'd seen the buck that day before the opening of the season as he made his way up through a stand of fir and aspen. It was the eve of deer season, and the buck knew it—he'd heard the parade of four-wheelers and all-terrain vehicles on the road two miles to the north and was moving to a safer place. I picked up his tracks the next morning and stayed with them for the better part of the following three days, returning to camp each night exhausted from the hiking and concentration. It was the longest I'd ever tracked anything. On the afternoon of the third day, as I was slowly following the tracks down into a steep, rugged canyon, I got a very strange feeling. I'd had the feeling before, so I knew better than to try and discount it. The best way I can describe it is as a feeling of anticipation—action-to-come. I moved up the canyon on the side slope, above the tracks in case he'd circled above his backtrail. A small four-point flushed from a patch of oak scrub and bounded into the canyon bottom and up the opposite slope. A bit farther on, a forkhorn and a doe repeated the maneuver. I continued up the canyon when suddenly the big buck flushed from somewhere down the slope, bounded the stream, and made his way up the opposite side. Three days of tension burst like a balloon. I was so excited that I missed clean with the first shot. On the second, I settled into that quiet, impersonal state you shoot from when you do it right. Like a wild bronc just out of the chute, the buck lowered his head and kicked with his hind legs. I knew that he was already dead, but I was taking no chances. I held ahead and a little above as he trotted across the slope, and hit him again. I wouldn't be surprised if he was the last trophy-size runner I'll take out of that country.

If you're hunting country that isn't true wilderness, as most of us are forced to do these days, adult bucks will typically be hiders. Don't waste time waiting for a trophy buck to feed out of a stand of timber into the open and then expect a nice, open broadside shot. It just doesn't happen that way much anymore. You may catch small bucks that way, or see does and fawns, but unless it happens to be during the rut, the big bucks are going to stay hidden and won't move during the daylight unless you just about step on them. Because the majority of hunting seasons occur before the rut, hunting trophy bucks means flushing them out of their beds and taking a quick shot, usually at close range.

Hiders behave more like whitetails, elk in timber,

or even black bears. Hiders will most often stay close to heavy brush or timber. When they do, they are difficult to approach. Mule deer bucks have perhaps the keenest hearing of any game on the continent—witness the large ears—and can smell at least as well as whitetails or elk. And they rely more heavily on eyesight. In other words, they're darn tough to stalk once they have bedded. It requires the stealth and silence of a leopard, the patience of Job, and the reflexes and shooting eye of Billy the Kid. In addition, hiders will not, as a rule, flush until they are absolutely certain they've been detected. They've learned that most humans can't find them if they lie absolutely still. Probably the best way to find hiders is to track them.

One season, I would consistently find large deer tracks in an open flat on a plateau. The flat was full of good deer feed—frost-dried forbs, wild rose, cliff rose, mahogany and sagebrush—but in spite of my dawn-to-dark vigils, I couldn't catch a glimpse of the buck. He would only feed at night, then return to the timber before first light. After about three days of waiting, I decided to follow his tracks down into the thick spruce and fir of the north-facing slope of a large canyon. Unfortunately, the tracks were heading downwind so if I stayed on his trail, he'd eventually smell me before I could get a shot. At that point in my hunting career, I'd already learned that under such situations, it was best to make loops on the downwind side of the trail, returning to it every 100 yards or so to make sure that I hadn't overshot the end of the trail. If I did overshoot it, I'd make smaller loops back in the direction of where I'd last seen the tracks. I also knew that typically, smart old bucks make a buttonhook on the downside of their trails when they bed so that they can smell, and usually see, their backtrail. I'd made several loops downwind of the trail as I moved along in the direction the buck had taken. I kept my rifle ready and my thumb on the safety because if I got a shot, it would have to be taken quickly. I moved slowly and quietly, keeping close watch on where I put my feet, and straining to see as far ahead into the gloom of timber as possible. I hadn't gone 200 yards into the timber when I saw something that didn't quite fit. I stared at it for several minutes. It seemed to be a large, dark knothole on a weathered deadfall that lay in a tangle of broken branches. It was just 30 feet ahead, and I stared at it for what seemed like hours. Then it blinked! At exactly that instant, the rifle came up and my thumb flicked off the safety. The buck was up and over a log as I fired. A few hairs drifted away in the breeze. The buck was a good one and very fat.

Sometimes, you'll find a hider on a relatively open slope, ridge or meadow. But they'll behave the

Hiders are more prevalent in heavily hunted areas. Some will refuse to spook. Wyman Meinzer photo.

same as one in thick brush. They won't move until they're sure they've been spotted. I hunted a particular buck for four straight seasons. The buck had a variety of tricks in his bag, and most of the time they worked on me or other hunters. Once, I had located the buck on an open slope across a wide canyon. He was bedded in a scrubby clump of maples and was too far away for a shot. A quarter–mile down the canyon, four hunters on horseback were heading straight for him. I was sure that they were about to kill "my" buck. I thought briefly of opening fire or shouting to scare the deer out of the country, but I figured that it would be unsporting. It probably wouldn't have worked anyway. The horsemen came on: 200 yards, 100, 50, 20. The buck had stretched out his neck and lay his head along the ground. Two horsemen rode above the clump of maples and two below, not 30 feet from the buck. He didn't move. When the hunters were far enough up the canyon to no longer pose a threat, I stood up. I'd reasoned that if the buck had let them pass so close without moving, he'd let me, too. And I knew where he was. But the moment I stood up, the buck saw me and stood up himself. Somehow he'd known that I'd detected him, and he trotted up the slope and over the ridge. Several years later I did manage to collect the buck, but that's another story. Sometimes, bucks may hide in places where you wouldn't think there was enough cover to conceal a fair-size prairie dog.

Once, my longtime hunting buddy Rick Lovell, a heavyweight wingshot, and I were hunting sage grouse across the top of a flat plateau in Weber County, Utah. The tallest vegetation on the plateau was shin-high stunted sagebrush. Much of it was little more than ankle-deep. We were working toward a small wind-tortured clump of fir not quite knee-high. At the most, we had maybe expected to flush some grouse from the scrub, but were startled nearly out of our shoes when a big buck bounced out and took off for the next canyon. He'd let us approach to within 20 or 25 feet.

Another time, in Wyoming's Red Desert, I was making a stalk on a nice antelope buck. He had a large harem, so I was stalking not just one pair of eyes but 25. I was on my belly and squirming my way up the last few yards of the rise where I could get a shot. I eased into a small gully, not even the size of a small irrigation ditch, when I came face to face with a good mule deer buck 15 feet away. We scared the pants off each other and he, not content with startling me out of five years of my life, also frightened off my antelope. He'd been hiding in a small depression where the scanty vegetation was scarcely a foot high.

There seems to be fewer good bucks in country that gets moderate to heavy hunting pressure. This only makes sense, because even hiders aren't invulnerable and the more hunters in a given area, the greater the odds that someone will stumble onto a good buck and collect him. So make sure that there are some good bucks in the country you're hunting.

The only way to do this is by pre-season scouting. If there aren't any runners around, you have to look for tracks. An adult buck's track is unlike the track of either a small buck or a doe. The hoofs of a big buck point outward somewhat, especially if he's just meandering along, as he'll almost always do unless he's frightened or after a doe. A large buck will usually leave drag marks between prints when he's ambling along in soft soil or snow, just as a fat man is more apt to shuffle than a lean, energetic younger man. Aside from track size, a big buck will sink more deeply in soft soil. The best way to learn to recognize deer tracks made by different age and sex-classes is to observe them during the summer. Because there are no hunters afield then, even big, old hiders are apt to revert back to their running behavior. Note where a big buck has walked, and then go and look at his tracks. How do they differ from those of the forkhorn you tracked?

Now that you know what a big buck's tracks looks like, see if you can find any in the area you are going to hunt. Don't do your scouting too far in advance of the hunt because changing seasons produce changes in feed plants, and bucks that were there in September may not be there in October. I usually do most of my scouting a week or so before the season opens.

Mule deer have changed since the day of the runners. They'll hide until they're nearly stepped on. Last season in western Colorado, I watched a group of hunters work up the canyon from the river bottoms of the Dolores River, pushing bucks as they came. Smaller bucks and does streamed up the trail just below where I was perched on a sandstone rimrock. Apparently, the hunters were inexperienced, because they'd posted no one above to intercept anything that might flush. One hunter was passing a small clump of tall sagebrush a few yards below me. I thought I saw something move in the sagebrush and put the glasses on it. It was a good buck, with a total of 11 points. He was standing and moving around some tall sagebrush to keep it between himself and the hunter. The hunter passed on by and moved up the canyon. Before long, another hunter walked by the sagebrush on the other side. The buck repeated the maneuver, then lay back down. I had my camera and managed to get a few photos of the maneuvering. After photographing and watching the buck, I didn't quite have the heart to shoot him.

Later in the day, I shot a small buck, dressed and dragged him toward the sagebrush where the big buck was hiding. I then sat at the edge of the sagebrush not 15 feet from him. It was several minutes before that buck flushed and bounded down into the canyon bottom and up the other side. The last I saw of him, he was topping out onto a timbered mesa. I guess he'll very likely die of old age. ![bird]

Hunting Alone, Comfortably

By Ed Park

Life can get no better than being alone in some remote desert canyon, enjoying an evening fire after a good hunt. My mule deer buck is hanging just up the ridge, cooling in the chill night air, while coyotes sing to the rising moon.

The next morning, I hike to my buck and bone out the meat. Then, I shoulder my pack and head for civilization, where I'll see another person for the first time in nearly a week: As I ease down the canyon, I'm aware that a solitary hunter returning with his kill has been a common scene throughout man's history, because man was once as much at home in the wilds as the animals he hunted. Some of us still hunt alone, so that we can enjoy great hunting as well as complete independence and peaceful solitude.

But isn't it dangerous? Who should consider it? If you decide to do it, how do you go about things? Where do you find uncrowded places? What equipment and precautions are necessary?

I know the answers for me, but for a broader view, I asked others.

"Don't do it," was Sgt. Terry Silbaugh's reply. Terry is head of the search-and-rescue section of the Deschutes County (Oregon) sheriff's department. "If you get hurt, who is going to help? If you suffer a major break, such as a leg, there is no self-help."

Terry is strongly opposed to hunting alone because he has directed too many searches for lost or injured hunters. He suggests that if you ignore his advice and go anyway, at least follow the search-and-rescue theme: location, duration, return.

Always let some responsible person know where you will be and when you'll be back, then notify that person when you do return. Search-and-rescue people get justifiably annoyed when they spend days looking for a hunter who is home.

Terry pointed out that during an average 10-day deer season, a dozen or so hunters will get lost, and there will be a serious injury about every other year. Everyone should consider what search-and-rescue agencies say about hunting alone. They say, "Don't do it."

But there is a breed of men who don't fit molds and who commonly travel or work alone. We call them explorers, pioneers, philosophers, hunters and writers.

Even as a kid, I took overnight hikes into the mountains, alone, and once hiked 100 miles across Oregon's Cascade Mountains to see the girl who is now my wife. Summer jobs included being a forest lookout, and also a stream guard on Kodiak Island, Alaska, where I lived alone in a tent. Then, as now, it was no big deal, as I was, and still am, comfortable alone.

The key word is "comfortable," and in exchanging thoughts with others, I learned that the common thread is a feeling of complete ease when being alone.

We, as those who enjoy hunting alone, also think that the danger is overplayed. "Most people hurt in gun accidents are hurt by others in their own party," said Bill McRae, a Montanan who is one of the country's top wildlife photographers and writ-

ers. "If you hunt alone, your buddy can't shoot you."

Judd Cooney of Colorado, a noted hunter, guide, outdoor writer, all-around great guy and modern-day equivalent of a mountain man, added, "I never could understand why people worry so much about safety in the woods. They drive cars on freeways."

In a half-century of hunting rough country, my only injury came as I stepped on a loose boulder. The rock rolled, I went down hard, and the boulder crushed my foot. Camp was two miles away, uphill, so it was a case of taking two steps, then crying a lot. X-rays showed that one major bone was broken into five pieces, plus chips.

If we listened to all of the "what-ifs," we would do nothing. As Bill expressed it, "It's been said that you sit as many risks as you run, and I'd much rather be out there running a risk than home sitting one."

Remembering the hunters he has guided, Judd said, "Although many say that safety is why they don't hunt alone, it's really a cop-out because they aren't comfortable. But those same people don't feel comfortable alone in *any* situation."

So, it's a personal thing, and solo hunts are only for those who appreciate solitude, who know themselves and who are content within themselves.

Do we get lonely? Jim Zumbo of Wyoming, who is an *Outdoor Life* Editor-at-Large and probably the country's best-known hunting writer today, and Judd simply said, "No."

Bill told me, "Sure, but I sometimes get lonely when I'm with people. I enjoy being alone with my thoughts and nature. Sometimes there is an abysmal loneliness, but in a way, I sort of enjoy it."

Fear is not a factor, because regardless of what television throws at us about supposed dangers from bears, cougars wolves, snakes, bats and other wildlife, the woods are far safer than any city.

"Probably your greatest enemy is fear," Bill said. "You never want to let yourself feel lost, even if you do not know where you are."

But those of us who hunt alone don't get lost. We have an idea of where we are at all times. Everyone who leaves the pavement should be an expert with a map and compass. This knowledge should automatically be part of every sportsman's education.

Part of why we hunt alone can never be explained but must be experienced and felt. At best, we can state our love of independence and solitude, and the desire for better hunting.

Unfortunately, most modern hunting too often resembles a riot. The result is that most hunters never learn the pleasures of solitude, as they find comfort only from close association with others. Al-though we loners enjoy camps shared with friends, we also know that solitary hunting is special.

As Bill said, "You always sacrifice part of your freedom if you're hunting with someone else. You have to be at a certain place at a certain time, and people worry about you."

We also hunt better alone. As Dwight Schuh, a noted writer, lecturer, photographer and superb, intense bowhunter from Idaho, noted, "When I'm with somebody else, I tend to be distracted because there's more than one reason for being out there. There's the companionship, the company, the social interaction. When I'm alone, it's pretty much the single purpose of hunting, and by far the best hunting success I've had has come when I've been alone, simply because I have concentrated more on what I was doing."

Independence is important, and Judd put it very well when he said, "I've got complete freedom about where I go and what I do. There's nothing to worry about. Either that, or you can sit down and worry all you want."

Naturally, you should hunt only those species you can take care of by yourself. For backpackers, this usually means nothing much larger than deer. For larger species, pack animals are usually required. Part of any hunting is knowing your limitations.

Continually preparing for solo hunting is simply a part of our nature. We collect gear that allows us to camp in relative comfort. For backpacking, this includes special attention to both quality and weight. Physical conditioning is important, and year-long exercise that considers strength, flexibility and endurance will not only allow you to go that extra mile, but it will also help protect you from injuries. Gaining knowledge of map and compass, first aid and survival skills will make you more self-confident.

As the earth gets bred to death, wild lands shrink, so searching out remote areas is also a continual activity. And because solitude is more of a philosophy than a location, you don't have to go to remote Western mountains, as you can find solitary hunting almost anywhere.

To find solitude, study "social filters." A social filter is anything that reduces human access, including inhospitable terrain, distance, ownership, and time. I use maps for most of my initial searching, because I know that careful study of maps will reveal good hunting country protected by social filters.

Excellent maps of our public lands are produced by the government agencies charged with managing those lands. National forests are found in 39 of our 50 states, and information can be obtained from the U.S. Forest Service, Box 96090, Washington, DC 20015. Public lands managed by the Bureau of Land Management are found mostly in our Western states, and information is available from the Bureau of Land Management, 18th and C Sts. NW, Washington, DC 20240.

No matter how far the trip, always take along the basics that would allow you to stay for several days. Tim Christie photo.

Man was once as much at home in the wilds as the animals he hunted. Some of us still hunt alone, so that we can enjoy the solitude. Leonard Lee Rue III photo.

In addition, states have public lands that are administered by state wildlife, forestry or other departments. Large timber companies often have lands open to public hunting, too. Telephone books will show many places to check.

The best maps are the topographic maps produced by the U.S. Geological Survey, Map Distribution, Box 25286, Denver, CO 80225. First ask for the free index and catalog for your state. These will give full details on available maps, prices and ordering instructions. You then order the individual quadrangles to cover the areas in which you are interested. Many libraries have files of topographic maps, so you may want to check these out before purchasing your own.

Begin with maps, then personally scout the areas. Any country that is difficult to get through or across is a wonderful social filter. Such areas might include rims, cliffs, ridges, canyons or water.

Many times, I've seen hunters drive to the rim of a particular canyon I hunt, get out of their vehicle,

walk to the edge, then get back in the rig and drive on, after noting what appears to be miles of unbroken vertical rimrock that blocks all access to that canyon.

Few know that if you hike upstream along that rim for about two miles, there is a break in the rimrock that allows fairly easy access to the canyon and to a ridge to the west that has no road access. That ridge has produced many fine deer for me, and I've yet to see another hunter there. I discovered that roadless ridge, and the break in the rimrock, by studying maps.

Other good hunting areas might be surrounded by swamps that require some tough slogging in hipboots to get across. Most hunters would not put out the effort, so that swamp becomes an ideal social filter. Good maps can reveal such areas.

Rivers are also social filters. I know a situation where a good highway follows one side of a river that has no roads on its other side. The roadless side holds a large basin that is surrounded by high, steep ridges. Hunters could approach by road on the backside of those ridges, but nobody does, because to hunt the basin they'd have to climb up over the ridges, then down into the basin. I've had excellent hunting by simply boating across the river from the highway.

In another case, I hunt public land that is accessible only by floating a river because all other access is blocked by a large ranch that allows no hunting. I put in upstream at a public boat launch, float down to that isolated public land, hunt, then float to another public launch several miles below. As with many such areas, I have the area all to myself.

This year, I hope to check out the hunting on the backside of a large lake. There is a road to the east of the lake, but the western side is a remote roadless area. I'll simply boat across the lake, and though I imagine that a few hunters hunt the far side by horseback, I don't expect to find many people.

Islands in rivers or lakes are other possibilities, and by using a boat, you can turn a social filter into an advantage.

Distance is another fine social filter, and solitude can usually be found if you are willing to walk farther than others. Drive to the end of the road, then start hiking. The first miles will eliminate most others; a few more miles will put you alone.

Finding solitude by distance is difficult in our more heavily populated states. It's just not possible to get two miles from a road in some areas. That's when the serious solitary hunter looks for difficult terrain or the social filter of land ownership.

Ownership maps are found in most county courthouses, and once you learn the value of these maps, you'll start visiting courthouses often. For example, I know of one particular tract of public land that is almost surrounded by posted private land. One narrow corridor of public land allows rightful access, but it is not common knowledge. A friend told me about the land, and a check of ownership maps confirmed it.

Access to or across private land is frequently a problem, but sometimes permission can be obtained with a polite inquiry that stresses the fact that you are a responsible sportsman. More than once, I've seen signs stating that hunting was not allowed, but I gained permission by simply asking. In one case, I was given directions to the far backside of a farm, an area the owner said nobody had hunted for years, and enjoyed complete solitude.

Others of like mind can help, and those who work outdoors, such as farmers, ranchers, foresters, and biologists, are often excellent sources of information on isolated areas. Sometimes, they are more willing to help once they learn you are interested in getting off by yourself and don't intend to take in a horde of fellow hunters. Others may appreciate your quest for solitude, even if they personally do not feel comfortable hunting alone.

Most hunters overlook time as a social filter, but some of us avoid opening weekends. And though not everyone can adjust schedules, consider the off-times, and hunt during midweek, or mid or late season.

Apply for controlled hunts that allow only a few hunters in rather large units. A classic example is Nevada. Because Nevada is our driest state, it cannot support large deer herds, so the entire state is divided into hunt units, each with a limited number of permits. For the state's 110,000 square miles, only about 40,000 deer tags are issued. That's fewer than three hunters per square mile. I've hunted for many days in Nevada without seeing another person. Similar opportunities can be found in other states having controlled units.

Hunting big game with high-powered rifles is the most popular method today, so consider hunts open only to bows, muzzle-loaders or handguns. Combine a mid- or late-season time period and a special-weapons season, and you may have the woods entirely to yourself.

When I asked Judd, Bill, Dwight and Jim what special preparations they make for solo hunts, each surprised me by replying, "None."

When pressed further, I learned, as Jim Zumbo put it, "Of course, I take along a map, compass, fire-starting stuff, shelter, food, water—the usual."

That's the key, "the usual." We make no *special* preparations, because whether we hunt alone or with others, near camp or 10 miles back in, we *always* take the basics that would allow us to stay out there for several days, alone, comfortably.

The exact equipment depends on the hunt, the area, the season, the weather, the type of game being pursued and other variables. Always include map and compass, items to build fires and shelters, first aid materials, food and water, and equipment to take care of your game. (And remember to let a responsible person know your destination and schedule.)

In expressing our respect for solitude, Dwight spoke for all when he said, "It heightens my sense of appreciation of what I'm doing when I'm by myself. When I'm with somebody, I'm more attuned to that other person—making conversation and doing things to please him. But when I'm by myself, I focus on the country, my own feelings and the game I'm hunting. So, I come back with a greater sense of appreciation for what I'm doing out there. Even if I'm not successful, I have a particular feeling for the hunt that I don't have when I'm with somebody else."

Hunting alone is certainly not for everyone, but the rewards can be tremendous if it is done properly. You can enjoy some of the greatest hunting there is and return home refreshed, relaxed, and rejuvenated. The bush or even the back 40 is a friendly place for those who have learned the pleasures of hunting alone, comfortably.

PART 3

ORDEALS

When Deer Become Dangerous

By Tom Huggler

Bill Bevins hunts for trophy deer from a ground blind in the farm country of Michigan's Thumb region. In the past 12 years, Bevins has shotgunned 10 bucks from that location while turning down dozens of smaller animals. Four years ago, however, his hunting season ended 30 minutes after daylight on the November 15 opener. That was the morning Bevins was attacked by a huge whitetail buck.

"I had built my blind from leafy saplings two weeks earlier so that the deer could get used to it," Bevins said "A buck had made a primary scrape just a few yards away. In branches above the scrape, I stuck a cotton ball soaked with doe-in-heat scent to attract him. Then, to mask my own odor, I placed several cotton balls containing fox urine in the forks of some willows right behind my blind."

With the aid of a trail timer, Bevins determined that the buck was checking his scrape shortly after daylight. One morning, the animal tripped the timer at 10 minutes to 8; another morning, at five minutes after 8. So, Bevins was in his blind at about 7 o'clock on opening morning. Soon, it began to grow light. A doe wandered by, sniffed the buck scent with upturned nose and then ambled over to the blind, where she began to chew on some remaining leaves. Knowing that the doe was a perfect decoy, Bevins sat motionless an arm's length away.

"Soon, I heard a muffled noise," he recalled, "like a mouse under snow-covered leaves [there were about 3 inches of snow on the ground]. Then, the noise grew louder, and I remember thinking that maybe a squirrel was coming closer." The doe moved off about the time that Bevins heard the noise for a third time, only now it seemed to be almost on top of him. He turned his head around slowly; 3 feet away, a massive buck stared back.

"He scared the hell out of me," Bevins said. "He started moving his head around, and his eyes rolled like he was crazy. He must have thought that I was another buck. My gun was sitting on a 5-gallon bucket next to me. I grabbed it and, lifting it over my head, took a big step to get out of the blind so that I could turn around for a shot from the hip. I figured that the deer would run back the way it came."

But instead of running away, the buck, with head down, lunged at Bevins, hitting the hunter just as he was twisting to face the deer for a shot. At that instant, Bevins' foot slipped into a hole. The buck hit him with such force that the ligaments in Bevins' leg snapped like rubber bands.

"I got hit by lightning once," Bevins said, "and was knocked unconscious for three hours. It felt like that, like thousands of volts of electricity passing through my body. Meanwhile, the buck ran off—I could hear branches striking his antlers. Had he decided to gore me, I might have been helpless unless I could have gotten off a shot."

In intense pain, Bevins lay in the snow for about 20 minutes. Then, he unloaded his gun and, nearly passing out, used it as a crutch until he could find a strong stick. It took him three hours, instead of the customary 20 minutes, to hobble to his hunting camp. Much later, when he finally arrived at a hospital, his swollen knee was 19½ inches in diameter because the kneecap was shattered, a tendon was torn in half and most of the cartilage in his leg had ripped. After nearly a year on crutches, he faced corrective surgery.

Bevins continues to hunt from the same blind where he was attacked, and last year killed a huge buck that dressed at 224 pounds. He figured the one that attacked him was that large or larger. Bevins also knows that he's lucky because deer have killed many people and injured scores of others. In fact, some observers estimate that whitetails and mule deer have killed more people in the United States than black bears and grizzly bears combined. In his recent book, *Bear Attacks,* Stephen Herrero documented 357 incidents of injury or aggression involving bears in the United States through 1980, including 41 deaths by grizzlies (22 in Alaska) and 21 by black bears. No one knows how many casualties have been caused by deer. Because there are more deer than bears, however, interactions between man and animal are more frequent. And deer can become highly aggressive, even with the slightest provocation from man.

During the rut, for example, bucks are unpredict-

Laid-back ears and tongue flick are sure signs of aggressive behavior in deer. Leonard Lee Rue III photo.

able and always potentially dangerous. This is especially true when they are kept in a captive situation. About six or seven years ago, Kim Heller, a staff photographer for the Ohio Department of Natural Resources, died of wounds inflicted by a rampaging buck. Heller, who was in his 30s, was working alone while photographing the animal at a sanctuary in east-central Ohio. Suddenly, the buck charged, hitting Heller and severely puncturing the photographer's chest with its sharp antlers. The wounded Heller ran to a nearby pond, where he plunged to safety. The enraged buck stalked back and forth for an hour, then finally walked away for long enough for Heller to escape. Two days later, he died of gangrene poisoning in the hospital.

"A captive whitetail buck is one of the most dangerous animals in North America," said Leonard Lee Rue III, one of the nation's premier wildlife photographers. Rue's travels have taken him all over the world in search of big-game animals to photograph. Many times, he has seen captive deer exhibit aggressive behavior. One day a few years ago, Rue was photographing deer in an eastern preserve. He knew that a certain buck appeared to be dangerous but momentarily forgot about the animal as he snapped pictures of other deer.

"That buck came looking for me," Rue said. "He sneaked up behind me and caught me by surprise. His ears were laid back, and his hair bristled." Before the buck could actually strike him, Rue belted him over the head with his camera and motor drive, stunning the animal long enough for the photographer to scale a fence to safety.

Contrary to what some believe, captive deer don't have to be in the rut to show aggressive, unpredictable behavior. One July day, Rue was photographing an antelope fawn on the Bison Range in Montana when a mule deer buck in velvet came up to investigate the photographer.

"I knew that he had no intention of using his antlers [the still-growing antlers would be tender]," Rue said, "but suddenly he stood on his hind legs and began to flail. I have no idea why." Rue slugged the buck in the head with his fist, hard enough to knock the animal off balance and allow Rue to get out of the enclosure.

Deer that have grown used to humans lose their fear of man and can become very dangerous with little or no warning. Many years ago, a Newberry, Michigan, man who had a state permit to pen a wild deer was found stomped to death inside the enclosure. More recently, the same thing occurred in Tyrone, Pennsylvania. At the Wildlife Research Station in Boone, Iowa, a buck in velvet reared up on his hind legs and struck a department of natural resources worker on the forehead. And Jeff Murray, *Outdoor Life's* Minnesota Editor, was photographing a nice buck on a farm when the deer suddenly pinned Murray's friend. Murray struck the animal repeatedly with a post-hole digger, to no avail. Meanwhile, his friend held on to the buck's antlers to avoid being gored while a neighbor called the police. When all alternatives to get the buck off failed, officers shot the animal.

Such stories occur more frequently than many people realize. Consider the tale of Dan DeLisle, a wildlife technician with the Michigan Department of Natural Resources.

DeLisle spent 18 years doing research with whitetails at the Cusino Wildlife Research Station near the Upper Peninsula town of Shingleton. Several times during that period, angry bucks chased him and other workers until they could find safety and in 1973, an ornery 10-pointer put DeLisle in the hospital. Dan was part of a team doing a controlled breeding study to determine the estrous cycles of does, and when early or late conception would produce male and female fawns. DeLisle's job was to run deer down any one of 16 chutes that were 50 feet wide by 100 feet long. Two inmates on loan from a state prison were helping him that fall morning.

"I walked into the pen containing the 10-pointer, which was standing about 70 feet away," DeLisle recalled. "I turned around to lock the gate, then turned back to face the deer. He was coming at a dead run—ears laid back and head down—and was already on top of me before I realized it."

The 250-pound buck smashed into DeLisle, who is slight of build. The circumference of the animal's rack was wide enough to go all around the DNR worker, but the long brow tines struck him in the chest. DeLisle grabbed the buck's antlers and hung on while trying to gain control and prevent further goring.

Meanwhile, one of the inmates went over the 12-foot-high fence in a panic. The other had a homemade club about the size of a baseball bat. He began striking the deer in the neck, but one blow glanced off and hit DeLisle between the eyes. Blood flowed, and DeLisle went down with the deer on top of him. Somehow, he still managed to hang on to those lethal antlers.

"You can't believe how powerful a big buck can be," DeLisle said. "The only thing you can do is grab hold of the antlers, and even then he'll throw you around like a flag on a stick. It was muddy, and I couldn't get my feet under me. Meanwhile, the buck was picking me up and throwing me down, two or three feet at a time, and he was stepping on me."

DeLisle yelled for the armed worker to start hitting the deer on the hindquarters to divert his attention. With all of his strength, DeLisle lifted the buck's rack off his chest and then twisted the animal's head to pry him away. But the crazed buck wanted one more shot at his opponent. As DeLisle turned the buck's head, a main antler beam scraped across his chest and drew more blood. At this point, the deer turned his attention to the inmate, who had found some temporary protection behind a feeder shelter and was striking the deer's backside.

Freed at last, DeLisle sprang for the gate, opened it and dashed outside, then hollered for the inmate to make a run for it. The worker also dived for the gate and made good his escape while the buck thrashed around, looking for more trouble. DeLisle needed stitches to close the wound in his face; he also suffered two black eyes and had nasty chest lacerations.

"The very next day, an 11-pointer cornered a doe in another pen," DeLisle recalled. "She wasn't ready to be bred, but that only seemed to enrage the buck, which impaled two tines through her lungs and killed her. We cut the antlers off both bucks [the rack of the one that gored him is hanging in De-Lisle's cabin, along with the club] and turned them loose the following spring. Most people just don't know how dangerous penned deer can be. Only recently, for example, I was talking with a fellow who recently got a permit to keep a captive buck. Already, he had been attacked."

What about deer in the wild? Are they dangerous, too? Hardly a week goes by that the editors of *Outdoor Life* do not receive a "This Happened To Me" story on the subject of close calls with deer. Bear attacks provide more spine-tingling reading, but deer attacks probably occur more often. Just ask Pennsylvania hunter Jim Dawson of Duncansville.

Several years ago, Dawson, now 39, had just gotten out of the service in time for the deer-hunting season. "I was hunting from a tree stand when a group of whitetails, including a six-point buck, went past in thick brush below," Dawson recalled. "I shot but figured that I had missed. Still, I got down to check because I don't like to wound game and then leave it unknowingly."

Dawson scoured the area around his blind for an hour, and although he kept hearing strange sounds in the brush, he could locate no sign of the deer. Suddenly, as he neared his blind, Dawson heard a commotion. Rushing into the brush, he found himself point blank in front of the buck. The animal whipped its head around to impale the inside of Dawson's left knee on a brow tine. Then, the buck picked the hunter up off his feet and threw him backward.

"He put his head down to come at me again," Dawson said. "Luckily, I hadn't let go of my gun and shot him before he could attack." Dawson said that he has a perfectly round hole in his leg as proof that wounded deer are dangerous.

In Utah, bowhunter Melvin Laws wounded a mule deer buck with a 25-yard shot, then got the shock of his life when the deer rushed him. Laws ran behind a quaking aspen as the buck buried his antlers in the trunk. Muzzleloader hunter Paul Mantz, also of Utah, shot a big 4 × 4 mule deer buck with a 28-inch spread while hunting in Montezuma Canyon. For two hours, Mantz trailed the wounded buck, which bled little and did not appear to be mortally injured. Eventually, Mantz got a glimpse of the buck going up a steep rise. He shot again but missed. While reloading his .54 caliber weapon, he suddenly found himself 30 yards from the angry buck, which apparently had had enough dogged pressure for one day.

"The buck whirled, put his head down and charged," Mantz explained. "There was no time to shoot. Had I not thrown my side forward, he would have hit my stomach with those big antlers. Even so, his antlers ripped through my clothing, pulling some of it off, and he pummeled my legs. I rolled down the hill, leaving my rifle behind."

Mantz was hurt, but not badly enough to scrap a $750 rifle. Of greater concern, perhaps, was the fact that he hadn't told anyone where he was hunting. His car was 5 miles away. Keeping trees between him and the buck, which stood off at a short distance, Mantz inched his way back to the rifle, finished reloading and killed the deer.

"I'll carry scars on my legs and back where his antlers cut me," he said. "Plus, I had some bad bone bruises on my legs, and he shredded my clothing. But I guess I'm lucky to be alive."

Bill Bevins' story at the beginning of this article is proof that deer don't always have to be wounded before they attack hunters. Consider, too, this tale told by M. S. North, a rancher/hunter in Nebraska's Sand Hills more than 100 years ago. The story is from North's unpublished journal, which I came across while on a recent hunting and research trip of my own to the Sand Hills.

"A little later that fall [1879], a party of hunters from the Republican River came out to hunt near the Dismal River. One night, one of the party failed to show up, and the next day the others started to hunt for him. They found where he had killed two deer within two miles of their camp."

North goes on to say that they hunted for the lost man, who was 63 years old, for several days without luck. More than a week later, the man's son and others returned to look further, and after several days found the old man's body on the back side of a sand hill.

"The signs showed that he had sat down just under the top of the hill, and that a buck deer had walked up the hill from the other side and, seeing him there, had attacked him, and after knocking him down had jumped on him and trampled him to death. There were only two empty shells in the man's belt, and they would account for the two deer he had killed. The deer must have attacked him without being wounded."

Earlier that fall, North himself was attacked by a deer that rushed him from a distance of a half-mile. He was riding the range one day when he happened to spot two deer grazing on a sidehill. When they disappeared over the crest, North left his horse behind and started a long stalk. He was partway there when a big buck suddenly stood up near the spot where North had last seen the feeding deer.

"I dropped down in the grass almost out of sight," North wrote, "and he started for me on a run. I waited until he was within about 150 yards of me, then raised my gun, thinking he would stop to look at me and I would get a shot at him while [he was] standing still. He kept coming as fast as he could run, and when he was about 50 yards away, I fired. He never slackened his speed, and I thought I had missed him. I tried to get a cartridge out of my belt, but my hands were so cold and numb that I was slow, and before I could load he had gotten to me. I jumped to one side and he went past me, striking me on the arm with his antler so hard that I thought he had broken it. He stopped as quickly as he could and turned back toward me, but as he again started for me, he stumbled and fell. I had hit him in the breast and the bullet had gone through him lengthwise, but he never slackened his speed at all."

Because deer are among the most researched animals on the continent, biologists have known for decades of their social hierarchy. Within groups, most aggressive encounters occur when higher-ranking members dominate subordinates. This happens among does and yearlings, both in and outside of family groups, and among bucks as the rut progresses. It also occurs in winter yarding areas where many animals congregate and compete for limited food resources.

The aggressive actions of deer usually form a pattern of certain postures that are used in sequence. For bucks, the least intense threat is called "ear drop," when the animal merely lays his ears along the neck. The second threatening posture is termed the "hard look," and occurs when the buck, with ears laid back, extends his head and neck and stares at an opponent. Sometimes, the buck's body hair will bristle, an effect of the erector pili muscles. If those actions don't cause the adversary to back down, the buck will likely "sidle," or tuck in his head and body and advance several steps. At this point, bristling is nearly always pronounced. If those actions do not provoke retreat, the animal normally employs "antler threat," in which he lowers his head and aims the antler tines toward the opponent. The "rush," or attack, is the final stage of aggression.

Does follow the pattern of ear drop, hard look and sidle—also in sequence—and then add "striking" with one or both feet while lunging at an adversary. The female's final aggressive action is called "flailing," and occurs when the animal stands on her hind legs while striking with her front feet. As we have seen, bucks in velvet will also flail. Other examples of aggressive behavior, though not necessarily in sequence, include lip curling, foot stamping and snorting. According to Leonard Rue, a buck that flicks his tongue up his nose is in an extreme state of aggression.

Two years ago, 13-year-old Chris Williamson of Burgettstown, Pennsylvania, was walking in the spring woods near his home when he saw a white-tail doe in some trees just off the road. He walked a bit farther and then heard a thumping noise. He spun around just in time to see a large buck about to charge from a distance of 10 feet. Chris fled, but the buck was on him in an instant, hooking an antler in the boy's shirt and catching the belt loop of his jeans. The buck flung its head back and forth, lifting Chris from the ground and shaking him like a rag doll. Only when the deer slammed him into a tree trunk was it able to free its antlers. The boy was in a state of shock but not severely injured.

Most of the incidents involving unruly deer and hunters result from the hunters' carelessness or lack of judgment. Listen to the fireside talk in any deer camp, and sooner or later you'll hear stories about someone getting the shock of his life when the deer that he thought was dead suddenly came to and started kicking. To avoid becoming the subject of a future horror story, always approach a downed animal from the side or rear, and never in the flight path should it try to escape. Look for the eyes to glaze, a telltale sign of death, or poke the deer with a stick or your gun barrel to be certain that it is dead. Never straddle a deer to begin the dressing operation until you are absolutely sure that the animal is dead—hoofs are lethal weapons. About 10 years ago, a Pennsylvania hunter lost his life when the doe that he thought he had shot dead near Everett suddenly came alive and kicked him to death.

Deer are not the cute, defenseless creatures that many people, many of them nonhunters, believe they are. Leonard Rue tells the story of a Blairstown, New Jersey, woman who is an animal protectionist and antihunter. One day, a wild buck attacked her in her backyard, knocking the woman down into a multiflora rose bush. And the attacks do not always involve bucks. Does are especially protective of their fawns for three to 15 hours after birth, according to Ed Langanau, Michigan DNR deer specialist. Langanau spent years of study at the DNR's Porter Ranch research facility near Houghton Lake. Many years ago, Viva Cunningham, the wife of one of the workers, was attacked by a doe when Viva tried to bottle-feed her fawns. The mother deer, which was unable to produce milk, went into a rage, knocking the woman unconscious, ripping her clothing and badly bruising her body.

There are many other stories, some of them tragic, involving deer that attack people. Just last month, for example, I was watching an outdoors show on television. Someone had found two large southern Michigan bucks with their antlers locked together in combat. A film crew taped away while a biologist and a veterinarian worked to disengage the battlers by sawing through their antler tines.

Suddenly, the bucks broke free, and one of them, probably the loser, took off for the woods. The other stood his ground, head down and antlers pointed menacingly at his benefactors. For a tense half-minute or so, the buck seemed undecided about what to do; finally, he turned tail and fled. It would not have surprised me, though, had that buck attacked the people at the scene. Why? Because deer can be dangerous.

A Valley Full of Memories

By Bill McRae

It was a bitter, drab November dawn—minus 5° and snowing—as Mike and I trudged up the old road along Recollection Creek. The white stuff lay 18 inches deep on the ground, and though deer tracks were everywhere, it was impossible, because of the new snow, to tell how fresh they were. After we had gone a couple of miles and crossed the creek for the fourth time, the forest opened up and we stopped to glass an opposite slope. I was steaming hot from exertion, but stabbing cold air gushed in as I slipped the binoculars from beneath my parka. "The visibility is poor," I thought, "but game should be easy to see against the white background."

The frigid snow had crunched and groaned beneath our feet, but now that we had stopped, a pervasive stillness closed in to engulf us. Suddenly, there was shouting—a man's voice saying, "Shoot, kids, he's coming straight at us!" Then, through a curtain of swirling snow, I saw it: a grizzly bear, half-running, half-rolling down the mountainside toward a man and two young boys. They must have been tempted to run, but instead the trio stood their ground and fired at the enraged mass of silver fur and muscle.

"Dad . . . hey, Dad!" Mike said, beckoning me back to reality. "Where was it that you, Tim, and Mark had the run-in with the grizzly?"

"On that hillside, just below the cliffs," I said, pointing. "See that lone fir tree? It was there that we hung Tim's deer, but we didn't hang it high enough and the bear got it. It's hard to realize that

it happened almost 20 years ago. You were pretty young at the time.''

The valley had been one of our favorite hunting spots for elk and mule deer, but this was the first time that I had set foot there in 15 years. I wondered why I had stayed away for so long. Perhaps it was because there are so many great places to hunt in Montana that one can't explore them all in a lifetime, and I do like new places. I had come back now because I wanted Mike to see the place; it was also a kind of sentimental journey. Maybe I was getting old, starting to live in the past, and wanted to relive the neat things that had happened there. The encounter with the grizzly bear was one of them.

Mike's older brothers, Tim and Mark, were 14 and 12, respectively, at the time. The deer, a two-point muley, was Tim's first. He had killed it at dusk in the calm preceding a storm front that was bearing down on us from the north, bringing with it heavy snow and cold. We dragged the buck for about a half-mile, and when it started to snow and get dark, we hung it from a tree and went on to camp. Tim expressed concern about leaving the

deer, but I assured him that nothing would bother it. How wrong I was!

The storm hit in force that night, and the following morning we turned our attention to finding a buck for Mark. Apparently, the deer had holed up because of the storm, and when we hadn't jumped any by noon we circled back to get Tim's buck. What we found was hair-raising! Some obviously formidable creature had pulled the buck down from the tree, breaking the very sturdy limb on which it had been hung. The animal had fed on it, consuming most of the hindquarters, and had covered it with debris. It was the kind of thing that starts you looking over your shoulder.

"What do you think did it?" Mark asked, the usual ruddiness of his cheeks replaced by somber gray.

"Snow has covered any tracks that might have been left, so there is no way of knowing for sure," I said. "It could have been a cougar, but more likely a bear and probably a grizzly!" I looked over my shoulder again.

"Boy, I'm mad," Tim said. "We've got to get even

with whatever it was." The idea of involving the kids in an altercation with a grizzly bear didn't appeal to me, but when you're trying to teach boys to be men, what do you do in a situation such as this one?

Whether or not I did the right thing is a moot question, but that evening we took a position about 100 yards from the deer and waited until we could no longer see the crosshairs in our riflescopes. Nothing showed, but we did hear a noise on the mountainside about us just at dark.

The boys both had spanking new Remington Model 600 rifles chambered for the then-new 6mm Remington cartridge. Mark's had a Weaver K2.5 scope and Tim's a 4× Lyman All-American. My rifle was a pre-1964 Winchester Model 70 in .30/06 with a 3× Lyman scope.

The streak of dawn found us pussyfooting back into the area. Snow hung heavily on the trees, giving them a surrealistic look. We almost jumped out of our skins when a golden eagle took off a few yards ahead of us. The fact that the eagle was in the area but not on the carcass seemed ominously

significant. When we got to where we had waited the night before, I could see through my binoculars that nothing was on the deer, but something had been there because the snow was packed down. A few yards farther on, we cut fresh grizzly tracks leading down from rock outcroppings high on the mountainside. The bear had moved the deer a short ways, eaten most of it, and then buried it again.

We followed a maze of bear tracks up the bottom of a draw. I thought of the possibility of there being more than one grizzly, but all of the tracks were the same size; besides, one animal can make a lot of tracks in 10 hours.

We found where the grizzly had lain down on the open mountainside 50 yards above the deer carcass, probably to watch and charge anything that tried to take it—a chilling thought! The grizzly had to be close. But where?

I looked behind us, back at the deer, and along the lower edge of the timber. Then, I looked up the mountain again. What I saw was a sight I'll never forget.

Every pine, fir and spruce, every rock and bush

wore a frosting of white snow. Low-hanging clouds shrouded the rock outcroppings at the top of the ridge. And there, just below the clouds and beside a small patch of brush, stood a beautiful silvertip grizzly—the abundant white hair on its head, sides and back giving it the same frosted appearance as that of the trees.

"There's our grizzly, kids," I said.

"It looks just like a big dog," Mark said.

It didn't look like any dog I'd ever seen, and it didn't look as though it was about to run away, either. With the bear being uphill from us and with our being between it and the deer, it looked like big trouble to me. I had seen grizzlies run, and I knew that the bear could be on us in seconds. "Get ready, kids," I warned. "It might charge."

I raised my rifle but then decided against trying to shoot offhand. There was a dead spruce about 30 feet to my left that would serve as a rest. Telling the boys to stay where they were, I walked to the tree. The bear moved in the same direction I did. I knelt down, rested the rifle on a branch and looked through the scope.

The grizzly stopped with its left shoulder pointing straight toward me, and I remember saying to myself, "You've got to make the first shot count. Bust the shoulder. Hold about 3 inches low for the bullet to rise. Hold your breath. Squeeze." Then, all hell seemed to break loose!

I don't know how many shots we fired before the grizzly lay dead at our feet, but only three of them connected. One of the rounds had hit the bear's paw. In a good-natured jab, I later asked Mark, "Why did you shoot him in the paw?"

Mark seriously examined the bear's wounds and said, "That should teach him not to hold his paw over his heart."

There were other hunts in the valley with the boys, with my brother John and with a favorite uncle, Tony Sotak. On one of the hunts with John and Tony, something with an almost mystical twist happened.

One evening from high on a ridge, I spotted, shot at, and subsequently wounded a fine muley buck. Because there were only intermittent patches of snow where tracks could be seen and the deer had left only an occasional drop of blood, I lost the trail when darkness fell.

I have never been able to take wounding and losing any animal lightly, and I hope that I never can. That night, I slept fitfully and dreamed that I went back to look for the deer and found him standing in a particular small park some distance from where I had lost his tracks.

The next morning, I left camp long before daylight, and because the park that I had dreamed about wasn't much out of the way, I decided to look there first—though I felt a bit foolish about doing so.

The game trail that I followed twisted its way up the side of a draw through thick timber, and my first glimpse of the park, which was on the opposite side of the draw, was through a small opening in the trees. At first, I saw nothing. Then, a faint movement about 100 yards away caught my eye, and a gray shadow materialized into a buck. He moved ahead a few yards, showing a definite limp. Then, he stopped and turned his head toward me, revealing his heavy antlers. There was no doubt: It was the buck that I had hit the evening before.

I couldn't see the buck from a sitting position nor could I find a rest, so I had to shoot offhand. Centering the crosshairs behind the deer's shoulder, I pulled the trigger. He lunged and headed for the brow of the hill at timber's edge about 40 yards away. As he disappeared, I feared for an instant that I had flubbed again. Then, I heard a crash and saw the top of a dead spruce sway violently. That was where I found him.

My shot had taken the buck right through the heart. I also found a superficial wound on his front leg where I had hit him the night before.

How do I account for what happened? I don't take a great deal of stock in psychic phenomena; rather, I believe that the incident was entirely coincidental. Because I was so troubled about wounding the deer and intended to go back and look for him in the morning, it wasn't strange that I should dream about doing so. And because I was familiar with the park and had in fact seen deer there before, it wasn't strange that I might dream about finding the buck there. However, I do wonder about it.

But there is more to the story. I dressed the deer and started to skin it, planning on taking the hindquarters to camp in one load and coming back later for the rest of the meat. The knife I was using was, as always, razor sharp. First, I cut the lower legs off, then began skinning out the gambrels. The hide was tough, and I foolishly turned the knife toward my hand. It slipped and hit my left index finger on the second joint. In the instant before the blood started to flow, I could see the bone.

I considered going straight to camp, where there was a first aid kit, but then I would have to come back twice for the meat. So, I tore off a strip of handkerchief, wrapped it around the finger a couple of times and knotted it tight.

It isn't easy to skin a deer without the use of your index finger, but I got the hindquarters skinned, tied them onto the pack and started for camp, which was two miles away. The finger was still bleeding badly, and about halfway there I noticed that the end was turning white.

John was in camp when I got there. I washed the cut in the cold, crystalline water of the creek and had John bandage the finger so that I couldn't bend it.

That afternoon, Tony went with me and finished skinning the deer, and we brought the rest of the meat to camp.

I don't remember how many days we stayed on and hunted, but when I got home and removed the bandage, the finger was completely healed.

Both John and Tony took bucks on that trip, which seemed important at the time, but there is so much more that goes into the making of warm memories. There was the companionship of people I cared about and times around cheery campfires when adventures of the day and of days gone by were shared and relived.

My uncle made three trips from Wisconsin, where he lived, to hunt with me in Montana, and between the first and second hunts he had a serious heart attack. One day, as we sat on a ridge and watched a snow squall swirl over a 9,000-foot escarpment and down into the valley, he said, "Do you know what I thought about most when I was in the hospital?"

"What?" I asked.

"Of course, I thought about my family," he explained. "But I didn't worry about the business or the farm. Instead, I thought about these mountains and I wondered whether I'd ever see them again." It has been 15 years since another heart attack took him. Perhaps his passing had something to do with my not hunting in the valley for so long.

We hunters are a pessimistic lot. We talk of the "good old days" and, rightly, worry about what the future holds. I recall one campfire conversation with Tony and John that centered around what would become of our beloved valley.

I am happy to report that it is a better place now than it was then. There used to be a four-wheel-drive road that wound and twisted for about three miles up Recollection Creek (which, incidentally, isn't its real name). Today, the road is gone. In 1975, there was a very bad flood in the mountains that did a lot of damage, but mostly to man's contrivances. The road was one of the casualties; near the mouth

of the valley, flood waters left the creek and ran straight down the middle of the road, cutting a deep and impassable gully. In the years since, nature has pretty well healed the scars, and young trees are growing where the road was. As Mike and I looked at what the flood had done, he commented, "It's enough to make one think that God must be a conservationist."

We didn't get a deer on that bitterly cold November day, but I didn't think that Mike was too disappointed (I suspect that he really came home to look after the old man, anyway), and I certainly wasn't. The valley had already given me so very much.

For our family, the "moving finger" has continued to write; a few months after the hunt with Mike, Tim was killed in a boating accident off Kodiak Island, Alaska. Mark and a daughter, Colleen, live in Texas, and Mike is in California.

PART 4

GUNS AND SHOOTING

Search for the Ideal Deer Rifle

By Paul A. Matthews

There isn't one deer hunter in 100 who doesn't have what he considers to be the "ideal" deer rifle, and there are many of us who, over the years, have changed from one ideal deer rifle to another that we considered "more" ideal.

About 50 years ago, when I was full of vinegar and could cover mile after mile with almost effortless ease, I swore by the little Winchester Model 94 chambered for the .32 Special and fitted with a Lyman tang sight. And why not? Every deer I ever shot with that little rifle was a one-shot kill. Who could ask for anything better than that?

Then, during the years immediately following World War II, the little .32 was no longer ideal. I had to have something better, with more power and longer range. I swapped the little carbine and, in quick succession, suffered dismal failures with a chrome-lined Arisaka 7.7 taken from an arsenal in Japan, and an amputated .30/40 Krag that had a barrel that looked as though it had been used as a water pipe.

I lost two bucks to the Arisaka because I insisted on using government ammunition that I had Sott-pointed with a file. I lost one buck to the .30/40 simply because the barrel had long since seen better days. Either rifle with proper sighting equipment, good ammunition and, in the case of the Krag, a new barrel would have been good on deer, though maybe not the ideal deer rifle.

I wanted something better. I wanted the supreme. And in 1949, I hocked everything except my wife and soul for a brand-new Winchester Model 70 .30/06 equipped with a Lyman 48WJS receiver sight.

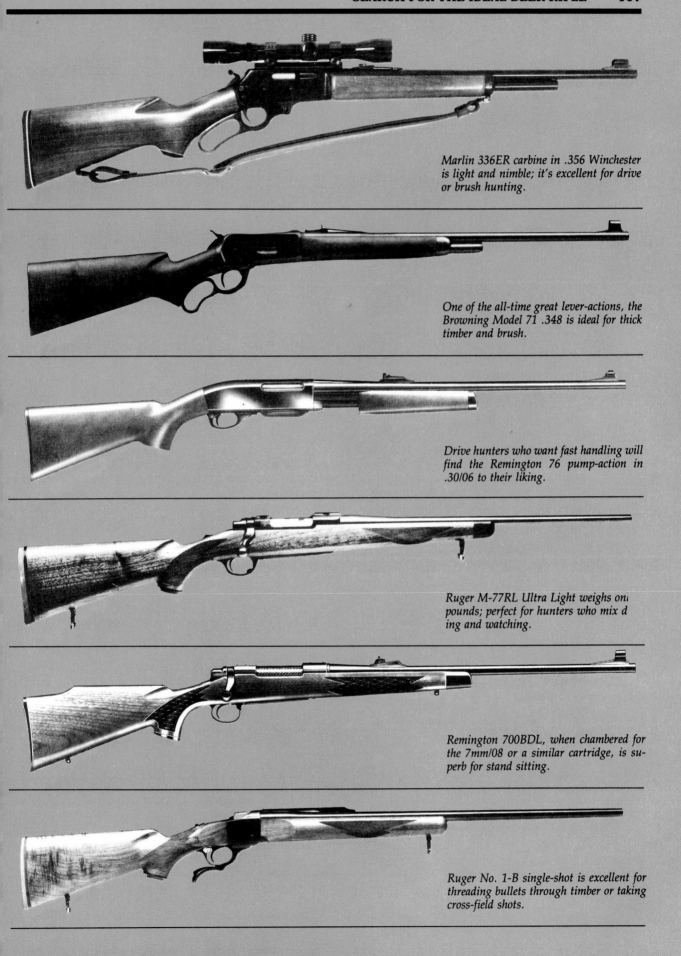

Marlin 336ER carbine in .356 Winchester is light and nimble; it's excellent for drive or brush hunting.

One of the all-time great lever-actions, the Browning Model 71 .348 is ideal for thick timber and brush.

Drive hunters who want fast handling will find the Remington 76 pump-action in .30/06 to their liking.

Ruger M-77RL Ultra Light weighs onl pounds; perfect for hunters who mix d ing and watching.

Remington 700BDL, when chambered for the 7mm/08 or a similar cartridge, is superb for stand sitting.

Ruger No. 1-B single-shot is excellent for threading bullets through timber or taking cross-field shots.

It was the best that the average man's money could buy.

Was it the ideal deer rifle? I thought so and proceeded to kill deer with it. I also began getting a cripple now and then, and I didn't like that. In fact, I used the rifle for only a few seasons.

Now, before we go any further, let's clarify a point about the .30/06. Col. Townsend Whelen once said that the .30/06 is never a mistake. It was, is and always will be a superb cartridge for almost anything that you want to hunt, provided you use the proper bullet for the game intended. That was my problem. For the way I hunted—on foot and in the brush—the '06 didn't turn out to be quite as ideal as I had hoped. This was not because the gun lacked power, but rather because the light bullets didn't work well on the occasional end-on shots, and the heavy bullets sometimes failed to expand on the crosswise shots.

Thus, my type of hunting demanded something different from what I was getting from the '06. It demanded deep penetration for raking shots and positive expansion for crosswise shots. That added up to a heavy bullet with lots of lead hanging off the front end, preferably with a large diameter to help compensate for those times when expansion was a bit slow. It added up to a .45/70.

I made a tour of the local secondhand stores and came up with a beautiful Winchester 1886 that had been rebarreled by P. O. Ackley and chambered for that venerable cartridge. It was one whale of a rifle. It shot where I pointed, and it pointed as naturally as my finger. It carried nicely in the woods, balanced perfectly and, despite its heavy weight, came to the shoulder with remarkable ease. It was my ideal deer rifle.

Or was it?

Remember, back then I covered a good many miles during the course of a day, some of those miles across open fields as I was working from one wooded area to another. And sometimes, when crossing those fields, I came into eye contact with legal deer.

Now, I like the .45/70. I've used it for years and consider it the greatest woods cartridge ever developed. But no matter how you slice it, the .45/70 is not the rifle to use for shooting across open fields at running deer. It is strictly a woods cartridge and should be used as such. Thus, after using it for a season or two, I again purchased another ideal deer rifle, one that would handle those cross-field shots as well as the south-end-headed-north, close-in brush shots.

I went whole-hog this time and came up with a new Winchester Model 70 chambered for the .375 H&H. Yes, I know that the .375 H&H is far more gun than necessary for deer; all of the experts will tell you that. But the .375 H&H remained my ideal deer cartridge for the next 23 years. For 17 of them, my rifle was the Winchester Model 70, easily the most accurate hunting rifle I had ever used, shooting consistently into less than an inch at 100 yards.

After better than 6,000 rounds through it, I switched to a Ruger No. 1 and promptly put another 2,200 rounds through that rifle in less than two years.

The .375 H&H was the best all-terrain cartridge I had ever used. With the 270-grain round-nose Hornady bullet at a modest 2,600 fps, it gave rapid expansion on crosswise shots yet retained sufficient weight for deep penetration on lengthwise shots. I made four successive neck shots with the cartridge, and in each instance the bullet gave ample expansion for an instant kill. The .375 H&H wasted far less meat than the .45/70 or the .30/06 by virtue of the fact that there was a relatively small bloodshot area around the wound. Never did I lose a deer hit with the .375, and only once did I have to use a second shot.

Would I recommend a .375 H&H for deer? No way! If you need a recommendation for this cartridge, you are not ready for it. And if you are ready for it, you don't need the recommendation.

Is the .375 H&H ideal for deer? For 23 years, it was ideal *for me*. I didn't mind carrying a heavy rifle, and I had the Winchester barrel cut back to 22 inches for fast handling in the brush. The heavy bullets sailed through the brush, and they gave me the trajectory of an '06 when I had to stretch the range a bit. All in all, it was just about as good a cartridge as I could get for the way I hunted and the country in which I hunted.

But all good things have a way of coming to an end. As the years went by, I found that the 8½-pound rifle seemed to double in weight during the course of a day; it became more difficult to handle on those fast shots, and I was no longer covering as much ground as I once had. In short, my ideal deer rifle was no longer ideal.

But this time, I didn't have to look for a new ideal. I analyzed how and where I hunted—slow-poking in the brush lots—and realized that for that set of conditions I needed something light, short and powerful. I needed a Ruger single-shot chambered for the .45/70. And that's what I got: two of them, a No. 1 and a No. 3.

Are they ideal deer rifles? For me, yes; for you, maybe.

Will these .45/70 Rugers remain my ideal deer rifles for the rest of my life? I expect so, but I wouldn't bet on it. The recoil with this cartridge in these light rifles, especially with heavy loads, is something to be reckoned with. So, when I hit 70, perhaps I'll use something with a little less kick on the back end, such as my Ruger No. 3 in .30/40.

In the final analysis, the ideal deer rifle is as elusive as the Holy Grail or Golden Fleece. It is an intangible goal, with a different image in the mind of each seeker. No gun writer, myself included, can define the ideal deer rifle for a given individual. As with a wife, this is a selection that has to be considered and made in the eye of the beholder. The best that the writer can do is to relate his own experiences and perhaps impart some idea of the factors you have to consider.

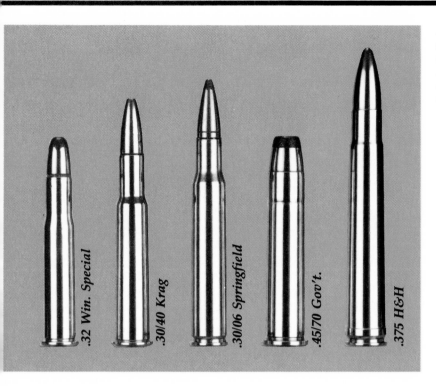

Some of the many cartridges used by the author in his 50-plus years of deer hunting. The .375 H&H was his "ideal" cartridge for 23 of those years, until he switched to the .45/70 in a Ruger single-shot. Stanley Trzoniec photo.

.32 Win. Special .30/40 Krag .30/06 Springfield .45/70 Gov't. .375 H&H

What are these factors?

The most important factor is how you hunt—do you do a lot of walking, or do you hunt mostly from a stand? And related to this is the second factor, where you hunt—is it in open country, woods, mountainous areas or fairly level terrain?

It's likely that 90 to 95 percent of eastern deer hunters hunt from a stand. They spot their game at a distance and can pick their own shot. If they are in a wooded area, the shot is usually made at less than 100 yards at a walking or standing deer. If they are hunting in an open area, the range is often greater and the deer is often running.

Here, it doesn't require a degree in engineering to determine that the critical elements are accuracy for threading a bullet through the brush, flat trajectory for the longer shots, and a fairly high velocity to reduce the amount of lead on a running deer. To me, these elements spell out a bolt-action rifle chambered for an inherently accurate cartridge such as the 7mm/08, .308, .257, .270 or .30/06. Further, the rifle should be topped with a good scope to utilize the full potential of the cartridge.

In addition to the standers, we have a group of hunters who divide their time between watching and standing. In fact, they might sometimes be involved in drive hunting—alternately standing watch and driving. But regardless of their methods, these men are faced with a different set of circumstances than those of the dedicated stand hunter.

Because about half of their time is spent walking, these men need a fairly lightweight, well-balanced, easy-handling rifle. They need a rifle that carries easily, comes up quickly for fast shots, and has the accuracy and trajectory needed for cross-field shots.

While walking, the odds are that these hunters are *not* going to be able to pick the shot. They have to take it as it is offered, crosswise or endwise, standing or running, and this requires a cartridge with enough punch and bullet weight to get to the vitals with a raking shot.

The rifle requirements for this type of hunting are well met by most lever-actions and single-shots, as well as some of the slim, lightweight bolt-actions made especially for the job. In the cartridge category, I strongly favor the .356 and .358 Winchester, and the .350 Remington Magnum. For sighting equipment, I would go for a 2½× or 3× scope, as short and light a scope as I could find. And I'd probably have a set of auxiliary iron sights for use in bad weather, preferably a good receiver sight and post front.

Now, we come to the minority of the deer hunting clan, those who prowl the brush lots hour after hour, with only an occasional stop to sit on a stump or log for long enough to eat a granola bar or rest tired feet. These men are almost never able to pick the shot. Every deer is a surprise, and usually a brief one at that. In a matter of just a few seconds, the brush hunter has to positively identify his deer as legal, pick out his spot on the game and drive the bullet home. As often as not, he's going to cut some brush in the process and the deer is not going to drop on the spot. If ever a specialized rifle were needed, it is for the brush hunter.

Rifles for this type of hunting must be short, lightweight and fast-handling. They must point as naturally as your finger, and they must fire a cartridge powerful enough to drive a heavy bullet through brush and into the vitals of a deer from behind the

SUGGESTED IDEAL DEER RIFLES

Following are suggested ideal deer rifles and calibers based on the different methods of hunting. This list contains the more common off-the-shelf models, but does not include all possible choices.

Between the time this was written and the time you read it, catalog listings may have changed, and some of the models and calibers listed may have disappeared from the catalog sheets. This does not mean that they are gone from dealers' shelves, or that your dealer cannot get exactly what you want by making a few phone calls.

Stand Hunting In Open Country
Remington 700ADL—.270, .308, .30/06
Remington 700 Classic—.270, .30/06
Remington 700BDL—7mm/08
Remington 78—.270, .308, .30/06
Ruger 77R—.308, .270, 7×57, .257, .280, .30/06, .25/06
Ruger 77RS—.270, 7×57, .30/06, .308, .25/06
Ruger 1A—.30/06, .270, 7×57
Ruger 1B—.30/06, .270, .280, .257, .25/06
Browning 1885—.270
Browning A-bolt—.25/06, .270, .30/06
Browning A-bolt (short)—.257, 7mm/08, .308
Savage 110C—.270, .30/06
Savage 110E—.270, .308, .30/06
Winchester 70XTR—.25/06, .270, .30/06, .264
Winchester 70XTR (short)—.308

Drive Hunting
Remington 7 Custom KS—.350 Remington Magnum (preferred models and calibers)

Browning BLR—.358 Winchester (preferred models and calibers)
Winchester 94 Angle Eject—.356 Winchester (preferred models and calibers)
Marlin .336 Extra Range Carbine—.356 Winchester (preferred models and calibers)
Remington 7—7mm/08, .308
Winchester Angle Eject—.307
Ruger 77RSI International—.308
Ruger 77RL Ultra Light—.270, .30/06, .308
Ruger 1RSI International—.270, .30/06, 7×57
Winchester 70XTR Featherweight—.270, .30/06, 6.5×55
Winchester 70XTR Featherweight (short)—.308
Browning BLR—.308
Savage 99—.308
Remington 6 (pump)—.270, .308, .30/06
Remington 76 (pump)—.30/06
Winchester Ranger Bolt Action—.270, .30/06

Brush Hunting (Jump Shooting)
Marlin 444SS—.444 Marlin
Marlin 1895SS—.45/70
Marlin 336CS—.35 Remington
Marlin 336 Extra Range Carbine—.356 Winchester
Winchester 94 Angle Eject—.356, .375 Winchester
Ruger No. 1A—.45/70
Browning 1885—.45/70
Browning 1886—.45/70
Browning 71—.348
Browning BLR—.358
Remington 7 Custom KS—.350 Remington Magnum, .35 Remington

---

ribs. Equally important, the bullet must be of sufficient diameter to ensure a blood trail. Wounds from small-diameter bullets close up and leave a poor trail.

Lever-action and single-shot rifles are the predominant favorites for the brush hunter, with cartridges ranging from the .348 Winchester up through the .350 Remington Magnum, the .356 and .358 Winchester, the .375 Winchester, the .444 Marlin and the prestigious .45/70.

If your sighting preference runs toward a scope, again get a 2½× or 3× scope. For this type of hunting, however, a good receiver sight with a bead or post front sight is hard to beat. When you consider that most brush-hunting shots are taken at less than 50 yards and sometimes at only a matter of feet, the extra weight of a scope, and the awkwardness it lends to carrying a rifle, is far more of a detriment than an advantage. Further, I've not yet seen the scope that is as fast in the brush as a good receiver sight, nor have I met the hunter who in stand-up, hind-leg shooting under hunting conditions can do

any better with a scope than with a good receiver sight. If you doubt that statement, try it sometime!

In summation, the ideal deer rifle, elusive as it may be, does exist—at least for a time. But before you buy that ideal rifle, sit down with a pencil and paper and jot down a description of the kind of country you hunt, how you hunt, and your physical capabilities. Then, select a cartridge, rifle, and sighting equipment that best meet the requirements for these various factors.

Mix a lot of common sense in with the energy figures that you see in the ballistics tables. Just as you can't haul concrete in an MG sports car, nor run the Grand Prix with a garden tractor, neither should you use a hotshot 6mm with a heavy 3×9 scope in the brush, nor a heavily loaded .45/70 for shooting across fields.

Select your ideal deer rifle based on the job for which it is to be used and how you are going to use it. To do otherwise is a disservice to yourself, your hunting partner and the game being hunted.

The Flight of the Bullet

By George H. Haas

In one of the original Buck Rogers comic strips, Dr. Huer, the scientific brain behind Buck Rogers, finally found a way to penetrate the enemy's defenses against "disintegrators." Both sides in those early space wars had discovered methods of nullifying the destructive rays. After wrestling with the problem, Dr. Huer simply mounted old-fashioned artillery on the good-guy spaceships. The antique shells were not subject to dissipation or diversion and penetrated the enemy's protective energy belts to such good effect that justice and virtue triumphed. The old had also triumphed over the new, which is very nice to see once in a while.

It was a clever idea for an exciting episode, but it did not mention one great advantage of firing old-fashioned artillery pieces and small arms in outer space. Out where the stars shine with great brilliance, there is no gravity, no atmospheric drag, and no wind to disturb the course of a shell or bullet. The projectile, once launched, would continue on its course in an absolutely straight line, and it would do so for eternity, provided it did not encounter the gravitational pull of some heavenly body. A gunner could aim right at any stationary target, fire, and be relatively sure of a hit before the shell or bullet arrived on target.

On earth we have problems. Our bullets do not travel in straight lines. The bullet's course is curved, and several forces impart that curvature.

GRAVITY AND DRAG

The most important of these forces is gravity—the pull of the earth's mass. This basic force is hard to characterize because it is present every day and is so much a part of everyday life that people are hardly aware of it. But gravity is the most important reason why bullets and other projectiles, such as golf balls, footballs, and arrows, follow a curved path (trajectory).

When a shooter holds a firearm solidly just before triggering a shot, he is resisting gravity, which tends to pull him and his gun downward. After the bullet leaves the muzzle, nothing supports it, and gravity begins to have its way. This is hard to imagine because most people know that the bullet's path is comparatively straight during the first few yards of travel. But the force soon makes itself apparent, and the bullet is eventually pulled down to its point of impact with the ground.

All bullets fall at the same rate of speed—an average of about 32 feet per second during a 3- or 4-foot drop, which is typically the distance between the rifle's muzzle and the ground. This cannot be changed. But if all bullets fall at the same rate of speed, why is it that some have a comparatively "flat" (straight) trajectory and others are quite curved? The primary reason for this is that typical modern cartridges drive bullets at higher rates of speed than others. This means the bullet travels farther during the time it takes to drop in response to gravity and hit the ground. Older loads drive bullets at slower speeds, and the projectile cannot travel as

Reprinted from The Outdoor Life Deer Hunter's Encyclopedia, *Outdoor Life Books.*

far during the time interval before impact. Time, specifically time of flight, is therefore a controlling factor in determining how far a bullet can travel horizontally.

Another major factor in determining the curve of a bullet's flight is atmospheric drag. At high speeds this is a very powerful inhibiting force, and the actual mechanism is friction. The energy of the bullet is diminished rapidly by friction with the atmosphere, and this force is at work slowing the bullet from the instant the cartridge is fired. A good illustration of the power of this force is a "shooting star," which is merely a chunk of rock flying through space. When it encounters the earth's atmosphere at tremendous speed, the friction is so great that the rock heats up and burns (oxygen now being present).

Put gravity and atmospheric drag together and it's easy to understand why a bullet's flight is not a perfect arc (segment of a circle). With the barrel horizontal, the bullet leaves the muzzle at, say, 3,000 feet per second, but it must resist both gravity and atmospheric drag from the outset. Gravity is constant over time and affects the bullet equally close to the muzzle or far from it. But drag slows the bullet. At first drag has little effect, but over the bullet's course, it slows the projectile more and more. Because the bullet travels slower, gravity has more *time* to pull it down during a given segment of flight. This downward pull therefore *seems* to increase the farther the bullet gets from the muzzle. Eventually the bullet reaches a point where it is moving comparatively slowly. Gravity now has a sharply increased effect, and the bullet's path curves steeply downward. At this point in the trajectory, it becomes very hard for a shooter to hit his target because he must compensate for that sudden downward curve.

The desire to overcome this gravity/friction effect has motivated improvements in cartridges since the late 1800s. Black-powder cartridges could not provide sufficient velocity to flatten the bullet's curved path very much. But modern smokeless powders have made it possible to drive bullets at such high speeds that, over the first few hundred yards, the downward curve is negligible, particularly when one is firing at a target as large as a deer's heart-lung area. Increased velocity is the principal means by which modern designers produce flat-shooting cartridges, but they cannot go too far along this path because recoil increases as well. Quite soon, a point is reached at which the recoil becomes intolerable.

Improved bullets. Because of this recoil penalty, every other imaginable way to achieve a flat trajectory has been thoroughly explored. The result has been a continuing trend toward increasingly streamlined bullets of a smaller and smaller diameter. The smaller the frontal area of the bullet, the less the effect of atmospheric drag, and if the bullet is also sharply pointed, the effect of drag is greatly reduced.

Old-fashioned, blunt-nosed bullets of large diameter cannot be driven at modern high velocities within the acceptable recoil barrier. Modern bullets are said to have a "good sectional density" or a desirable "coefficient of form" when they are comparatively long, are of small diameter, and have a pointed aerodynamic shape. The mathematics involved in these descriptions of bullet form are too complex to be of interest to most hunters. An upcoming ballistics table provides information on bullets and the trajectories of almost all hunting cartridges. The table can be used to determine which cartridges are useful for any particular form of hunting.

CORRECTED TRAJECTORY

A new rifle complete with iron sights or scope must be sighted-in to take the best possible advantage of the bullet's trajectory. Sights and scopes are usually not adjusted at the factory or shop, though some gunsmiths will bore sight a rifle or use an optical instrument (collimator) to adjust the sights so that they are parallel with the bore. Even if this has been done, the shooter must sight-in the rifle himself to suit his particular needs.

Whether he realizes it or not, the shooter "corrects" the trajectory of his rifle to take the best possible advantage of the bullet's curved flight. If a rifle is held in a perfectly horizontal position and fired, the bullet immediately starts to drop in flight. In fact

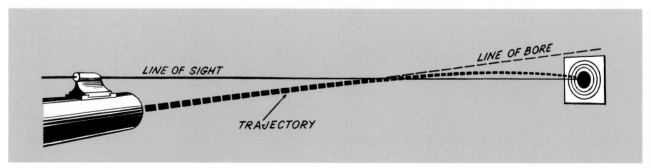

The trajectory or path of the bullet never rises above the line of bore but crosses the line of sight. To compensate for bullet drop, the bore must be pointed upward, done by adjusting the rear sight so that it is higher than the front sight. Lloyd Birmingham drawing.

the bullet drops below line of bore after such a short flight that the rifle is only useful for shooting at very close range. To make consistent hits at longer ranges, the shooter must adjust his sights to tilt the bore slightly upward. In doing so, he corrects for the trajectory resulting from gravitational pull.

The accompanying drawing shows how this is done. The line of sight, with iron sights or through a rifle-scope, is simply adjusted so that the curved trajectory of the bullet intersects it at the desired range. The line of bore, of course, just points off into the distance in a straight line. The bullet's flight intersects the line of sight at two different points: at the target and at a short distance from the muzzle—about 25 yards—where the flight of the bullet is angled slightly upward.

The upward angle of the bore provides corrected trajectory. This is why, in shooter's language, a bullet is said to rise on exit from the muzzle. In reality, a bullet actually starts to drop below the line of the bore as soon as it exits the gun. It cannot fail to do so because there is no denying the laws of gravity.

SIGHTING-IN PRELIMINARIES

The first step is to make sure that the sights are firmly in place and that the rifle is solid in the stock. Unscrew the guard screws and take the barreled action of a bolt gun right out of the stock and check the barrel channel and other inletting. If it has not been done at the factory, coat the barrel channel with two or three coats of waterproof synthetic varnish or rub in a fairly thick coating of good furniture wax. This keeps moisture out of the wood and prevents warping. You don't want to go to all the trouble of sighting-in and then have your zero "wander" because the stock has warped and exerted varying pressure on the barrel.

After the stock is ready, put the barreled action back in the stock and tighten the guard screws. You'll need a screwdriver that fits the screws perfectly. Don't attempt to do this unless you have that all-important screwdriver. To get a perfect fit, it is sometimes necessary to grind down an oversize screwdriver so that it fits the slots perfectly. Rifles with two-piece stocks can usually be left as is because the buttstock is secured to the receiver with a massive throughbolt that pushes the wood against the receiver so firmly that very little moisture can enter. Check the forend attachment to make sure that it is solid, and if screws are used to secure it to the rifle, tighten them.

Check all sight- or scope-mounting screws for looseness. If you find one that remains loose even after pressure with the screwdriver has been applied, remove it and put a drop of Loc-Tite on the threads. Then tighten it down. Loc-Tite holds the screw in place, but not so solidly that it cannot be removed later, if need arises. If this commercial product is not available, use a drop of synthetic varnish.

The rifle bore should be clean and dry when you start out. If it is a new rifle, use your cleaning gear and solvent to remove the protective coating that is usually applied to the bore at the factory.

FIGURING DEAD-ON RANGE

The purpose of sighting-in is to make best possible use of the rifle for the kind of shooting the hunter intends to do. To accomplish this, the hunter usually sights-in to be dead on target (zeroed) at fairly long range. With most modern deer loads, that is about 200 yards or a little beyond. The dead-on range should not be too great because that could cause mid-range misses. Obviously, if the rifle is dead on at 200 yards, the bullet will be high at half that. If that half-range height is too great, and the hunter does not allow for it by holding a little low, the bullet could miss by passing above a deer's back.

To this, of course, must be added errors made by the hunter—flinching, poor sight alignment when aiming, jerky trigger control, and so forth. For most deer hunters, therefore, the midrange trajectory height of a deer rifle should be no more than 3 inches. Expert shooters can increase that midrange height a bit because they know how to hold low for midrange shots, but for most hunters 3 inches is the maximum.

The following description of the sighting-in process is for a bolt-action centerfire rifle with a scope. Variations on this method that apply to other kinds of rifles are discussed afterward.

To begin, suppose you select the 150-grain .30/06 bronze-point, a good long-range deer round. If this is zeroed at 200 yards, the bullet is 2 inches high at 100 yards, 1.7 inches low at 250 yards, 8 inches low at 300 yards, 23.3 inches low at 400, and a fantastic 47.5 inches low at 500 yards. On a target as large as a deer's heart-lung area, we can therefore conclude that a rifle sighted-in to be dead on at 200 yards will make a good hit (*not* taking human error into account) out of 275 yards. In fact, the shooter can hold dead on out to that range, and for midrange shots there is no need to make a special allowance either. Beyond 275 yards, the hunter has to allow for bullet drop by holding a little high (or a great deal at extreme range). The maximum range at which no allowance is needed for drop is known as the "point-blank" range.

Modern flat-shooting cartridges have certain advantages. With many older rounds, the point-blank range is only 100 yards. If one of these older rounds is sighted-in to be dead on at 200 yards or a bit farther, the midrange trajectory height is often 8 inches or even more—surely enough to cause a miss or wounding shot.

SETTING UP

Sight-in your rifle on a clear day with good light but little glare and when the wind is completely absent or blowing at no more than 4 or 5 mph. Your pur-

HOW TO SIGHT-IN A RIFLE

1. *If the bolt can be removed from rifle, center the target in the bore as shown and then adjust the iron sight or scope to center on the same impact point. This is a coarse adjustment, best done at 25 yards or a bit more.*

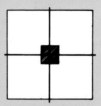

2. *With three rounds loaded and a steady rest, carefully aim at the target (a 1-inch black square is best with a scope, larger with iron sights) and fire three shots.*

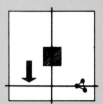

3. *Aim precisely at the black square again, and holding rifle steady, move the sight vertically until the crosshairs move into line vertically with the group of bullet holes.*

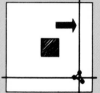

4. *Then move the crosshairs horizontally so they center in the shot group. In effect, you move the sight to the point where the rifle is shooting.*

5. *You are now sighted-in to be dead on at 25 yards. Since the bullet, as shown in an earlier drawing, crosses the line of sight twice, at 25 yards or a bit more and again at a bit over 200 yards, you are also sighted-in to be dead on at about 225 yards. Your bullet will be 2 or 3 inches high at 100 yards. Fire at 100, 200, and longer ranges to check. Make fine adjustments, if needed.*

pose is to find out what the rifle can do without variations caused by the wind or human error. You want to know where the rifle and cartridge will hit at various ranges before adding other variables.

Don't forget to bring along protective earplugs or muffs, or both. In any fairly long shooting session, you need good ear protection, and many shooters wear both plugs and muffs. Shatterproof shooting glasses are also a source of mental calm. Your ammunition should be the same loads you intend to use for hunting, here Remington 150-grain bronzepoints. Never sight-in with one load and then hunt with another. Even if the bullet weight is the same, point-of-impact variations can result from differences in the bullet shape, differences among manufacturers in loading a given cartridge, and other factors. This should also tell you that you must sight-in again if you do change loads—for example, to go varmint hunting in the spring with a 125-grain or 130-grain bullet instead of a deer-hunting .30/06 load.

To eliminate human error as much as possible, the rifle should be supported very solidly. If you have access to a rifle range and solidly anchored

shooting benches where you can sit while firing, by all means take advantage of that fortunate situation. If a shooter's benchrest pedestal and sandbag are available, do use them. But you can set up on the hood of your car or even shoot prone from a rest and do fairly well.

You must have a firm, but not hard, rest for your rifle and a flat, unobstructed piece of ground over which to shoot. You must also have a good backstop, such as the side of hill, to halt your bullets. Some shooters use a heavy cardboard box and make cutouts at its ends in which to rest the rifle's fore-end and the stock just in front of the trigger guard. A tightly rolled coat or blanket is just as good, if less convenient. Never take a rest against a hard object unless you put your hand between the rest and stock. On firing, a rifle bounces away from a hard object and causes wild shooting.

BORE SIGHTING

Set up an aiming point 25 yards from the firing point. For a rifle with a fairly powerful scope, the best aiming point is a 1-inch square of black tape stuck on a white sheet of paper. Use a big sheet of paper or mount a smaller sheet on a large piece of cardboard. A big cardboard box of the kind used to ship refrigerators or washing machines is excellent. It stands up by itself without stakes and provides a big surface so that you can see where all shots go, even if some of them are way off at only 25 yards. Of course, if you are shooting at a formal rifle range, you will have to use the target frames provided.

Remove the screw-on covers from the windage (horizontal) and elevation adjustment dials of your scope and take the bolt out of the rifle as shown. Sight through the bore and maneuver the rifle on your rest until the black square is dead center in the bore. Now hold the rifle steady and use the windage adjustment to move the scope's crosshairs so that the vertical wire cuts the square into two halves. Then move the horizontal crosshair up or down so that the black aiming point is exactly quartered by the scope's crosshairs. In doing this, you are moving the sight so that it points exactly where the rifle's bore is pointing. If it is done with care, bore sighting should put your first few shots right on the aiming point, or close to it.

It is difficult to adjust the elevation and windage dials (or knobs) while you're holding the rifle, but if you're careful and have a good rest, you can hold the stock at the pistol grip with one hand and use a screwdriver or coin to turn the dials with the other. An easier way is to hold the rifle solidly with both hands and have someone else adjust the scope in response to your directions.

Firing at 25 yards. After bore sighting, replace the bolt in the rifle and wait a bit so that you will be steady. Practice a bit by dry-firing at the aiming point, again quartering the black square with your crosshairs. This is particularly important if the rifle is new and you are not used to the trigger pull.

Take your time and fire three shots with the crosshairs perfectly on target, using the steadiest hold and best trigger control you can muster. The goal is shot-to-shot consistency.

Sighting-in at 100 yards. If the group is dead on, congratulate yourself heartily and go on to shooting at 100 yards. But for one reason or another, you may find that the three-shot group of bullet holes is a few inches away from the aiming point.

In this case, put another 1-inch square of tape over the group of bullet holes so that you will be able to see it clearly through your scope. By the way, the bullet holes in a three-shot group at 25 yards should all be within a 1-inch-square area. If a rifle won't hold a 1-inch group at 25 yards, something is terribly wrong with it, the scope, the ammunition, or the shooter's technique.

Now steady your rifle again and put the crosshairs on the *first* aiming point. Then walk the crosshairs across the paper onto the *new* black square, holding the rifle very steadily while doing so. This time you have moved the sight so that it points at the exact place where the rifle is shooting.

As we have already seen, a bullet intersects the line of sight at two points—close to the muzzle and out at long range. The first point of intersection with scopes mounted 1½ inches above the bore line (the most common mounting height for powerful scopes) is 25 yards from muzzle, or close to it, and that is why bore sighting and preliminary shooting is done at that range. Because you are dead on at 25 yards, you should also be close to the plotted trajectory of your chosen load out at longer ranges.

But this is the real world, and rifles do vary from the ideal for many reasons. Therefore, set up a new aiming point at 100 yards and fire a three-shot group from a steady rest as before.

Walk down to the target and place a new black square over the center of the three-shot group. If two holes are close together and one is quite distant, ignore the "flier." Out-of-group shots like that are usually the result of shooter's error, not the rifle's. You may have jerked the trigger, for instance. Again, walk the crosshairs across the paper from the first aiming point to the new one so that they quarter the new aiming point, vertical adjustment first, then the horizontal. You are now sighted-in to be dead on at 100 yards. With a new aiming point, fire another three-shot group to make sure.

But to take the best possible advantage of our 150-grain .30/06 load, you should be 2 inches high at 200 yards, not dead on. It's simple to make this adjustment. Put up a new 1-inch aiming point exactly 2 inches below your dead-on 100-yard group center. Measure center to center on the squares. Hold the rifle solidly, aim at the original square, and then move the crosshairs down to the new one. The point of impact is now 2 inches higher than the crosshairs indicate.

Finally, you should be able to aim confidently at new aiming points and have all your shots hit 2 inches high, or very close to it, in a tight group. Fire a few groups to make sure. Be as precise as you can at this short range. Remember that groups open up as the range increases and that a small error at 100 yards becomes much greater at longer ranges.

This method of sighting-in is convenient and easy. You don't have to worry about the adjustment markings on your scope's dials or knobs, and that's very comforting, because it's easy to make mistakes when reading them. For most hunters, this method is much better than the usual system of making on-target measurements with a ruler and then adjusting the scope up or down by the necessary number of "clicks."

In any long shooting session, sighting-in or practice, remember that you are working with a hunting rifle. Don't fire too rapidly, because that could heat the barrel a great deal and cause it to expand, changing the point of impact. When you see a buck in the woods, you'll fire maybe two shots, at most three, and that doesn't heat the barrel of most rifles enough to cause trouble. Target shooters fire rapidly in some matches and need to know where their shots will go when fired from a hot barrel.

Long-range. If you think your sighting-in is all done, you are mistaken. You must fire at longer ranges to make sure of what your rifle will do way out there. In this case with the 150-grain loads, the objective is to have a 200-yard zero. Set up a target at that range and fire a group. You should be dead on. If not, and it's entirely possible, put up a second aiming point on your group and walk the sights across the paper just as you did at 100 yards. Normally, you will only have to work with the elevation adjustment because windage remains the same, no matter what the range. Of course, you should be doing all this long-range shooting on a windless day.

You should also fire at 250 yards and 300 yards to check the exact curvature of the bullet's path. For many different reasons, a bullet may drop more quickly than the ideal curve in the ballistics table, and if that is true, you should know about it. Write the exact impacts (how many inches low) at 250 and 300 yards (closer intervals if you so desire) on a piece of tape and stick it on the rifle's stock for ready reference during practice. After a while you should have these figures memorized.

The reference mark. Most scopes have a reference mark that can be moved to register the zero of your rifle. After making sure that you are dead on at long range (200 yards in this case), move this reference mark to the 0 marked on the vertical adjustment dial and leave it there. Then do the same with the windage dial or knob. This is your 200-yard zero. If you do make minor adjustments in elevation or windage at some future time, always "return to zero" after you are through.

Most scope adjustments are graduated in minutes of angle and parts thereof. Directions furnished with your scope will tell you what markings on your scope adjustments actually mean. A minute of angle, for all practical purposes, is 1 inch at 100 yards, 2 inches at 200, 3 inches at 300, 4 inches at 400, and so forth. If the scope is graduated in quarter-minute "clicks" (the most common graduation), it is necessary to change the scope adjustment by four clicks to move point of impact on target 1 inch at 100 yards, eight clicks for 2 inches, and so forth. This information may come in handy if you have to make temporary minor adjustments, but it's really not important if you sight-in as described previously by moving the crosshairs to point of impact.

To sight-in any other cartridge, first look up its trajectory in the table to determine how high you should be at 100 yards and what the long-range zero should be. Then sight-in accordingly. For instance, it's usually thought best to sight-in the 150-grain .300 Winchester Magnum so that it is dead on at 250 yards. To do that, you need to be 2.6 inches high at 100 yards. With less-powerful rounds, the zero range is shorter, and the 100-yard impact point varies too.

OTHER RIFLES AND SIGHTS

With iron sights, it's usually best to use a square 4-inch, or even larger, aiming point so that you can see it clearly. But the sighting-in process is much the same, except that it's best to start out with the preliminary bore sighting and shooting at only 12½ yards. This applies also to low-power, low-mounted scopes that are less than 1 inch above line of bore (center to center). The bullet's path intersects the line of sight closer to the muzzle with low-mounted sights of any kind.

Iron sights are almost always used at fairly close range when hunting. With most short-range rifles and loads, it's usually enough to be able to keep your shots within a 4-inch area at 100 yards when using iron sights. A bullet's trajectory and the nature of its downward curve at long range are of very little interest to a deer hunter if he hunts in heavy cover. In typical whitetail habitat, most deer are shot at only 50 or 60 yards. Some are taken at only 50 *feet* or less, particularly when shooting from a tree stand over or near an established deer runway or scrape. For this kind of hunting, it's almost always best to sight-in to be dead on at 100 yards to

If the bolt of the rifle cannot be conveniently removed, a bore-sighting device such as this Bushnell Bore Sighter is useful. The stud enters the barrel to keep the optical tube parallel to the bore. The shooter looks through scope and lines up on a grid to adjust the sight and barrel to the same point of impact. Several different types are sold. These bore-sighting devices are also useful to check sight setting without firing after the rifle has been zeroed. A check can be made without firing shots that might alarm game. This shooter's setup for sighting-in includes a cardboard box with cutouts to hold the rifle steady. It works, but it is not as good as a solid shooting bench anchored in the ground and a shooter's pedestal or sandbags. Vin Sparano photo.

Shooting at a 45-degree angle, up or down, you should hold for 70 percent of the indicated visual and actual range, as explained in detail in accompanying text.

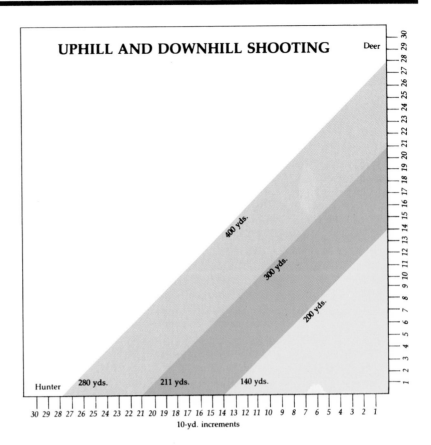

UPHILL AND DOWNHILL SHOOTING

Deer

400 yds.

300 yds.

200 yds.

Hunter   280 yds.   211 yds.   140 yds.

30 29 28 27 26 25 24 23 22 21 20 19 18 17 16 15 14 13 12 11 10 9 8 7 6 5 4 3 2 1

10-yd. increments

allow for moderately long shots that may come along and let it go at that. Many lever-action rifles and other short-range guns really don't shoot within 4 inches at 100 yards anyway; so there's little use in trying for precision.

It's easy to remove the bolt from a bolt-action rifle so that it can be bore sighted as a preliminary step, but bolts or breechblocks of other kinds of rifles are difficult or impossible to remove. If this is the case with your rifle, a gunsmith can use his collimator to adjust sights or scope so that the line of sight is parallel to the bore. This usually puts you nicely on paper at only 12½ yards.

Inexpensive bore periscopes are available. You simply open the rifle's action, slip the periscope into the breech end of the barrel, and do your bore sighting by peering through the instrument. After bore sighting, you proceed as with a bolt-action rifle, using the periscope when you walk your crosshairs across the paper. Yes, you *need* adjustable sights.

UPHILL AND DOWN

Obviously, any bullet's flight is curved to the greatest degree when the barrel is horizontal or close to it. If the barrel is elevated more and more toward the vertical, the effect of gravity is lessened because the horizontal flight is shorter and shorter. If the barrel were exactly vertical (very unsafe), gravity would only act on the bullet to slow it down, and atmospheric drag would do the same. The bullet's flight would be perfectly straight. Surprisingly, the

same thing is true if a hunter is firing downhill at a fairly steep angle. If the rifle's bore were exactly vertical, and the bullet came straight down out of the sky toward the earth, it's flight would again be perfectly straight. Gravity and drag could only speed up the bullet.

This concept is difficult for many hunters, but it is true that a steep downhill *and* a steep uphill shot elevates the point of impact a bit higher than the normal point of impact when firing horizontal shots. In other words, for a steep downhill or a steep uphill shot, hold a bit lower than normal in order to compensate. The question is, how much? In hilly country, this becomes a matter of some importance.

People judge range mostly by the apparent sizes of objects. The farther away something is from you, the smaller it looks, and that is what allows you to estimate the range fairly accurately. This process is largely unconscious, but most hunters do quite well at range estimation. If you cannot, you need practice or eyeglasses.

Assume that you are in the bottom of a valley and spot a mule deer buck on the crest of the sloping valley wall. The upward angle is 45 degrees and the buck appears to be 300 yards away.

You are, of course, using the same ammunition that you used when you sighted your rifle in—the 150-grain Remington bronze-point load. You know that you are dead on at 200 yards, and carefully memorized numbers tell you that the bullet will impact 8 inches low at 300 yards. You therefore hold 8 inches to compensate and then fire. If you do that, the bullet will almost surely fly over the animal or merely crease his back because you failed to take the steep upward angle into account.

The 70 percent rule. It's possible to calculate the effect of shooting uphill or downhill (Kentucky elevation) with pencil and paper, provided you have time to do it or you can use a computer. Doing either is impossible when you are hunting, but there is a simple way to compensate.

Imagine how far away the target would be if it were on the same horizontal plane as yourself. If you drop the mule deer buck (seen at a 45-degree upward angle) straight down to your own level, you will find that he is only 210 yards away.

It may help to refer to the diagram on the previous page. It shows a right triangle with one short side horizontal and the shooter at its base angle. The deer is at the top of the triangle above the hunter. If the distance to the deer is 300 yards, the distance along the horizontal leg is 210 yards—70 percent. The buck looks 300 yards away because of his diminished apparent size and that is the actual distance the bullet must travel, but you hold for the 210-yard (70 percent) range with your 150-grain load. Remember that you are sighted-in to be dead on at 200 yards! Ten yards is too small a distance to worry about, so you hold dead on the center of the buck's chest, just behind the shoulder, and drop him in his tracks.

This 70 percent rule would apply uphill or downhill for shots of 45-degree angle, and holds for all ranges. For instance, if the upward-angled range is 400 yards, the hold is for 280 yards—again 70 percent. Anything flatter or steeper technically requires a different percentage, and you could work out a whole set of numbers to cover all the angles. In actuality, just keep 70 percent in mind for quite steep shots and hold pretty much as usual for anything less steep. If you ever get a shot steeper than 45 degrees, you will have to hold even lower. It seems unlikely that you will even fire straight up at a deer since they cannot fly. Besides, all shots should be backstopped for safety's sake. It is also unlikely that you would ever shoot straight down.

THE WIND

In woods hunting at a maximum range of 100 yards or so, allowance for the wind is not important. The close range and damping effect of vegetation diminish the importance of wind. But for long-range shots a hunter must allow for wind, which can move a bullet off a straight course to an astonishing degree. Take an extreme example: the old-fashioned .32 Winchester Special with its 170-grain round-nose bullet. If the wind is blowing 10 mph at right angles to the bullet's path, the bullet will curve off course by about 9 inches at 200 yards. That's often enough to cause a complete miss. Double the wind velocity and the deflection more than doubles, causing a sure miss if you hold dead on. To give an example

at the opposite extreme, the fast-stepping .300 Weatherby Magnum with a 180-grain bullet is only deflected 2½ inches at 200 yards by a 10 mph crosswind.

Kentucky Windage. It's obvious that a modern fast-moving cartridge lessens the allowance that must be made for wind. Hunters do not have the time to "click off" their sights to allow for wind deflection like target shooters. Instead, they hold into the wind to compensate. This is known as "Kentucky windage."

The chief stumbling block in allowing for wind by holding off is estimating the wind velocity. But experienced hunters are seldom really aware of the wind in terms of miles per hour. They adjust their shooting by the feel of the wind on their face and hands and by how much it moves bushes and grass. Using one rifle and one load over a long period both in practice and when hunting provides a largely unconscious scale of allowances for wind.

The angle at which the wind impinges on the bullet varies a great deal, and most experienced hunters constantly register wind direction without really thinking about it. Wind blowing from straight ahead or directly behind has little or no effect on a bullet. At a slight angle, the wind is not really important either, though you might hold off a few inches to compensate for a strong breeze. In practical terms, most hunters stillhunt game by approaching into the wind because downwind approach would allow game to pick up human scent at long distances. In most circumstances, therefore, the wind is blowing toward the hunter, and its effect on the bullet's path is mild. It only lowers the point of impact slightly.

Tables of wind deflection for sporting cartridges are not readily available, though they do appear in some reloading manuals. Glancing through these tables is useful because it gives the shooter a general idea of how much wind affects bullet flight, but these tables are calculated in terms of wind blowing at right angles to the bullet's path. The shooter must determine what the effect would be at other angles. Another problem is that wind can fishtail across a considerable arc in a very short time. It's also true that the perfect right-angle wind is seldom encountered.

You must also estimate the wind velocity, no matter what its angle. For a hunter, anxious to get off a shot at a distant deer, conscious estimation and calculation is impossible. One is forced to the conclusion that only patient practice provides the skill needed to make accurate allowances for wind.

If you refuse to take shots at extreme range, you cut down on the need for wind allowance, especially if you use a load with high velocity. Do both and you have few problems. But high velocity in deer-killing calibers means a hard kicker, and anticipation of heavy recoil could throw your shot off more than any wind that ever blew, short of a hurricane. Every factor in shooting accurately is subject to some sort of compromise.

The Right Bullet for Deer

By Paul A. Matthews

There is no question that bullet placement is the most important factor in taking a deer. The problem is that the deer bullet is rarely placed exactly where we want it, and it is then that the type and weight of bullet become all-important.

Looking back across 50 years of deer hunting, I recall a gentleman from Nanticoke, Pennsylvania, who hunted with us one year near the old lumbering town of Laquin. The man carried a beautiful 8mm Mauser sporter with side panels and double set triggers. He had hunted for 16 years and had never killed a buck despite having taken several shots.

On this day, he finally connected with a large, heavy buck with a gnarled rack that bespoke years of staying out of sight. Yet, as we rolled that buck over, looking for the entrance and exit holes made by the bullet, it seemed that the buck was unmarked; not a visible wound nor drop of blood. Finally, in roughing up the hair along the neck, we found a small pencil-size hole in one side and out the other. And then we discovered that the gentleman in question had been using old military ammunition for his entire hunting career. A classic case of the wrong bullet properly placed.

Though the use of military ammunition in the woods today is rare, if not illegal, we still have any number of examples of the use of the wrong bullet on deer. Five or six seasons ago, my nephew was using a .300 Winchester Magnum in the deer woods

and put four shots through the chest area of a buck with no apparent reaction from the animal. Not a single bullet expanded. And why should they? They were designed for game heavier than deer.

If you are going to kill deer consistently and reliably, you have to use a bullet that expands rapidly yet retains enough weight to ensure penetration from a raking shot.

This is quite an order, one that is very difficult to fulfill, especially in these days of velocity consciousness. Think about it for a moment. The higher the velocity, the more difficult it is to design a bullet that functions properly on both heavy and light game, at short and long ranges. In fact, it's almost an impossibility to design a jacketed bullet that will expand well on both deer and elk and still retain the weight necessary to drive through to the vitals of the elk. Conversely, if the bullet structure is strong enough to drive through the elk after expansion, chances are that it will not expand on deer.

So, which bullet is best for deer? To answer that, you have to give some consideration to how you hunt and the terrain on which you are hunting. But first, let's take a look at the deer itself.

I have read many times that deer are extremely fragile, highly nervous animals that are easily killed with almost any reasonable high-velocity bullet. This may be so—in certain areas of the nation where the country is open and expansive. But in the woodlots of the East, Pennsylvania in particular, I've seen

119

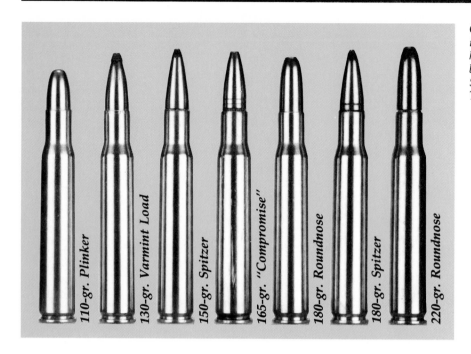

110-gr. Plinker   130-gr. Varmint Load   150-gr. Spitzer   165-gr. "Compromise"   180-gr. Roundnose   180-gr. Spitzer   220-gr. Roundnose

Choosing a proper bullet is nearly as important as making a good shot. For hunting whitetails with a .30/06, the best choice is a 180-grain round-nose. Stanley Trzoniec photo (left). Opposite, Tim Christie photo.

a few deer soak up a lot of lead and keep going. I've seen a lot of them drop at one shot, too. In almost every case, however, the deer that dropped in their tracks were those that were standing, at a slow walk, or shot in the spine. In short, a whitetail deer pumped up with adrenaline requires a lot more horsepower than one that is at ease with the world.

A prime example of this was an experience I had close to 40 years ago when I was using the .30/06. At that time, the late Jack O'Connor had written that his favorite deer and antelope load for the '06 was the 150-grain Remington bronze-point bullet loaded with 52 grains of IMR 4320 powder. In my Winchester Model 70, this load was deadly accurate, and the first deer I shot with it was at about 175 yards across an open field. The deer was feeding, and when the bullet struck she dropped like a stone. I was elated.

The next three deer I shot with that load were all running hard, and much as I hate to put it on paper, two of them were cripples. We owe our deer something better than that!

Oh yes, had the bullets been placed exactly right, there would have been no cripples—the deer would have dropped. And had they been standing quietly at the shot, they probably would have dropped, too. The facts are that they were being driven on adrenaline in the timber, where exact shot placement is more by accident than intention. Under these conditions, I needed more bullet to open up a longer wound channel and destroy more tissue.

Now, let's go back to how we hunt and its relationship to the bullet required.

A large majority of today's deer hunters do their hunting from a stand. That is, they sit on a stump or in a tree stand, or stand with their back to a tree. Most of the deer taken by stand hunters are shot as the animals cautiously poke their way through the timber or are at a standstill. In either case, the hunter usually has the opportunity to take his time, pick his shot and thread the bullet through to a precise point on impact. Under these conditions, a man can do little better than to use one of the mid-weight bullets for the caliber in question. For a .30 caliber rifle—which has more oomph than the .30/30—I would opt for the 150- to 165-grain bullet; in .270 caliber, I would take the 130-grain bullet; and in 7mm, I would go to the 140-grainer. For the .30/30, I would stick to the traditional 170-grain bullet.

Practically all mid-weight bullets are structured for lighter game such as deer and antelope. Thus, the stand hunter is pretty well fixed when it comes to bullet choice, just as long as he doesn't try to drive these same bullets from behind the ribs on a diagonal path forward into the lung cavity. Few mid-weight bullets are capable of the journey.

The ballistic features that attract us to the mid-weight bullet are velocity, flat trajectory and a high energy figure—all worthwhile factors to consider. However, under certain conditions they can work against us, for just as energy is based on the square of the velocity, so is resistance. Another way of saying this is that the faster an expanding bullet is traveling when it hits, the faster it stops and the more shallow is its penetration. The slowdown is greatly enhanced by rapid expansion and sometimes almost-total disintegration of the bullet. Some will argue that such rapid expansion dissipates most of the bullet energy or transfers it to the deer. My opinion—and it is only an opinion—is that the bullet itself absorbs most of the energy during the expansion process.

Of late, bullet manufacturers have done a lot to prevent bullet breakup and still retain rapid expan-

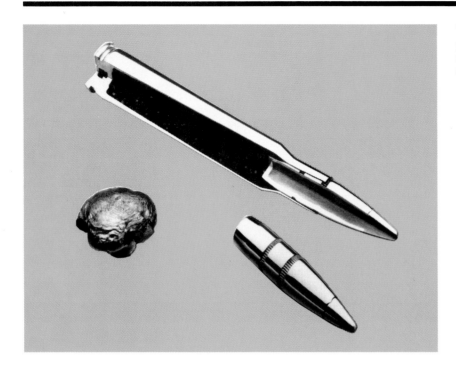

The Winchester Silvertip is a protected-point bullet. The point is covered by an aluminum alloy cap that dissipates on impact, allowing optimal expansion.

sion. But the fact remains that if a bullet retains 50 or 60 percent of its weight in one piece, it's doing well. And 50 or 60 percent of a 150- or 165-grain bullet is not very much, not enough for deep penetration on a raking shot.

There is a small segment of deer hunters today who hunt on their feet, either by the drive method or by skulking the brush lots and laurel thickets. In either case, they are faced with an entirely different set of problems than those confronting the stand hunter. First, though they may get some of the same kind of shooting as the stand hunter—that is, standing or slowly walking deer—they also have to take some shots at running deer, quite often from a rear angle that puts the bullet behind the ribs, where it has to range forward into the chest.

For this kind of hunting—and I'm the kind who likes to poke around the brush—I am a firm believer in a heavier bullet that has a lot of lead exposure and is driven at a more modest velocity. The problem that arises here is the fact that many of the heavier bullets are structured for heavier game, especially those bullets normally used in the high-velocity magnums such as the .300 Winchester and 7mm Remington. You can't expect the heavier bullets in these calibers to expand on deer when both the cartridge and bullet are designed for elk and bears.

Winchester's new CXP cartridge selector clearly shows that though the 180-grain Power Point for the .30/06 is the bullet recommended for deer, antelope and black bears, the same weight and type of bullet for the .300 Winchester Magnum is recommended for elk, moose and brown bears. It also shows that the 180-grain Silvertip Boattail for the .30/06 is the recommended cartridge for elk, moose, and brown bears instead of for deer.

Thus, when it comes to the heavier bullets in the more powerful cartridges, you have to exercise a lot more care in bullet selection. In fact, with cartridges especially developed for heavy game, unless you are a handloader, you may have to go with the mid-weight bullet regardless of how you hunt. For the .300 Winchester Magnum, the Winchester CXP cartridge selector does not recommend any bullet of more than 150 grains for deer. The same is true for

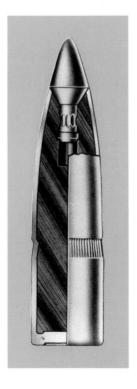

The 150-grain Remington Bronze Point features a bronze tip inserted into the lead bullet to provide good aerodynamic shape. The bronze point is driven into the lead on impact, helping the bullet to expand or mushroom.

The popular Nosler Partition bullet is a high-velocity pointed bullet that mushrooms quickly due to the thin jacket walls but does not fragment during penetration. The "partitioned" rear section holds the bullet together.

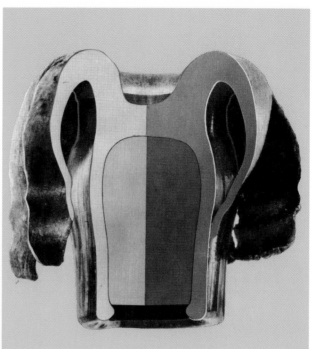

the 7mm Remington Magnum cartridges, though for the less powerful 7 × 57 Mauser, Winchester recommends a 175-grain softpoint.

I can remember when Silvertip bullets first came on the market. I was using them with total satisfaction in a .32 Winchester Special, and my dad was using them with equal satisfaction in the .300 Savage. But more than one hunter using the early 180-grain Silvertips in the .30/06 found that he was punching holes clean through his deer with no expansion.

Again, in selecting a bullet for the hunter who is on his feet and prowling the brush lots, or taking part in drive hunting, go for the heavier bullets of the caliber used, preferably of a round-nose, softpoint design. For this type of hunting, a flat trajectory out to 200 yards is of little advantage. You are interested in rapid expansion and deep penetration.

More than one authority has written that the round-nose bullet is as obsolete as the Model T Ford. Though the statement may be accurate for the Ford, there is nothing obsolete about the round-nose bullet. It will expand more rapidly than the pointed soft-nose bullet for three reasons:

● There is a broader frontal area of exposed lead.
● In the swaging operation, the jacket of the round-nose bullet is not closed in as much as that of the pointed bullet.
● The structural shape of the bullet jacket aft of the exposed lead on the round-nose bullet lends itself to expansion far better than does the structural shape of the pointed bullet.

If just one of these three reasons is valid, it's reason enough for me to go with the round-nose for the type of hunting described.

Many hunters favor lighter bullets because these bullets yield more-spectacular kills. And there is no denying it—lighter bullets driven at a higher velocity do give spectacular one-shot kills. But I wonder whether this is because of the superiority of the lighter bullets, or because of the way the game is being taken—a standing or slow-walking shot as opposed to a running shot. Use a heavier bullet on the first two shots, and you will get the same results. Use a lighter bullet on a raking shot, and your chances of not finding your deer are multiplied.

Even with heavier bullets on raking shots, don't expect your deer to pile up on the spot. He probably won't. But with the heavier bullet, your chances of reaching the boiler room are greatly improved, as are your chances of an exit wound and subsequent blood trail.

If your shots at deer will be at long range, similar to what a western mule deer hunter will encounter, bullet choice should be different. For long shots—out to, say, 350 yards—hunters need bullets with sharp points and boattails, which allow the bullet to slip through the air with a minimal amount of drag. These bullets are designed to mushroom more reliably at long ranges. They therefore do not work well at close range because they either blow up or pass through the deer. Select a load that will develop 2,200 fps remaining velocity at 300 and, preferably, at 400 yards. And practice until most of your three-shot groups impact within a 2-inch circle at 100 yards.

Whatever your choice, the next time you purchase a box of ammunition for your favorite deer rifle, give some thought to the type and weight of the little bullet that does your job.

Deer Stand Guns

By Tim Jones

Ultra-lightweight rifles for deer hunting have certainly been getting a lot of attention recently from hunters and gun writers—and with good reason. In certain situations, they make superb deer killing weapons.

Last fall, for example, I showed up for a hunt for trophy whitetail bucks in the Moser River country of Nova Scotia, toting a brand new Ruger M-77 RSL ultralight in .308 caliber. With a compact Swarovski 3×-to-9× variable scope, a nylon sling and five rounds of Federal Premium ammo with 165-grain boattails, it weighs an honest 6 pounds 10 ounces. Not the lightest rifle on the market, but certainly no heavyweight, either.

In the vast, glacier-scoured, up-and-down country, you hunt on your own two feet. Though you may sit morning and evening, you spend your days walking. In my case, I walked constantly because a hurricane arrived at the same time I did and stayed for the duration. The deer weren't moving, so I spent the entire week walking, looking for deer that were hiding better than any proverbial needle in a very large haystack. I never found them.

By the end of that frustrating week, I appreciated every ounce that my rifle *didn't* weigh. So did my guide, Kevin Findley of Sheet Harbour. His Remington Model 700 ADL .308 with a Bushnell 3×-to-9× scope topped out at more than nine pounds. Findley's a good guide and tough as a tree root, but dragging that ordnance up and down steep, wet, spruce-choked hills took its toll on him. Along about midweek, I began to fear that he was going to murder me in my sleep to get my rifle.

The more you have to walk, the steeper the terrain you're covering, and the thicker the woods, the more you appreciate a lightweight, short, fast-handling rifle. That's why the handy Winchester and Marlin lever guns have been so popular for so long, why the Remington Model 600 bolt-action carbines are as scarce on the used-gun market as fur coats at an animal-rights meeting, and why the new lightweights are getting so much attention.

But what about the opposite situation, when your day's hunting consists of walking a few hundred yards from camp or pickup truck, plunking your butt down in an elevated stand or ground blind and staying put, waiting for the deer to come to you? That's the way more and more hunters, especially those east of the Mississippi, are bringing home their winter's venison these days, and it's as good a way as I know to ensure success with whitetails. But is a lightweight rifle the best gun for that type of hunting? My answer is a resounding no!

The advantages of a lightweight rifle—easy portability and fast handling—just don't mean that much to a stand hunter. Once you are on stand with your rifle set across your knees or with the butt resting on the ground or your stand platform, it doesn't matter how much your gun weighs. And fast handling just isn't that critical in most stand-hunting situations. If you stay alert and keep your senses sharp, you usually have time to prepare for a shot.

For the stand hunter, bringing home venison is a matter of choosing a stand that is likely to offer a shooting opportunity, toughing it out on that stand until the deer shows, and then shooting straight once the opportunity presents itself. Frequently, at least on the stands I hunt, those shooting opportunities are less than perfect.

I prefer deer stands that are set up along an edge

Lightweight rifles are great when you need to climb, but for sitting on stand, a solid, heavy, accurate rifle is best for bagging a buck. Joe Albea photo.

of some sort. Usually, it's where thick brush or conifers break out into open hardwoods, swales, clearcuts, power lines or agricultural land. The deer travel these edges in the security of the thicker cover, so I frequently have the opportunity for close-in shots. But very often, the deer I shoot at are either moving, partially screened by brush or trees, or both. The ranges may be short, but the shots are rarely easy.

In these edge stands, however, there is always the chance that the deer will show themselves in the open to feed or fight, or on whatever whim causes deer to do what they sometimes do. I therefore have to be prepared for some far-and-fine shooting, whether that's 150 yards through open hardwoods or 300 yards across a field or clearing. Long shots are always a challenge to me.

Given these variables of stand hunting, I find that I bring home more venison with a rifle that I shoot well than with one that's easy to carry. I suspect that's true for most stand hunters.

I would argue, therefore, that a good stand rifle needs to be chosen as carefully as the rifle you'd pick for sneak-and-pause whitetail hunting in heavy cover, or for chasing up and down mountainsides. Not that any deer rifle—or shotgun, for that matter—won't work on a deer stand. I've shot deer from stands with everything from a 20-gauge shotgun to a .44 Magnum carbine to a .30/30 to a 7mm Remington Magnum, so I'm not about to get into the trap of arguing that you *must* have a special stand rifle. It's just that a carefully chosen firearm that you shoot well may just give you the edge when conditions are less than perfect.

The choice stand rifle for me, and for most of the really successful stand hunters I know, is a bolt-action weighing between 9 and 11 pounds fully dressed; sporting a 24- or 26-inch barrel of standard weight or heavier; chambered for a fast, accurate round; and equipped with a good sling and a portable variable-power scope. A stand rifle purchased today will probably also have a synthetic or laminated stock—though there are many perfectly functional rifles with wood handles on stands around the countryside. A few stand hunters will substitute a high-quality modern single-shot, such as those made by Ruger, Browning or Thompson/Center, for the bolt-action. But otherwise, the specs will remain about the same.

My favorite stand rifle is a Ruger M-77R in 7mm Remington Magnum with a Swarovski 2.2-to-9×42mm scope, a laminated wood stock and a leather Whelen-type sling. I feed it Federal Premium loads with either 150-grain boattails or 140-grain Nosler partitions. Fully dressed and loaded, it weighs 9 pounds 9 ounces. I'm thinking of having it outfitted with a heavy target barrel to increase the weight. Incidentally, this rifle is such an effective deer killer that I've nicknamed it "Thumper," after Bambi's best friend.

Why these choices? Let's take it step by step and look at the reasoning. Maybe I can convince you that a stand rifle is a necessary part of your deer hunting.

First, the action. I have a soft spot in my heart for lever guns, perhaps because I've killed more deer with an ancient, inherited .300 Savage Model 99 than with any other rifle in my small arsenal. And there are probably lots of good-to-great stand hunters who swear by pumps and autoloaders. But I'll argue all night around any fireside you care to invite me to that bolt guns make the best stand rifles. They do so for the same reason they make the best target rifles—accuracy.

Bolt actions, both Mauser-type and other variations on the turnbolt idea, produce more accuracy than do levers, pumps and autoloaders. Their only rival in strength and accuracy is the modern single-shot. The mass of steel in bolt actions and the solid lockup of the turnbolt help make these actions extremely rigid. The more rigid a rifle is, and the less the action flexes under the tremendous pressures generated by modern rifle cartridges, the higher the degree of inherent accuracy in the rifle.

Also, most modern bolt guns, even the military models, come with either sharp, crisp triggers or triggers that can be improved with a little knowledgeable gunsmithing. I was skeptical about the importance of good trigger control to accuracy until I started doing a lot of practice shooting offhand and in various field positions. I was using two rifles, a bolt-action .308 and the lever-action .300 Savage, that delivered roughly comparable accuracy from the bench; in fact, the lever was even a bit more accurate. Both guns weighed about eight pounds. The bolt gun had a crisp 4½-pound trigger; the lever had a 5½-pound trigger that was very good for a lever gun but not as good as the bolt's. I thought that the two were comparable rifles until I lifted them off the

Accuracy, and power, make a bolt-action tops for stand hunting. Richard P. Smith photo.

sandbags and started shooting at targets offhand, kneeling, sitting and with various field rests. All comparisons disappeared. The bolt gun was much easier to hit with.

Any of the great, standard-weight bolt-actions now on the market as new or used guns has the capability to be a highly accurate stand rifle. The Winchester Model 70, Remington Model 700, Ruger M-77, Sako, Savage Model 110, Mauser Mark X, Weatherby Mark V, Browning A-Bolt and BBR, and the various military Mausers, including the '98 and the Springfield, are all time-proven deer killers, and each has the inherent accuracy to make a great stand rifle.

Why all of the concern about accuracy? After all, a rifle that holds its shots to within 4 or 5 inches of center at 100 yards or so is accurate enough for most deer hunting. Isn't a fast follow-up shot, available from a lever gun, more important than minute-of-angle accuracy with a bolt rifle?

No, not really. Maybe my experience is unusual, but most of my successful stand hunts in 20 years of chasing whitetails from Canada to Georgia, with many stops in between, have been concluded with a single, well-placed shot. Sometimes, that has meant slipping a bullet through a tiny opening in the brush; sometimes it has meant reaching out several hundred yards across a field or clear-cut. Firepower just hasn't been nearly as important as accuracy.

If a bolt-action or single-shot is the way to go, why not just settle for one of the new lightweight bolt guns and use it on stand and for stretch-your-legs hunting? You can go that route, all right, but you'll be handicapping yourself for stand hunting. As stated above, a stand rifle ought to weigh somewhere between 9 and 11 pounds in full dress. That may seem like a lot of excess avoirdupois, but it really isn't.

Many of the modern lightweights scrimp on the barrel to save weight. Lightweight barrels are inherently less accurate than heavier models, due primarily to their flexibility. But that isn't the main reason why a heavier barrel is better on a stand rifle.

As noted above with trigger pulls, there's a significant difference between accuracy from a sandbagged benchrest and accuracy in field shooting conditions. The difference between a light barrel and a heavy one for the first shot (which is the one that really counts) may be only a fraction of an inch. But none of my deer stands has ever come equipped with a benchrest, and even if it did, the deer usually didn't come at an angle where I could have used it. The simple fact is that shooting from a sitting position, or from a standing position with some sort of improvised rest—as is most often the case with stand hunters—is easier with a heavy-barreled rifle. Inertia helps keep that long, heavy tube steadier.

If you choose a standard-weight action and a regular barrel for your stand rifle, and then add a scope, mounts, sling and swivels, and a magazine full of ammo, you will find that the rig weighs nine pounds or so. The weight may be a little less with a Kevlar stock, a little more with dense wood or wood laminate. Add a heavy barrel, and you'll push the weight up over 10. That's right where a stand rifle should be.

The heavier weight and longer barrel of your stand rifle are going to help you make the most of the modern, high-performance caliber for which it's chambered. The 24- or 26-inch tube will help you get every last foot-per-second of velocity out of either factory ammo or handloads. And the extra heft is going to help you tolerate the extra recoil of the high-performance loads. Heavy rifles kick less sharply than do lightweights. Guns that kick less are less likely to cause a shooter to flinch.

Why choose a high-performance load for your stand rifle? Why not? Just because countless whitetails have been killed with .30/30-class rifles doesn't mean that there aren't better alternatives for a stand rifle.

When hunting whitetails from a stand, especially in wooded country, you may never see a deer at 300 or 400 yards. And even if you did, you might not feel capable of shooting at that range, though with practice, most shooters are capable of shooting accurately at long ranges.

But long-range deer cartridges—loads with enough retained energy to kill a deer at more than 300 yards—also make superb cartridges at medium ranges. High-energy cartridges achieve their extra killing power with extra velocity, and extra velocity translates into flatter trajectory. Flatter trajectory makes it easier to place a killing shot, even at normal ranges.

Let me give you an example. Two years ago, I was sitting on a deer stand in Vermont. A classic edge stand, this one sat on the border of some heavy conifer cover, overlooking a clearing that contained several apple trees that bear fruit in most years. The distance across the clearing was just shy of 200 yards.

When a spikehorn wandered into a lower edge of this long, narrow clearing on the last morning of my hunt, it took me a minute to pick out his spikes in the gray early morning light. By then, he was almost to safety in the woods on the other side. My only hope for a shot was to shoot between two small saplings and *under* an overhanging apple branch. I had only about a 6-inch opening at 100 yards through which to slide the bullet, with the deer 75 yards beyond that. Fortunately, there was no wind, and the stand I was sitting on had a solid 2 × 4 crossbar for a rest. The 150-grain boattail from my 7mm Remington Magnum struck within 2 inches of where I wanted it, just in front of the buck's last rib as he angled away from me. With the rainbow trajectory of a slower cartridge, I'd either have hit the buck too low for a killing shot or nailed the overhanging apple branch fair and square.

What constitutes a good cartridge for a stand rifle? I'd say that any cartridge that launches a bullet of 115 grains or more at anything close to 3,000 fps is ideal. That eliminates the popular .243 and 6mm

The author's own stand rifle is a Ruger Model 77R in 7mm Remington Magnum with laminated stock and Swarovski variable scope. Weight is less than 10 pounds.

Remington cartridges, which normally use 100-grain bullets for deer.

A partial list of excellent stand-rifle cartridges would include the .25/06 and .257 Weatherby with 117- to 120-grain bullets; the .264 Winchester with 140-grain loads; the classic .270 Winchester and the .270 Weatherby with 130-grain bullets; the .280 Remington, 140-grain load; the 7mm Remington Magnum and 7mm Weatherby with 140 or 150-grain bullets; and the .30/06 with 150-grain bullets, especially in handloads.

Some stand hunters use much hotter calibers. The .300 Winchester and .300 Weatherby magnums with 150-grain bullets are tremendous long-range deer calibers. I know soybean-field hunters in Georgia who use these big cartridges to their maximum potential, regularly making killing shots at 500 yards. And I've heard of a small cadre of long-range enthusiasts in Pennsylvania who use wildcats such as the .375 H&H Magnum necked down to .30 caliber to take deer at outlandish ranges. But for most stand hunters, cartridges such as the ones listed above, or anything similar, are more than adequate. Hunters shouldn't chance a shot beyond 300 yards unless they've had a great deal of long-range practice.

The truth of stand hunting is that a stand sitter is often as likely to get a shot measured in feet as in yards. Too fast a cartridge will zip right through a close-range deer without the bullet expanding, or it may blow up and only wound.

It's this potential for close-range as well as long-range shots while stand hunting that dictates not only the best caliber choices for a stand rifle, but also the best choice of optics. By far the best sighting equipment for a stand rifle is a big variable scope, such as a 3×-to-9× or a 2×-to-8×, with an objective-lens diameter of 36mm or larger.

The reasoning behind this choice of optics is simple. Sitting on stand with the variable screwed down to its lowest setting, you are ready for fast action if a deer comes in close. Also, it's easy to pick up a running deer in the wide field of view at the low-power setting. But when a longer shot offers, you usually have time to screw the power ring up to a higher setting for more precise shot placement.

The large objective lens is needed to improve the light-gathering power of the scope in those critical first few minutes of light at dawn and the last few minutes of light at dusk. Normally, the only reason to avoid large optics is to save weight. On a stand rifle, however, a heavy scope is no penalty at all.

If the trend toward lightweight rifles has produced anything of value for the stand rifle, it's the synthetic stock. A good stand hunter stays on his stand all day long, come hell or high water. A synthetic stock, whether it's fiberglass, Kevlar, molded plastic or resin-impregnated laminated wood, can take a lot more hell *and* more high water than even a well-sealed wood handle, and keep on shooting straight. I chose laminated wood for my stand rifle because it looks better to my eye, feels better in my hand and weighs more than most synthetics. That's personal choice. The issue only becomes critical when the buck of a lifetime shows up after you've spent the day sitting in the pouring rain. In that situation, I'll take the stability of a synthetic stock over the beauty of non-laminated wood any day.

The final element in the perfect stand rifle is a sling. A sling is absolutely necessary for toting such heavy artillery to and from your stand. For that, a simple lightweight nylon or oiled-leather sling is fine. But a sling can serve another purpose. Though most of today's riflemen seem to have gotten out of the habit of using one, a sling is a great aid to shooting accuracy, especially in the offhand, kneeling and sitting positions. For this type of shooting, a two-part military Whelen-type sling with keepers is far superior to the simple strap.

Learning to use a military sling takes a little time (if you need instruction, there's an excellent series of photographs in the Outdoor Life Book Club's *Deer Hunter's Encyclopedia*), but it's well worth the effort. You'll shoot better.

It really doesn't matter whether your favorite deer stand is situated in the sawgrass of south Florida or the woodlands of Maine, overlooking a crop field somewhere in Wisconsin or deep in the Texas brush country. The principles always remain the same—pick a good stand site, stay put until the deer show up, and then shoot straight. That last step is a lot easier to accomplish if you've got the right rifle in your hands. Pick up a lightweight when you have to walk. Get a stand rifle when you're ready to put venison in the freezer. 🦌

Big Game on the Run

By Norm Nelson

When my uncle topped the low ridge, a big whitetail buck below him broke from a clump of black spruce and started running all-out across the snowy muskeg. Down the ridge a ways, I heard the bark of the long-barreled .30/30 rifle, followed shortly by a summoning whistle.

When I joined my uncle, he pointed to the fallen buck out in the swamp. Like any boy, I knew how long a 100-yard football field looked. The buck looked farther, maybe 150 yards.

Uncle Ralph said that it was no more than 80 to 100 yards. Pacing it off wasn't possible on the wet ground, but after years of making distance tallies while cruising timber as a U.S. forester, his estimate was probably close. It was still a long one-shot kill for an open-sighted .30/30. Bounding high and changing course to clear the snow-capped clumps of sphagnum moss and Labrador tea, that buck was no easy target.

I asked Uncle Ralph how far he had led the deer. He had no idea but said that it was far enough.

That was my introduction to the tricky business of hitting big game on the run, and the experience didn't teach me much at the time. Only later did I realize that three important lessons were there for me if I had been ready for them. The passage of 48 hunting seasons has borne them out.

The first lesson is that most hunters overestimate the range at which they're shooting, just as I did in eyeballing the range at which my uncle shot that muskeg buck.

The second lesson is that the best shot a hunter gets on running game is usually the first one. Sometimes, it's his *only* chance. If the shooter knows his business, he doesn't need to fire more than once.

The third lesson is that you can't learn exactly how to hit game on the run by listening to what a successful shooter tells you. He probably remem-

bers some kind of sight picture, but he usually cannot tell you whether he was spot-shooting at a fixed point ahead of the buck, swinging with a maintained lead, or using a fast swing that overhauls the target and goes past it.

The last is sometimes called the "paintbrush technique" by shotgunners. It gives the illusion of shooting just a short distance ahead of a crossing target. However, by the time the gun goes off, that very fast, "painting out" lead has actually swung the muzzle farther ahead than the shooter usually realizes. When a successful shooter says that he shot barely ahead of a fast-moving target or even right at it, be it animal or bird, my guess is that he was using the paintbrush technique and that the lead was much greater than he believes.

I *think* that's what I did on a 350-pace crossing shot. The big cow elk was scared and moving fast in low bounds across a small opening between patches of timber. It's in my mind that the crosshairs were only about one elk-length ahead of her nose when my .340 Weatherby went off. With a maintained lead and the muzzle moving at the same speed as the target, I don't think that would have been enough. Whatever method I did use, the elk's sojourn to the home freezer was instantly ensured when the 210-grain Nosler completely destroyed heart and adjoining lung tissue.

Today's hard-hunted, spooky game is often first seen when on the run. Hitting these fast-moving targets, particularly at a 90-degree crossing angle, is an art, not a science. No math equation, regardless of how well you memorize it, can solve the marksmanship problem when a spooked buck rips out of cover. There simply isn't time enough to consciously calculate the needed lead.

Nor can any formula factor in such variables as the hunter's sight-and-shoot reaction time, which may be very fast at 8 A.M. and much slower at 4 P.M. the same day, thanks to weariness or even relaxed boredom just before the quarry breaks cover. Most shooters must rely on experience when such a moment arrives. The trouble is that few target ranges have a moving-target setup. Even so, conventional practice with stationary targets helps. Only through such practice can you master the fundamentals of sight picture, breath control and trigger squeeze.

If these are nearly automatic or subconscious actions, the conscious part of your brain is free to deal with all of the other problems. What's the range? Do I have to hold over? How fast is the game moving, and at what angle? Will it stay on that course? What obstacles are there, such as trees, rocks or even accompanying animals, that I don't want to hit?

All of this seems pretty awesome. Brooding about such things, a beginner might well believe that no one ever hits running game except by accident. True, there are problems, but they can be solved.

Let's examine them, starting with range estimation. Even the close-range woods hunter has to allow for the range, not to compensate for bullet drop, obviously. If the hunter thinks that a running buck or bull is 50 yards away and it turns out to be 75 yards, bullet drop can be ignored.

Yet, the *additional* time of bullet flight for the extra 25 yards will be from 2/100 to 3/100 of a second, depending on the cartridge. In that time, a deer doing 25 mph, or about 37 feet per second, moves 9 to 13 inches. With relatively slow loads such as the .44 Magnum, heavy black-powder loads or shotgun slugs, time of flight is longer and the required lead is slightly greater.

Nine or 10 inches of bullet-placement error won't cause a complete miss by itself, but it may well mean a paunch hit rather than a killing shot in the chest cavity.

At longer distances, of course, range estimation becomes extremely important, but not necessarily because of trajectory problems. Out to about 250 yards on antelope, 300 yards with big muleys, and 350 or so on elk and moose, the flat trajectories of most modern rifle calibers are very forgiving of range-estimation errors *if* the rifle has been properly sighted in to be dead on at, say, 200 to 225 yards. If, however, the hunter is unwise enough to sight in for 100 yards, he may undershoot game at 200 yards or beyond if he fails to hold high.

Time of bullet flight is really important at long ranges. Let's take the most demanding scenario—a 90-degree crossing shot. You're using a typical high-velocity rifle and a good pointed bullet that retains velocity at long range. You estimate the lead perfectly for a shot at 200 yards, but the game is really 300 yards away. Could you miss for that reason alone? You bet you could.

Traveling that additional 100 yards takes a typical high-velocity bullet about an extra 1/10 of a second.

If your target is a pronghorn antelope going all-out at 60 mph (80 fps), your bullet will kick up dust 8 or 9 feet behind the speeding animal. That's two antelope lengths. Even with a relatively slow mule deer covering about 30 to 40 fps, you'll either shoot behind or put a bullet through the hindquarters.

The moral is: When in doubt, shoot somewhat farther ahead. Broadside shots at running game are rarely missed by shooting too far in front. The late Jack O'Connor once wrote that in watching lots of shooters at a range that boasted a running deer target, he had yet . . . "to see anyone miss by shooting in front."

Even game moving at a trot is often going fast enough so that you'd have to run to keep up with it. With whitetails, the deer's tail is the warning signal. If a trotting buck runs up his big, white flag all the way, he's going to let the hammer down to full speed. For whitetails, that is up to 37 mph, according to my own automobile-speedometer clocking of frightened deer running on a level, unobstructed surface. That's about 54 fps.

Worse yet, running game is often doing a lot more than just running. On flat, clear ground, a whitetail makes top speed in long, low bounds. Because whitetails are dense-cover lovers, the typical fleeing buck is clearing brush, logs and windfalls in high leaps, and he often steers a zigzag course to avoid taller obstacles.

Elk are much faster than generally realized. Researcher Olaus Murie credited them with more than 40 mph. Seven big bulls were once clocked doing 34 mph over 1½ miles. Ernest Thompson Seton, the great naturalist, once clocked trotting elk that covered a mile of level ground in 3½ minutes. That is about 17 mph. Brush and timber don't slow them down a great deal.

What blows the beginning elk hunter's mind is seeing how far an animal that hefty can jump. I think, but I'm not sure, that an elk can leap as far horizontally as a whitetail—up to 20 or 25 feet, and probably more down a slope. Elk sail over ordinary cattle fences, and the New Mexico Department of Game and Fish reported one that jumped an eightfoot live-trap fence and did so "easily."

Mule deer and blacktails leave the starting gate in what researchers call the "stotting gait"—rhythmic, springy high bounds. They're not moving as fast as a whitetail in linear distance, but those high-trajectory bounds make for difficult shooting.

After too many misses, I long ago concluded that a muley is just too hard to hit when he's up in the air. I've done my best shooting at stotting mule deer by trying to hit the animal just as it comes back down to earth after a leap.

The buck often runs an erratic course to pick the best route through sagebrush or rocks, but when

A buck bounds away. Should you shoot him at the top of the rise or when he's down? Judd Cooney photo.

airborne, the deer can't change direction. You can tell about where it will land. The trick is to make a bullet arrive in the same space just when the buck touches down.

To each his own, however. Some experienced shooters prefer to shoot at bounding game when it is in the air. My father shot scores of northern forest whitetails. He argued that at the peak of the leap, the deer slows a bit, though gravity speeds it up a little on the downhill side of the parabola. Chewing that over, I decided that Dad might be right. Years ago, as a budding sports photographer, I learned that a fast-moving athlete is easiest to "freeze" with a camera at what photogs call the "peak of action." Watch hurdle runners, and you'll see that they slow down noticeably at the top of the trajectory.

Game running through brush and trees seems to be going much faster than it really is. This illusion often panics the shooter into firing too quickly. Not that he can waste time, but the best system in this situation is to pick an opening in the cover ahead of the animal and shoot just before the target arrives. That's an insufficient description, admittedly. The truth is, that kind of shooting just about has to be learned by practice and field experience. It's tougher than hitting a smoothly moving deer target at an unobstructed rifle range. Taking crossing shots at low-flying ruffed grouse in the woods is one training mode, however.

Speaking of optical illusions, I'm sure that many misses on running game in timber are caused by shooting too high, particularly when using open sights. The bounds of a deer or elk at full speed make the animal appear to be higher than it really is. Except at the peak of the leap, the animal is much closer to the ground during *most* of its bounding cycle.

That fact cost me a big buck in a snowstorm. From a stand, I was covering some deer trail junctions near a small marsh. My father jumped two bucks out of their evergreen storm shelter a few hundred yards away. When the gray bodies, with antlered heads held high, loped into view about 70 yards away across the marsh, I took a swinging shot at the bigger buck. Both deer poured on the coal, heads and necks low and straight out, and vanished.

Trailing in snow indicated that I'd missed cleanly, probably by overshooting. The bucks were partly masked by snow-bent cattails when I first saw them. Their head-high gait rhythmically bobbed them up and down beyond the cattail screen and made them appear misleadingly tall. I think this tricked me into shooting too high. At the time, I thought that the horizontal lead was about right. When a shooter has that feeling based on prior experience, it's correct.

What's the best preseason shooting practice that will help hit game on the run? Many hunters say that jackrabbit and cottontail shooting with a .22 rifle is invaluable. However, that's true only on dry ground, which clues you in on where you missed with a puff of dust. I've done a lot of winter jackrab-bit, snowshoe and cottontail shooting. It was fun, but not very educational. Most of the time, the snow swallows the bullet without a trace.

Years ago, I mounted cardboard in old tires and had my kids—safely placed behind a rise—roll them down the steep side of an abandoned gravel pit. Gaining speed, the tires often out-bounded any deer or elk that ever lived. But shooting in a rock-studded gravel pit is inherently unsafe. I dropped the whole drill when a bullet-chipped granite fragment flew at least 60 yards in my direction with enough force to chip the paint on my pickup's hood. On soft, dry ground and safely backstopped, however, it's good practice.

Shotgun wingshooting teaches a great deal about gauging target speed and instant estimation of leads and angles, and it also speeds up reaction time. The variety of shots offered by upland birds and waterfowl is good schooling. But even clay-target games help. Successful wingshooting is a great confidence builder, and that's important in itself.

A scope is better than open sights at long ranges. A low-power scope is usually fastest in the timber if it has a wide field and plenty of eye relief, and if the rifle is stocked for scope use. Today's duplex crosshairs are hard to beat. Most dots are far too small for quick aiming at close range, particularly in dim light. If running shots are expected, carry your rifle with both hands so that you can get on target fast. Spare yourself the panic that ensues when game erupts from the cover on the run and you're holding your rifle with only one hand.

Prone shooting is rarely feasible with running game. Usually, there's no time to get into position. And you can't swing quickly in the prone position. Sitting is better. For timber hunting, do lots of offhand practice because you'll rarely have a chance to use any other position. For most shooters, 75 or 100 yards is maximum hitting range when shooting offhand. That covers a lot of hunting situations. Using a hasty sling helps to stabilize offhand shooting, but sometimes you can't be hasty enough.

Remember that your first shot is likely to be your best. Just don't get caught with a shoulder-slung rifle when the buck breaks cover.

If you don't do your homework, you should never shoot at moving big game. It's all too easy to fire hastily and inaccurately at a moving big-game animal and wound it, never to be recovered. In this day of many hunters and scarce big game in many areas, that's not only cruel, it's also a terrible waste. Practice and hunt small game until you are quite sure that you can hit moving game consistently. Unless you can do that, confine yourself to shooting at standing big game or animals that are moving very slowly. Many experienced hunters do so because even after lots of practice, they know that they remain very poor shots when the game is up, up and away. These men deserve everyone's respect because of their restraint.

The Latest Slugs and Slug Guns

By L. P. Brezny

Most smoothbore shotguns firing slugs cannot be described as accurate, to say the least. At 50 yards, the vast majority of them produce groups that average 5 inches, extreme spread, and now and then a flyer fails to hit the target paper at all for reasons that mystify the shooter. In the late 1970s, however, several gun-cranks set out to improve slug-shooting accuracy, and their efforts have achieved great success.

Slug-shooting target competitions are now held regularly. At these events, top-flight practitioners of the art have astonished the gallery with 1½-inch groups, again extreme spread, at 100 yards. That's better than the 100-yard accuracy of many centerfire deer rifles, particularly older lever-action carbines.

Of course, groups shot unhurriedly at formal matches over level ground at ranges known in advance are not representative of the accuracy a deer hunter can expect to achieve. Nevertheless, slug guns and improved ammunition that can increase the effective (aimed) range of a hunter are now available. Their use could cut down on the number of wounded deer and may also enhance safety because the shooter is more likely to hit what he's aiming at instead of sending a wild shot into the woods.

The very finest results have been obtained with *rifled* shotgun barrels, and this leads to a controversy. If the barrel of a shotgun is rifled, has the shotgun become a rifle? If the answer is yes, should the firearm be prohibited in special areas (and some entire states) in which only shotguns are legal for big-game hunting? Shotgun-only zones are set up

Cutaways reveal Foster slug (separate wad) and BRI saboted bullet. Two-part sabot of BRI falls away on exit from the muzzle, leaving the .50 caliber spindle-shaped projectile to continue its flight toward the target.

in heavily settled areas, where the use of high-power rifles is dangerous because of their very great accidental killing and wounding range. Does using a rifled tube and improved shotgun slugs increase the gun's accidental killing and wounding range to the point where it is logical to forbid their use in shotgun-only zones as well? The answer to that question, so far, is a clear negative, but caution should be exercised in the future to make sure that this remains true, as will be demonstrated later in this article.

To understand the new wave in slug-gunning, it's best to have the characteristics of the older guns and ammunition clearly in mind.

Hollow-base Foster slugs are most common in the United States and are made of soft pure lead. Regardless of the manufacturer, Foster-type slugs utilize angled vanes on their exteriors to rotate and stabilize the stubby lead projectiles in flight.

European-style slugs, like Foster slugs, are most often constructed with angled vanes and a hollow base, but they also have some form of permanently attached wad that is carried along by the slug during its flight. The wad acts as a gas seal in the barrel upon firing. The compression system reduces deformation of the soft lead slug itself. The hollow-base Foster slugs are expanded by powder gases to seal the bore.

Because the European-type slug utilizes retained wads, the projectile also retains more weight in flight and on contact with the target. The European slug therefore produces somewhat deeper penetration and more uniform mushrooming of the projectile, which also makes for deeper penetration. During extensive penetration studies I conducted, I found that the European-style slugs tended to attain better levels of penetration at all workable hunting ranges when compared with Foster slugs.

The final type is the sabot slug. In effect, it is not a slug at all, but rather a spindle-shaped .50 caliber bullet encased in a two-piece plastic retainer (sabot).

Rifled-bore shotguns offer better accuracy than smoothbores but are illegal in some states. Steve Maslowski photo.

The two-piece, longitudinally divided sabot drops away from the projectile shortly after exit from the muzzle.

Saboted bullets or slugs are associated with a very high degree of accuracy, and are much preferred among competition slug-gunning target shooters. Of late, this high degree of accuracy has been closely linked with the use of rifled shotgun barrels, though these loads can also be used in smoothbore barrels.

You can design the best slug, but if you lack a suitable shotgun, the effort would be a waste of time. Slug guns are of three basic types. The first type is the ordinary bird gun turned into a deer gun for a few days each year. The second is more specialized, and uses a special smoothbore slug barrel. The final type consists of shotguns equipped with rifled barrels.

The ordinary bird gun is the worst possible choice. As a rule, these guns finish dead last in any type of competition. I say "as a rule" because once in a blue moon we do find one that performs beautifully with slugs. The lucky owner of an accurate slug-throwing bird gun has, in most cases, stumbled onto a choke-and-ammunition match that works well.

Smoothbore, specialized slug barrels are a different story. Regardless of gauge, these slug-shooting barrels range from 20 to 24 inches in length and are always equipped with barrel-mounted open sights or bases for a scope. Just by the addition of some form of adjustable sights, the slug barrel is vastly improved over the bird-shooting barrel.

The rifled bore is in a class by itself. To take advantage of the improved accuracy, these guns are almost always equipped with a low-power scope.

To determine the comparative performance levels of slugs and slug guns, I did a great deal of ballistics testing and compared the results with those of other researchers.

I test-fired a wide variety of slug loads in several different slug guns. One of the test guns was a Remington Model 870 fired with a 20-inch factory slug barrel and a Hastings Paradox 24 rifled slug barrel. By using these two barrels in the same Remington receiver, a very clear comparison of accuracy could be made.

Slug ammunition was supplied by Winchester, Remington, Federal and Dan/Arms. Also tested was the BRI .500 Sabot. All tests were conducted with 12-gauge ammunition.

The extensive velocity tests were conducted with double chronograph units, the first at the muzzle and the second at the target. I was amazed to find that regardless of the manufacturer or slug design, *all* of the slugs reached the 100-yard mark at about the same velocity. Foster slugs, European slugs and the saboted bullets all tended to fall off uniformly to less than 1,000 fps after reaching the 100-yard mark.

I started one set of tests with the Remington smoothbore slug barrel and then switched to the Hastings rifled barrel, thinking that I would observe

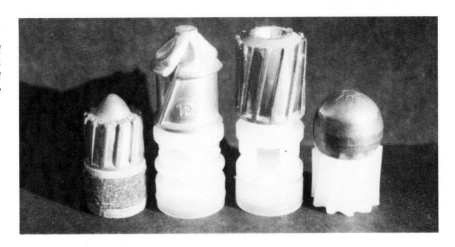

At right are four "European-type" slugs, all with typical attached wads: Brenneke, Gualandi, Cervo and AQ. Attached wad seals bore against powder gas without distorting lead portion of projectile. Attached wad also aids in penetration. The Brenneke slug has been used for 90 years.

increased levels of retained velocity. I was wrong. The change to the rifled tube, with its extra four inches of barrel length, had little effect on velocity. In fact, with one type of ammunition, the 24-inch rifled barrel actually produced a slightly lower muzzle velocity than its counterpart smoothbore barrel.

See the table on the next page for velocity figures. Looking across the table provides the reader with the speeds of the different slug loads at various ranges out to 150 yards.

I contacted my fellow ballistics researcher Tom Armbrust of Ballistic Research in McHenry, Illinois. I asked Tom whether he could run a few velocity tests so that I would be able to make comparisons. Tom did so and also provided test data produced by his massive commercial pressure gun. These guns, also called "static guns," are used within the industry to measure the pressure of various types of ammunition in the chamber. They are not manually fired but are instead mounted on a solid bench. A static gun lacks all of the error factors humans incorporate into hand-held shooting, including shooting from a benchrest. When Tom's data arrived, I found that his results confirmed my velocity recordings. But by using the static gun, Tom also provided some very important additional information on slug behavior at very long ranges. Tom's results are included in the velocity table.

The velocity measurements answered a number of questions. Most important, the European-type slugs, the Foster slugs and the saboted bullets are still traveling at much the same velocity even beyond 100 yards. On the use of rifled barrels, the hunter who believes that using one increases effective range because he harvested a deer with a one-shot kill at long range is wrong. Because all of the tested slugs weigh about the same and travel at much the same speed, it is likely that enhanced accuracy made the one-shot kill possible, not increased velocity, which does not, in fact, exist.

For all practical purposes, any form of 12-gauge shotgun slug currently in production and used in a quality specialized barrel will harvest game quite accurately to a maximum range of 100 yards. Better

shooters may be able to extend effective aimed range on deer to 125 yards, but that's the absolute maximum.

In the static gun with its 12-gauge, 30-inch cylinder-bored pressure barrel, slugs could be quite accurately fired to maximum range of 187 yards. The best group size at that range was 7¾ inches. However, a hunter with a hand-held shotgun could never do as well. The 7¾-inch group was shot with Gualandi slugs in handloads. I was impressed by the fact that regardless of the type of slug tested, long-range performance was always better than what I had expected. When groups were fired with the static gun (smoothbore barrel) and factory one-ounce Foster slugs at 50 yards, 1½-inch groups were produced, and very tight 3-inch groups were common at 100 yards.

To get a handle on the longest distance that a slug can travel, I first obtained some data compiled by the U.S. Army. The government testing of 12-gauge Foster slugs showed that when a smoothbore shotgun barrel is elevated to an angle of 28 degrees to 30 degrees, which is best for maximum range, the slugs contact level ground at about 930 yards. This information is of no practical value to the hunter because the angle of barrel elevation is so great that game cannot even be seen.

With this information in mind, I followed up on the Army tests. Setting up on an airfield during a typical Minnesota winter day, I fired slugs downrange into compacted snow.

With a target at 100 yards, and gun and aiming point at the same height, I fired both Foster and European-type slugs from a benchrest. As was the case during my first velocity tests, I used smoothbores and the rifled barrel.

After firing each series of three rounds, I searched for the points at which the spent slugs had hit the snow. I discovered that the slugs did not dig in, but rather skipped off the compacted snow and covered an additional 150 yards before hitting and skipping again. These skips continued until the slugs reached resting points on top of the snow that were an average of 634 yards from the firing point. This told me

TERMINAL VELOCITY OF 12-GAUGE SHOTGUN SLUGS

(In Feet Per Second)

	Brand	*Muzzle Velocity*	*30 Yds.*	*50 Yds.*	*75 Yds.*	*100 Yds.*	*125 Yds.*	*150 Yds.*
R	BRI Sabot 2¾-inch 445 grain	1,256	1,142	1,056	1,009	875	862	n.a.
R	BRI Sabot 3-inch 445 grain	1,436	n.a.	1,253	1,157	1,016	997	939
S	BRI Gualandi 2¾-inch 1⅛ ounces	1,592	1,362	1,196	1,047	846	790	n.a.
S	Federal 2¾-inch 1¼ ounces	1,495	1,313	1,165	n.a.	940	925	888
S	Federal 3-inch	1,480	n.a.	1,215	1,105	1,000	905	n.a.
S	Federal 2¾-inch 1 ounce	1,516	1,291	1,149	1,015	890	780	n.a.
S	Dan/Arms 2¾-inch Cervo 1⅛ ounces	1,333	1,190	1,111	1,006	918	835	765
S	Remington 2¾-inch 1 ounce	1,554	1,330	1,190	1,077	n.a.	890	952
S	Remington 2¾-inch 1 ounce	1,652	n.a.	1,269	1,112	966	847	n.a.
S	Winchester 2¾-inch 1 ounce	1,665	1,434	1,254	1,132	944	n.a.	772

S: smoothbore 20-inch Remington slug barrel; R: rifled-bore 24-inch Hastings Paradox, n.a.: not available. Data from: L.P. Brezny (author); Tom Armbrust, Ballistic Research, McHenry, Illinois; Ross Metzger, Shotdata Systems, New Brighton, Minnesota.

GROUP SIZES OF RIFLED SLUGS: RIFLED BORE VS. SMOOTHBORE

(Test Gun: Remington Model 870)

		Hastings Paradox 24-inch Rifled-Bore Barrel			*Remington 20-inch Smoothbore Barrel*	
Dan/Arms 1⅛ ounces	50 yds.	2½″ max.	1⅞″ min.	50 yds.	5½″ max.	3⅞″ min.
	100 yds.	3⅞″ max.	2″ min.	100 yds.	9⅜″ max.	3⅞″ min.
Federal 1 ounce	50 yds.	2 6/8″ max.	1⅝″ min.	50 yds.	4⅜″ max.	3⅝″ min.
	100 yds.	4⅛″ max.	3⅞″ min.	100 yds.	10⅜″ max.	5⅜″ min.
Winchester 1 ounce	50 yds.	2″ max.	1⅝″ min.	50 yds.	3⅛″ max.	2⅞″ min.
	100 yds.	4⅜″ max.	3⅝″ min.	100 yds.	6½″ max.	5⅛″ min.
Remington 1 ounce	50 yds.	3⅜″ max.	3″ min.	50 yds.	9⅛″ max.	3⅞″ min.
	100 yds.	4 2/8″ max.	4⅛″ min.	100 yds.	11″ max.	5⅜″ min.
BRI .500 Sabot	50 yds.	2⅛″ max.	1⅞″ min.	50 yds.	3″ max.	2⅞″ min.
	100 yds.	4″ max.	3⅛″ min.	100 yds.	5⅛″ max.	4¼″ min.

PENETRATION OF 12-GAUGE SHOTGUN SLUGS

(Medium: 97-Pound Wet Paper Blocked Into Layers, 5/16 Inch Per Layer)

	Number of Layers Penetrated		*Percentage Of Retained Lead*	
Slug Type And Brand	*50 Yards*	*100 Yards*	*50 Yards*	*100 Yards*
Federal 12-gauge 2¾-inch 1 ounce Foster	6	8.5	87	97
Federal 12-gauge 2¾-inch 1¼ ounce Foster	6.5	9	93.2	98.5
Dan/Arms 12-gauge 2¾-inch 1¼ ounce European	6	9	83.3	99.6
Winchester 12-gauge 2¾-inch 1 ounce Foster	5	8.5	92.8	94.6
Remington 2¾-inch 1 ounce Foster	6	9	78.5	95.3
BRI Sabot Bullet 50-cal.	6	12	43.5	78.2

that many hunters underestimate the retained velocity of shotgun slugs. A good deal of special attention should be paid to the safety of standers during deer drives in cornfields, even when "short range" slugs are used. Slugs can cover long distances before coming to rest.

After observing the shallow marks left by the slugs in the snow, I also concluded that both Foster and European-type slugs do actually rotate during flight. If the slugs had not been stabilized by rotation, they would have contacted the snow at varying angles, and there probably would have been deeper penetration in the snow. In every case, the slugs were found with their noses pointing downrange in line with the muzzle of the test gun. I conclude that all shotgun slugs retain a good deal of velocity and rotation even at long range and after skipping off the surface. Though most of the slugs made first contact with the snow at about 275 yards, we can safely assume that they were moving quite fast.

I also noted that when using the rifled barrel, I could not find any measurable increase in the range of first contact with the level surface.

My penetration testing also turned up some startling information. The various slug loads were fired into wet-paper block layers at 50 yards and 100 yards, with the results shown in the accompanying table. To sum it all up, all varieties of slugs penetrate more deeply at 100 yards than they do at 50. They also retain more weight after penetration is complete at 100 yards than at 50 yards. The reason for this was pinned down by recovering the slugs or their fragments from the paper test medium. At 50 yards, the slugs are traveling at comparatively high speed. When they hit, they mushroom a great deal, and very often they fragment into many pieces. The mushrooming and fragmentation both inhibit penetration. At 100 yards, the slug has slowed down a great deal, as shown by my velocity figures. When the slug hits, it does not mushroom so much and fragmentation is minimized. Having greater mass, the projectile maintains its momentum and penetrates more deeply.

Realistically, the future of slug gunning depends on how much responsibility the manufacturers and the hunters are willing to assume. Foster slugs and European slugs with attached wads are designed to be used within comparatively short, safe ranges. Sabot designs, though currently also short-range propositions, have almost limitless possibilities for increased range.

What if the velocities of various new forms of saboted slugs fired from rifled bores were greatly increased? What if the projectile shapes were improved to enable the bullet within the sabot to cover very long distances while retaining very high energy? For instance, how about a 150-grain saboted bullet in a 20-gauge magnum case? And there are many other possibilities.

I conducted a survey of various states about legal firearms in shotgun-only hunting zones. The reply I received from Ohio is especially interesting. According to the Ohio Department of Natural Resources, a slug gun with a rifled barrel is regarded simply as a rifle and is forbidden for deer hunting. The greatest concern voiced by the Ohio spokesmen involved handloaders who could wildcat shotgun ammunition comparable to high-powered rifle shells. Ohio does not permit the use of high-power rifles for big-game hunting anywhere in the state. The Ohio authorities have concluded, in effect, that shotguns with rifled bores are really rifles.

My home state of Minnesota has now zoned about half of its land for shotgun and rifled-slug big-game hunting. If the range of shotgun slugs is increased beyond the current maximum, a real problem could result. The portion of the state now open only to big-game hunters using shotguns could be closed entirely to firearms big-game hunting.

The whole thing boils down to the fact that any great increase in shotgun-slug range would probably result in the closure of vast areas in many states to *all* forms of big-game hunting with any kind of shotgun.

Many states do not currently bar the use of rifled shotgun barrels in shotgun-only areas, and I believe that this is so because up to now we have not had

any increase in the range of the guns. The shotgun zones were intended to allow hunters to go on harvesting deer in areas of high human-population density with a reasonable degree of safety. If the range increases, these zones may well disappear.

A few states have conducted studies of current slug guns and loads and have concluded that they pose no increased threat to safety. A very few others simply outlaw the rifled guns in special zones.

Massachusetts, for instance, has determined that according to *Webster's Third New International Dictionary*, shotguns with any form of rifled barrel are classified as rifles and are prohibited for big-game hunting in the entire state.

The Connecticut Department of Environmental Protection has determined that the use of rifled shotgun barrels only increases the accuracy of slugs and makes for swifter and cleaner kills. The officials in my home state of Minnesota feel exactly the same way. Wisconsin, after detailed studies of the newer forms of slug shooting, decided that these developments only aid in the clean harvest of big game.

In any state, however, check the regulations carefully before you hunt with a rifled shotgun. The regulations could change swiftly at any time.

By the use of some very complex computer-based ballistic profile processing, I have been able to verify that if the restraint were removed from the development of rifled barrels and improved ammunition, some loads would equal the performance of high-power-rifle ammo. So far, the manufacturers of rifled shotgun barrels and suitable ammunition have not overstepped the boundary of what is reasonable and within the intent of the law. Let's hope that this line is never crossed. If it is, American hunters could lose a lot of territory.

Another alternative is open to the authorities. They could avoid abolishing shotgun-only zones by allowing the use of buckshot while prohibiting slugs. Only a few years ago, only buckshot-loaded shotguns were legal for deer hunting in New Jersey. Then, slugs were legalized, and now hunters may legally use either one. If the range of slugs were greatly increased, New Jersey could go back to the old law, and so could other states. This would also be very disadvantageous to hunters. If 100 yards is a realistic range for an accurate, scope-equipped rifled slug gun, the maximum effective range of heavy buckshot loads is much less—say, 55 yards for 000 Buck in a 12-gauge 3-inch shell, and 40 yards or so for the garden-variety 00 Buck load in the 2¾-inch loading. Cutting effective aimed range by half or even more is not a happy prospect for deer hunters.

The notion that slug gunning with rifled bores provides a good market for equipment was recently demonstrated when Mossberg introduced a rifled barrel for the Model 500 Trophy Slugster. Ithaca's Deerslayer II also has a rifled barrel. Complete shotguns with rifled bores are also available from Ballistic Research Industries, 2825 S. Rodeo Gulch Rd., Soquel, CA 95073, and from Pennsylvania Arms Co., Box 128, Duryea, PA 18642.

Sights for Slug Guns

By Bob Bell

A half-century ago, the vast majority of shooters had never seen a scoped gun, and most of the few who had were full of misgivings. Everybody knew that glass was fragile, so how could a sight with glass lenses be expected to hang together on a hard-kicking outfit? And even if it did, how would it be possible to find moving game in that little area you saw—field of view, some called it—when you peered into the back end of the tube?

Fifty-plus years have proved the naysayers wrong. Millions of hunters have lugged scoped rifles into the world's harshest environments and used them to take countless heads of game. Yes, scopes are durable, and they're getting better every year.

No one has ever denied their superior aiming quality, but some still wonder whether they're fast enough for rapidly moving targets at close range. The question is becoming more important with the growing popularity of today's efficient slug-shooting shotguns.

Actually, the question was answered in the 1930s in west Texas when a lean transplanted Kentuckian put a low-power scope on his Model 12 and powdered countless skeet birds. Of course, he knew more about scopes than the average shooter because his name was Bill Weaver, and he had built the one he was using. Eventually, the company he created produced more scopes than any other manufacturer in the world. Nevertheless, his early results proved that a "fragile glass sight" had the durability to take a lot of recoil and the optical characteristics needed to handle fast targets even at close range—Station 8 birds, for example.

Admittedly, few clay-bird shooters or small-game hunters have any interest in scoping their shotguns, but there is a growing interest in scoping slug guns for deer hunting. It simply makes the guns more efficient. The number of areas where shotguns are the only legal firearms for big-game hunting is increasing constantly because of the expansion of densely populated suburbs. The usual quarry in such cases is the whitetail deer. This species adapts easily to humans and can survive in woodlots, brushy fence rows and even in big, overgrown yards. These deer are usually shot at reasonable ranges and can easily be taken by a medium-power load. The rifled slug can do the job if the hunter does his.

A hunter new to this situation tends to buy a batch of slugs, reach for his pet pheasant gun and head for the brush. After a moment's thought, though, he usually concludes that he should see whether his smoothbore will put slugs somewhere near his point of aim. So, he drives to the range, puts up a target at 100 yards, as he always did with his .270, and learns that his shotgun's big front bead completely covers it. Further thought makes it obvious that the rifled slug's muzzle velocity of 1,500 fps determines that its effective aimed range, due to a trajectory that's far from flat, is probably only 60 to 75 yards. He moves the target up to 50 yards and does some shooting.

If he's lucky, he's somewhere on the paper. Much depends upon the gun. A slide-action or autoloader or any kind of single-barrel shotgun, from a one banger rabbit gun to a high-grade trap model, has a greater tendency to put slugs fairly close to the aiming point than does any doublebarreled shotgun. A Remington Model 870 belonging to Dave Wise, a young friend, consistently places three shots just above the front bead at 50 yards, and Dave can easily cover most groups with his hand.

Remington 870 with smoothbore slug barrel and rifle shot 3- to 5-inch groups (three shots) at 50 yards. With 2½× scope, the same gun shot same-size groups. The advantage of a scope is increased light gathering and image clarity in dim light of typical deer woods.

Things don't usually work out that well, though. They almost never do with double-barreled guns. The two tubes sometimes don't even center their shot patterns, let alone slugs. Over/unders usually work better than side-by-sides, but even they tend to deliver separate groups from the two barrels, and the groups are often 6 inches or more apart at 50 yards. Side-by-sides are far worse. Because their barrels are in a horizontal rather than a vertical plane, recoil moves them in different directions, so groups tend to spread apart. Sometimes, one barrel will put its slugs fairly close to point of aim, but it's rare for both to do so.

In the end, anyone choosing a gun for rifled slugs would be wise to go with a single-barrel repeater, and 12-gauge is best. The 12-gauge slug is significantly heavier and makes a bigger hole than slugs in the smaller gauges. Also, ammunition in this gauge is easier to find when you need it in a hurry.

A new slug hunter will doubtless start with his small-game gun. He already has it and thinks it will do as well as anything. That's not necessarily true. Some tests have indicated that Foster-type slugs as factory-loaded by Federal, Remington and Winchester group best out of a wide-open bore, and a hunting gun may have any choke from cylinder to full.

However, my own shooting of hundreds of American and Brenneke slugs indicates that any choke can give acceptable woods accuracy. For example, numerous three-shot groups fired from the bench at 50 yards gave the following averages; improved cylinder, 4.3 inches; modified, 6.1 inches; improved modified, 4.1 inches; and full choke, 4.5 inches. By comparison, Remington's smoothbore slug barrel on a Model 870 gave a 3.6-inch average spread in 39 three-shot groups at 50 yards and an 8-inch average for six groups at 100 yards. Thus, the replacement slug barrel did prove better than any choked barrel, but it's questionable whether the difference could be noted on a deer's rib cage. It's always a good idea for a hunter to try his current smoothbore before buying a special slug gun or a replacement slug barrel for his small-game gun.

When buying a gun specifically for slug use, it's logical to choose one with the special barrel as original equipment. Even if choke isn't highly important, the slug barrel has rifle sights, and that's a great advantage. It's also worth keeping in mind that these short, open-choke barrels work well with shotshells for most upland hunting, a fact that almost never gets mentioned.

Special slug barrels aren't new. More than two

The SKB over/under made good groups at 50 yards—three shots from each barrel. Most doubles don't do so well because each barrel shoots to a different center of impact. The Action Arms Mark V sight projects an illuminated red dot that the hunter uses to aim.

decades ago, Ithaca brought out the Model 37 Deerslayer, Remington the Model 870 Brushmaster and Model 1100 Deer Gun, and Browning its Auto-5 Buck Special. Today's replacement slug barrels for most popular shotguns are readily available. Almost all slug guns have short, open-choked barrels and V-type rear sights. Considerable research has been done in this area, and the diameters of the bores and the projectiles seem to have gotten closer together, which aids accuracy. Slug diameters still probably vary more than bores, though. A small random sample of 12-gauge slugs we miked varied from .690 to .734 inch, which is a spread of .044. That's a lot compared with the variations in hunting bullets, but perhaps it's not too important to the game ranges at which slugs are used.

All of this is complicated if you use inefficient sighting equipment. A field shotgun's large front bead works fine with shot on flying game but not with slugs. Sometimes, a smaller bead is installed midway on a shotgun rib, the idea being to "figure-eight" the big front bead atop it when aligning the gun. That sometimes helps a bit with an over/under, but rarely with a side-by-side.

What is needed is an adjustable sight that permits you to zero in the slug gun just as you would a rifle. The most accurate benchrest rifle in the world would be useless without sights, so it should be obvious that they are necessary on slug guns, too. The slug shooter has the same basic options as the rifleman: open sights, aperture sights, electronic sights and scopes.

Open sights, reasonably adjustable, come on factory slug barrels. They are currently available on the following autoloader and slide-action smoothbores: Beretta A-302, Browning B80 and BPS, FIE/Franchi 48AL, Mossberg Model 712 and Model 500, Remington Model 1100, Model 11-87 and Model 870, Stevens 67VR, Weatherby 82 and 92, and doubtless

others I can't recall. All have barrels in the 18½- to 24-inch bracket. Of course, most shotgun makers have a model with a 26-inch improved cylinder barrel on which a gunsmith probably can mount the Williams Guide Open Sight or something similar. These sights are adjustable for both windage and elevation. The Williams Fool Proof and 5D models are adjustable aperture ("peep") sights.

For the specialists who really take their slug shooting seriously, there's the autoloading BRI/Benelli 123-SL-80 *rifled* shotgun, seemingly a contradiction in terms. As the name suggests, its 24-inch barrel is rifled, and its interior dimensions are optimum for an unusual slug developed by Ballistics Research Industries. This is a .5 caliber, wasp-waisted projectile enclosed in a plastic sabot of the proper diameter to tightly engage the rifling in the 12-gauge bore. The sabot is shed after exiting the muzzle, but the BRI slug continues its rotating course, which greatly improves stability and thus accuracy. The BRI/Benelli gun has neither open nor aperture sights but is drilled and tapped for a scope mount.

For those who like the rifled bore idea but don't want to buy a complete gun, the Hastings Company of Clay Center, Kansas, is supplying replacement barrels for the Remington Model 1100, Model 11-87 and Model 870, the Auto-5 Browning, Franchi AL/48 and Ithaca 37. These rifled tubes can be had with or without scope mount bases, so the user has a choice of systems. A scope is recommended for BRI-slug use in a rifled bore, as this combination is the most accurate of any we've tested. With a Hastings barrel in a Remington Model 870 and using a 2½× scope, six groups at 50 yards averaged 1.8 inches, and several 100-yard groups were less than 4 inches. However, conventional Foster-type slugs did no better out of the rifled barrel than they did from the smoothbore Remington slug gun.

Also, Ithaca's new Deerslayer II has a rifled barrel. And Mossberg has introduced a rifled slug barrel for the Model 500 Trophy Slugster. Unfortunately, I did not have time to test-fire these new items. Check your state and local regulations to find out whether use of a *rifled* slug barrel for deer hunting in shotgun-only territory is legal.

If a scope is to be installed on the shotgun barrel, it must be one of the long-eye-relief models that were primarily designed for handgun use. To get that characteristic, magnification must be kept low, usually 1½× or 2×, and even so, much field of view is sacrificed. With scopes of these magnifying powers that have a conventional 3½-inch eye relief, fields of view are about 65 to 45 feet at 100 yards. With the long-eye-relief models, the fields are in the 20- to 15-foot bracket. That doesn't seem like enough for fast-moving game in the brush, yet it tends to work out okay. The scope's far-forward position on the barrel makes it easy to shoot with both eyes open, in effect widening the field significantly because the hunter is also seeing the game with the non-sighting eye. The low power of such scopes, particularly the 1½×, means that the images seen with both eyes are so similar in size that they tend to blend together.

There are two other advantages of a barrel-mounted scope. It makes the gun easy to carry with one hand because there's nothing above the action to get in the way. More important, because with most repeating shotguns the barrel is not permanently screwed into the action, it's at least theoretically possible for the interrelationship of the barrel and action to vary somewhat from shot to shot. If the scope is mounted on the barrel, it will move right along with any change, whereas an action-mounted scope stays rigidly with that unit if the barrel moves. It is possible to permanently install the barrel by welding or by using fiberglass cement, and a few specialized slug guns have permanently installed barrels.

The action-mounted scope is the other alterna-

tive, of course. I like it better, perhaps because I've spent 50 years peering into rifle scopes mounted in that position. Nothing else seems right. This also permits using a scope of conventional design, so that the field of view is full size.

There was a time when it was difficult to mount a scope on a shotgun. The action had to be drilled and tapped, and that's usually a job for a gunsmith. Also, the thickness of the receiver was far less than that of the receiver ring on, say, a 98 Mauser. In some cases, therefore, the number of threads was scanty, and it was sometimes hard to keep a heavy scope in place. But for years now, installing a scope mount on many repeaters has been simple, at least with mount designs such as the B-Square, Weaver/Omark, Aimpoint and Kwik Mount. It's just a matter of driving out the two pins that hold the trigger group in the action, slipping on the basic mount unit, and snugging it tight to the action with two substitute locking pins. Regular rings are used to attach the scope to the base, and zeroing is done just as it is with a rifle.

Such mounts position the scope reasonably low on a shotgun, though not as low as is possible with numerous rifle mounts. For those who want the immediate availability of barrel-mounted open sights, raised figure-eight rings are available in Jerry Holden's Ironsighter and Kwik-Site's see-through mounts. These require drilling and tapping holes in the top surface of the action, and they raise the scope even higher. They therefore reduce face support on the stock while aiming. That's a disadvantage, but on the other hand, these high mounts provide instantaneous backup sighting if for any reason the scope becomes unusable. You pay your money to take your choice.

An interesting and useful mounting system for Remington's Model 870 and Model 1100 vent-rib guns is offered by Millett for use with long-eye-relief scopes. The scope rings are machined to straddle the rib and are secured by Allen-screws. The top

Tasco scope mount attaches to a shotgun by means of mounting pins that replace the gun's original trigger-group pins. Mounts of this type are made to fit many shotguns.

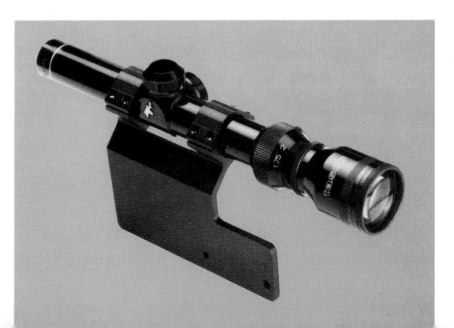

Mossberg 500 Slugster with Holden Wide Ironsighter mounts. This versatile rig permits the instant use of iron sights if the scope fails. The gun can be purchased with a rifled barrel.

halves of the rings serve as bases for emergency open sights. This is unusual but practical.

When it comes to the sighting units themselves, several other systems are available. Battery-powered electronic sights such as the well-known Aimpoint, Tasco's new Pro-Point, Action Arms' Mark V and others are available. All are small units that sit low on the gun and produce a bright red dot that serves as an aiming point. They don't magnify, so when used with both eyes open," as they should be, the field is essentially unlimited, as is the eye relief.

All of the big scope makers offer intermediate or long-eye-relief models for handgun use, and these also function well as barrel-mounted shotgun scopes. For installation on the action (receiver), any low-power rifle scope will serve, and all scope makers supply them. The rifled slug has a comparatively short aimed effective range, some 60 to 125 yards. This gear is used to hunt deer, wild boar or larger animals, so 2½× is plenty of magnification. Some may question the need for any scope if its power is to be kept so low and the gun's effective range is so short. As with a woods rifle, however, the scope makes it possible to zero in precisely and provides a bright aiming area so that the slug can be placed accurately when conditions are gloomy and the quarry would be almost invisible through metallic sights.

In choosing a scope specifically for a slug gun, I would lean toward a compact variable in the 1½×-to-4½× class, mainly to get the big field at the lowest power. Perhaps even better would be the new Weaver/Omark 1×-to-3× V3, which has a field of 95 feet at 100 yards with 1× magnification, or Tasco's new World Class Wide Angle 1×-to-3½×, which provides 115 feet of field at the bottom power. If you do get a standing shot at 150 yards or so, the top power may be very helpful. For the fellow who prefers to keep things simple, single-power 2½×20 shotgun scopes are available from Burris, Bushnell, Simmons and others. Those who prefer a single-power scope can get a Tasco 1×20

WA with a 97-foot field, a Hakko Shoji with 68-foot field, or even the Zeiss Diatal-C 1½×12 with a 78-foot field.

To answer the original question of whether a scoped shotgun can handle fast targets at close range, we put a 2½× Fullfield (55 feet) Burris scope on a short-barreled Model 870 and took it out in back of the barn. It seemed reasonable to assume that if we could break clay birds out of a Trius trap with shotshells, we ought to be able to do okay on a bouncing buck with slugs. Out of the cylinder bore, shotshells would be most effective at less than 30 yards. If we could hit with some consistency, it would mean that we were getting on fast-moving targets when the field of view was less than 20 feet.

Well, we busted them pretty well, Bob and Dave Wise and I. Going-away shots were easy, incomers more difficult because the field was constantly decreasing. At those ranges, the targets were also dropping fast, a shot that always seems unnatural to me. Still, we hit a lot more than we missed, and that was actually using the scope—swinging the reticle through the target, not ignoring it altogether and relying on the big pattern to do everything. Of course, the angles were minor, so we decided to make things tougher by throwing the birds to cross at right angles some 12 to 15 yards in front of the shooter. Again, it was possible to find the bird in the field and, a good percentage of the time, to break it. And why not? As we said, Bill Weaver did it regularly a half-century ago. Of course, he was better with a shotgun than we are.

In the end, the question of what's the best sighting arrangement for a slug gun can be answered in several ways. If the shooter is young and his eyes are excellent, open sights serve reasonably well in the woods, though aperture sights are better. But if one's eyes can use some help or ambient light conditions during hunting season are usually bad, an electronic unit or low-power scope is as useful on a slug gun as it is on a rifle. Which is to say, it's the best possible rig. 🦌

The Muzzleloader's Checklist

By Rick Hacker

After consulting his checklist, the author was totally prepared to take this nice buck.

When you hear someone shouting, "Let's go deer hunting!" you don't need a calendar to know that it's autumn. Yet, for a special breed of hunter, deer season means something more than just running down to the local sporting-goods store to buy a tag and then making sure that no new cobwebs have grown in the rifle's bore. For the hunter who has decided to enjoy the added challenge and thrills of bagging a buck with black powder, deer season is the culmination of an annual ritual that includes getting guns and gear in shape and gathering a plethora of paraphernalia that is necessary for hunting season.

Of course, even self-contained metallic-cartridge hunters go through this preparatory exercise, but for them, it is an unconscious activity that is rarely fraught with catastrophe. For example, if these hunters forget cartridges for the old .30/30, chances are pretty good and that the local sporting-goods store in their hunting area will have a box.

But it is usually an entirely different story for the man who hunts with a muzzleloader. After all, muzzleloaders are specialized rifles that have specialized needs. Of course, for those who were hunting in the 19th century, supplies were not much of a problem, but today, chances are that the local gun emporium won't have the exact size of roundball that you need. Heck, it's likely that the person behind the counter won't even know what a roundball is, for that matter. And the store may not carry a can of 2F black powder, or a tin of caps that are the proper size for your percussion rifle.

Therefore, the black-powder hunter quickly learns to make a yearly checklist in which he details exactly what he does and does not need for his deer hunt. This is not as simple as it sounds, for it often takes many seasons of trial and error for a hunter to finally settle on exactly the right formula to ensure a successful hunt. (Assuming, of course, that the deer, weather and Lady Luck all cooperate, too.)

Yet, even the most experienced of us often learn the hard way. I have been hunting with a muzzleloader for more than three decades, but it was only two years ago that I found myself in whitetail country at the height of the rut with a .54 caliber Hawken and a bag full of .50 caliber bullets! In my haste to depart from civilization, I had picked up the wrong bullet bag and never stopped to check its contents until it was too late. To illustrate my idiocy even further, my frustration was so great (there seemed to be bucks with hat-rack-size antlers leaping over my head at every step through the brush) that I actually tried triple-patching one of the .50 caliber balls so that it would fit tightly down the bore of my rifle. Of course, my moment of truth came at sundown on the last day of the hunt, when I finally spotted a forkhorn sneaking through the manzanita a mere 50 yards in front of me. Using the set triggers, I carefully aimed and squeezed off the shot, and sent that undersize roundball screaming off into who-knows-where country. The unscathed buck blithely executed a 90-degree change of direction and headed over the hill.

I have since devised a black-powder checklist to help me remember all of the necessary gear. And it works! Never again will I find myself in a deer hunter's heaven without everything I need to turn that weekend into a successful hunt.

Of course, the obvious question is: "Why do you need something as formal as a checklist in the first place?" The simple truth is that our minds are not what they used to be. (At least mine isn't.) I forget things, such as locking the car door or bringing in the cat. But I'll never forget that extra cleaning jag for my ramrod, or the right-size flints for my Kentucky rifle, because they're on my checklist.

The validity for taking the time to make a checklist was brought home to me just last deer season, when a bumpy pickup ride to my campsite somehow managed to jostle my rifle's front sight around in its dovetail track. I would not have ordinarily known this, but I had scratched the correct windage position of the front sight on the barrel flat with a Swiss file, and by looking at the sight, I could see that the blade had moved to the left. Normally, this would have meant re-zeroing my rifle at the campsite and possibly spooking game. (Either that or leaving the sight be, all the time dreading the thought of taking a shot at a trophy buck and having to rely on Kentucky windage.) Luckily, all of this was avoided, as I happened to have a small

brass-tipped hammer with me and was able to simply tap the sight back to its original position. Most hunters do not usually carry small hammers to camp, but I did, only because it was on my checklist. And, two days later I was able to get within 80 yards of a six-point buck, and I managed to drop him with one shot that hit where it was aimed.

Of course, in the days of Kit Carson and Jim Bridger, checklists were not necessary because longgun hunters and mountain men carried everything they needed with them when they ventured out onto the frontier. Just as we always carry our credit cards and car keys with us today, they brought their muzzleloader supplies. But most of us today do not carry pre-measured powder charges and extra flints with us to work. As modern black-powder hunters, we tend to need these items only once or twice a year. Thus, it has become easy to forget even the most necessary but mundane things, such as powder measures or nipple picks. But without these items, your hunt could be ruined should you or your frontloader encounter hard times.

Developing a muzzleloader checklist takes time, and the items on it are best assembled as a result of your own experiences. For example, I never thought about wearing an Army-style poncho until I was caught in a drenching downpour while on stand. The ordinary hunter's raincoat, which has sleeves, does absolutely nothing to keep rainwater off your smokepole. An all-encompassing, all-cover-

You might want to bring to camp a box in which to carry items for cleaning or repair purposes.

MUZZLELOADER CHECKLIST

Here is a part of the list that has helped me out so much on black-powder hunts. My complete list includes items of clothing, camping gear, photographic equipment, first aid materials, and so on. Of course, your list may differ as a result of your own experiences and needs, but this one has worked for me, and it should serve as a good base for yours.

- Rifle
- Extra rifle for backup
- Black powder/Pyrodex (make sure that you have the correct granule designation: 3F for calibers up to .50; 2F for .54 caliber and above; 4F for priming only)
- 10 pre-measured charges (20 for longer hunts)
- 10 bullets (20 for longer hunts)
- "Possibles" bag (if needed)
- Emergency kit for your muzzleloader (screwdriver, nipple wrench and pick, extra nipple, small brass hammer, "worm" and so on)
- Short starter
- Capper (for percussion guns)
- Bullet/patch lube
- Caps or flints (be sure to pack extras)
- Cleaning equipment (solvent, rod, patches, jags, bore and breech brushes, cotton swabs, extra rags, oil)

ing cape-like poncho, however, not only keeps you dry, but it can be used to cover your muzzleloader as well. Deer are often moving during a light rain or mist, and when one is spotted, your chances of taking it are much better if your powder is dry.

Likewise, I never thought much about carrying a screwdriver until an extended galloping session on horseback caused a test rifle I was hunting with to "shake loose" as the lockplate began to separate from the stock. A couple of hefty twists, and I was back in operation with a tight-fitting action that at least had the hammer lining up with the nipple.

Personal preference and experience has led me to favor some hunting accouterments over others. For example, I never carry powder horns in the field because they are cumbersome and downright dangerous—especially around the campfire at night. Instead, I carry individual pre-measured charges of powder and ball, which I carefully prepare at home before I get involved in the excitement and distractions of hunting camp.

When the situation permits, I often take not one but two muzzleloading rifles with me into camp. One is used as my main hunting rifle, and the other serves as a backup. Very often, one muzzleloader is a flintlock and the other is percussion. I use the flinter on calm days, but if inclement weather is looming above, the more sure-fire caplock comes into play. Also, should one frontstuffer somehow be knocked out of commission, I have another rifle with which to continue the hunt. To avoid confusion, both of my rifles are the same caliber, and they are both zeroed in to hit on target with the same powder charge and lead projectile. (This makes it unnecessary to have two different sets of pre-measured charges.) Of course, having more than one blackpowder hunting rifle is a luxury, and as an alternative, you might consider purchasing an extra lock and a spare ramrod for the frontloader you have. Any muzzleloader can be repaired back in civilization, but in the wilds, your checklist should at least ensure that your hunt will go on.

Your checklist should not only tell you what to take, but how much to take. I will never forget the story told to me by a close friend who is an experienced black-powder hunter. He had worked for years to be able to go on a fairchase buffalo hunt—one in which the herd was actually stalked on foot. For him, it was the hunt of a lifetime. Yet, he had only brought three lead balls for his rifle! Buffalo are hard to kill under any circumstance, but for him, it turned out to be impossible, as his first two shots missed and his third shot only wounded the bull. The animal had to be killed by another hunter, and this took away a lot of the thrill of the hunt.

It is true that when most of us spot a deer within range, we only need to shoot our frontloaders once. Yet, why take chances? What if we miss? Or what if a quick follow-up shot is necessary? Or what if we are fortunate enough to be hunting in an area where we can take more than one deer? Because of this, make sure that your checklist does not just read "pre-measured charges of powder and ball"; instead, have it read "*10* pre-measured charges of powder and ball." This is the *minimum* for any big-game hunt. And when venturing far from home on an extended elk hunt, for example, I always take a minimum of 20 pre-measured charges. With a muzzleloader, you cannot over-prepare yourself for any big-game adventure.

When making out your checklist, it will pay to be as detailed as possible. This means that your list can be as individual as you are. Moreover, don't be afraid to change and update the items as each new deer season brings new knowledge and new products. After all, this checklist is the culmination of your experiences, and it will eventually be as valuable as your muzzleloading rifle. Not only will it save you time and anguish, but it might just help you bag a black-powder buck next season.

For further reading on hunting with muzzleloaders, see Rick Hacker's The Muzzleloading Hunter, *revised and updated (Outdoor Life Books 1988).*

Do You Savvy Gunspeak?

By Tim Jones

Think you can hold your own when it comes to talkin' guns? Well, take your best shot at this quiz, and be prepared for some loaded questions and double-barreled answers.

QUESTIONS

1. Good sportsmanship is determined by: **a)** using the smallest caliber or gauge that ensures clean kills; **b)** using a large enough gauge or caliber to guarantee clean kills under any circumstances; **c)** using only primitive weapons to give the game a better chance; **d)** knowing the limitations of your weapon and your shooting abilities, and not exceeding either of them.

2. In shotgunning terminology, "fences" are: **a)** criminals who buy stolen weapons for resale; **b)** things for which you should unload your gun before jumping over; **c)** parts of the breech on a side-by-side double; **d)** all of the above; **e)** none of the above.

3. True or false: A collimator is a device that will let you sight-in your hunting rifle without ever firing a shot.

4. True or false: The .357 Magnum is an exceptional deer cartridge for handgun hunters.

5. The snaphaunce on this flintlock mechanism is which piece? **a)**; **b)**; **c)**; **d)**; **e)** none of the above.

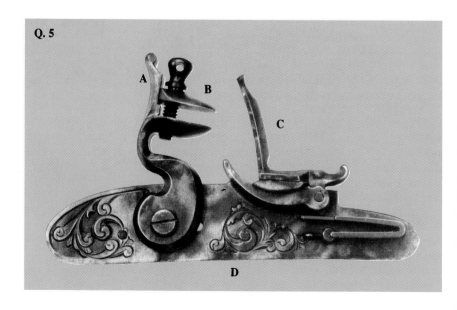

Q. 5

6. The way to vary the pattern in a hunting shotgun is to change: **a)** the choke; **b)** shot size; **c)** load; **d)** shot composition; **e)** all of the above.

7. True or false: A fired 2¾-inch shotgun shell measures 2¾ inches long.

8. What one factor, more than any other, contributes to clean kills on game animals? **a)** proper caliber; **b)** velocity and shocking power; **c)** bullet construction; **d)** bullet placement.

9. Selective ejectors are found in: **a)** bolt-action rifles; **b)** double-barrel shotguns; **c)** jet fighter planes; **d)** James Bond's Aston Martin; **e)** none of the above.

10. When shooting at an animal at a steep uphill or downhill angle, your point of aim should be: **a)** high on uphill shots, low on downhill shots; **b)** high for both; **c)** low for both; **d)** dead on because angle doesn't make any difference.

11. True or false: The famed Springfield military bolt-action used in so many sporter rifles is really just a modified Mauser.

12. Which of these hunting calibers did *not* serve as a U.S. military cartridge: **a)** .45/70; **b)** .30/40 Krag; **c)** .30 Remington; **d)** .30/06; **e)** .308 Winchester; **f)** .223 Remington.

13. 1964 was a bad year for gun buffs because: **a)** Winchester "revised" (many say ruined) the Model 70; **b)** Winchester discontinued the Model 12 pump shotgun; **c)** Winchester began using stamped parts in the Model 94; **d)** all of the above.

14. A heavy-barreled, target-style .22 Rimfire is an excellent choice for: **a)** target shooting; **b)** squirrel hunting in open hardwoods; **c)** woodchucks and prairie dogs out to 75 yards; **d)** plinking and general shooting practice for rifle hunting; **e)** all of the above.

15. True or false: The best way to carry a hunting handgun is in your hand.

16. True or false: Twenty-gauge shotguns should not be used for waterfowl hunting.

17. Many states outlaw the use of .22 Centerfire rifles for deer hunting because: **a)** they lack sufficient velocity; **b)** they are not accurate enough; **c)** energy-at-target levels are too low to ensure clean kills; **d)** lightweight bullets cannot be relied upon to penetrate to a deer's vitals from any angle.

18. "Choking" to a shotgunner means: **a)** barrel construction for pattern control; **b)** missing a shooting opportunity; **c)** wanting to throttle your hunting partner for shooting better than you.

19. True or false: Single-shot rifles are obsolete for hunting.

20. True or false: A black-powder hunter would not be upset to find a worm in his possibles kit.

21. True or false: The .22 Short cartridges are inherently less accurate in most rifles than .22 Long Rifle cartridges.

22. True or false: A hunter shooting a wildcat may be seeking a feline trophy.

23. The .25/06 Remington, .270 Winchester, .280 Remington and .35 Whelen are all: **a)** good deer cartridges; **b)** factory-loaded and chambered in factory rifles; **c)** based on the .30/06 case; **d)** all of the above.

24. A rifled shotgun is: **a)** nonexistent; **b)** the most accurate way to shoot saboted rifle slugs; **c)** an oxymoron; **d)** a Paradox; **e)** none of the above.

25. True or false: The .250 Savage was the first factory cartridge to produce a muzzle velocity of 3,000 fps. It remains an excellent choice for deer and varmints.

26. True or false: Full choke is always best for buckshot.

27. A .36 caliber muzzleloader shooting patched roundballs with 60 grains of FFFg powder would be about right for hunting: **a)** deer; **b)** mid-size varmints such as foxes and coyotes; **c)** turkeys; **d)** nothing larger than squirrels.

28. Hunting this type of pigeon with your field shotgun is: **a)** an exercise in frustration; **b)** darned good practice for game shooting; **c)** a waste of time because they don't fly like birds, and besides, they're tough and don't taste very good.

Q. 28

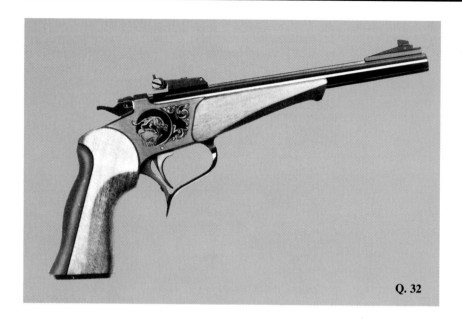

Q. 32

29. Trajectory is best defined as: **a)** the rise and fall of a bullet in relation to the line of sight; **b)** the fall of the bullet below line of bore; **c)** neither of the above.

30. Twelve-gauge shotshells are made in several lengths, including: **a)** 2½-inch; **b)** 2¾-inch; **c)** 3-inch; **d)** 3½-inch; **e)** all of the above.

31. The U.S. government's Civilian Arms Proof Laboratory is located in: **a)** Quantico, Virginia; **b)** New Haven, Connecticut; **c)** Springfield, Massachusetts; **d)** Denver, Colorado; **e)** none of the above.

32. Single-shot handguns are very popular for hunting because: **a)** they can be chambered for more powerful cartridges; **b)** they are inherently more accurate than repeaters; **c)** most can be fitted easily with a scope; **d)** one good shot is all you need; **e)** all of the above.

33. True or false: Weatherby Magnum cartridges are chambered only in Weatherby and custom rifles.

34. True or false: The proof marks on a firearm's barrel indicate that it has been tested to withstand greater pressures than are generated in firing normal loads.

35. To a black-powder hunter, pulling a charge means: **a)** unloading a muzzleloader without firing it; **b)** participating in a historical battle reenactment; **c)** running to get within shooting range of game; **d)** paying for supplies with a credit card; **e)** none of the above.

36. The first factory-loaded cartridge to exceed 4,000 fps muzzle velocity was the: **a)** .220 Swift; **b)** .22/250; **c)** .17 Remington; **d)** .224 Weatherby; **e)** no factory cartridge has exceeded the 4,000 fps mark.

37. True or false: Unlike rifle bullets, which can be blown off target, a shot charge in flight is not affected by wind.

38. The .284 Winchester is: **a)** an excellent, though often unappreciated, deer cartridge; **b)** the only American factory round with a rebated case; **c)** designed for short-action rifles; **d)** all of the above; **e)** none of the above.

39. Which one of the following cartridge designations reflects the actual diameter of the bullet used? **a)** the .300 Weatherby; **b)** the .303 Savage; **c)** the .307 Winchester; **d)** the .308 Norma Magnum.

40. True or false: The following .30 caliber hunting cartridges are correctly ranked in descending order of power: .300 Weatherby Magnum, .300 Winchester Magnum, .30/06 Springfield, .308 Winchester, .30/40 Krag, .300 Savage, .30/30 Winchester, .30 Remington, .30 Carbine.

41. True or false: The .303 British and the obsolete .303 Jeffery are both exceptional .30 calibers.

42. Double-barreled shotguns are frequently preferred over repeaters in heavy cover because of: **a)** their shorter overall length; **b)** quicker follow-up shot; **c)** instantaneous choke selection; **d)** all of the above.

43. True or false: Anything more than 50 yards is a long shot for a handgun hunter.

44. True or false: Gas-operated autoloading shotguns and rifles have less recoil than other designs.

45. True or false: No matter where he hunts, a deer hunter can't really go wrong with one of the following proven deer killers: .270 Winchester, .280 Remington, .308 Winchester, or .30/06.

46. True or false: Integral scope bases, such as those featured on Ruger and Sako rifles, are inherently stronger than other scope-mounting systems.

47. True or false: "Minute-of-angle" accuracy means that a rifle is capable of putting three shots into the bull's-eye within one minute, from any angle.

48. True or false: Minute-of-angle accuracy is not necessary in most hunting rifles.

ANSWERS

1. d) A sportsman owes it to the game to know both himself and his weapon, and to not exceed the abilities of either.

2. c) The often ornately engraved rounded swellings on a double that provide strength in the breech area are called fences.

3. False. A collimator is a useful piece of optical equipment that might put your first shot on target at 50 yards, but to properly sight in a rifle, you must shoot it.

4. False. Though the .357 Magnum may be adequate for short-range deer hunting in the hands of an expert marksman, the best Remington factory loads produce only an anemic 570 foot-pounds of energy at the muzzle. Choose a more powerful cartridge.

5. e) None of the above. **a)** is the cock, or, incorrectly, hammer; **b)** are the jaws, which hold the flint (missing in this picture); **c)** is the frizzen, which incorporates both the battery (steel) and the pan cover; **d)** is the pan (as in "flash-in-the-pan"). A snaphaunce was an older, more complicated mechanism in which the frizzen and flash pan cover were two separate parts.

6. e) Steel shot, copper-plated shot, high-antimony shot and buffered loads all pattern tighter than soft-lead target loads.

7. True. The nominal length of shotgun shells is measured after firing.

8. d) All are important, and no sportsman should hunt with too little gun, but bullet placement is the most critical of all.

9. b) Selective ejectors throw out only fired shells when the action on a double gun is opened.

10. c) Bullets shot at a steep uphill or downhill angle strike high.

11. True. The action is based on the Model 1898 Mauser. In fact, the U.S. government actually paid more than $1 million in royalties to Mauser for the rights to this design.

12. c) The .30 Remington was that company's answer to the .30/30 Winchester—a pure hunting cartridge.

13. d) 1964 was a *bad* year.

14. e) A .22 with the weight and trigger control of a good centerfire rifle is a most useful weapon.

15. False. Unless you've got forearms like Popeye, a heavy hunting handgun rides more comfortably in a shoulder holster.

16. False. In the hands of a good shot, a 20-gauge gun is just as deadly on close-range decoyed ducks as any magnum 12, and it is perhaps *more* effective at close range because lighter weight makes it easier to point and swing. But you have to be a *good* shot.

17. d) The 55-grain bullet from a .22/250, for example, is still traveling at more than 3,000 fps at 100 yards, and it has a retained energy level of more than 1,200 foot-pounds at that range, but the light-weight bullets lack adequate mass to reliably penetrate to vital areas through bone or heavy muscle.

18. a) Unless you shoot as well as I do, then **c)** is often correct, too.

19. False. The beautiful single-shots currently manufactured by Ruger, Browning and Thompson/Center, as examples, are deadly accurate, functional hunting weapons. After all, it's the first shot that counts most.

20. True. Though it depends on the kind of worm. The device that threads onto the ramrod and retrieves patches stuck in the bore is most useful at times.

21. True. But not because their velocity is lower, as most shooters would suppose. In rifles with chambers designed for the .22 Long Rifle, the long distance that the Short's bullet must travel before it engages the rifling affects accuracy.

22. True. Lots of hunters use non-standard "wildcat" cartridges to hunt all sorts of game.

23. d) All four excellent deer cartridges are based on

TERMS MENTIONED IN TEXT

Choke: A system of unknown origin whereby the muzzle of a shotgun barrel is constricted to control the spread of shot. Choked barrels were known before 1835, and there are indications that they may have been used as much as 100 years earlier.

Regardless of when or by whom the shotgun choke was first used, credit for its further development generally goes to Fred Kimble, of Peoria, IL, and to W. W. Greener, noted British gunmaker, for their efforts in the 1870s.

Collimator: A very precise instrument for checking alignment of optical elements for use in the assembly or repair of optical instruments, such as scope sights. As applied to guns, a small, simple optical device attached to the muzzle by means of which the sights may be brought into proper alignment with the bore.

Typical of the type is the Sweany Sight-A-Line which is fitted with an interchangeable, offset, precision-ground rod or "spud" of bore diameter. In use, the proper spud to suit the caliber is installed on the collimator and inserted into the muzzle. This action aligns the collimator parallel to the muzzle portion of the bore. Then, looking through the sights on the gun at the reticle image within the collimator, the sights are adjusted until aligned precisely on the center of the reticle. This adjustment makes the line of sight parallel with the bore at the muzzle, and from that point any desired shift to compensate for drop or other effects can be made.

Minute of Angle (MOA): The angular unit of measure generally used to describe the accuracy capability of ammunition and guns. It equals $\frac{1}{60}$ of a degree, making 21,600 minutes in circle. One minute of angle subtends 1.047 inches at 100 yards, twice that amount (2.094 inches) at 200 yards, and so on. For all practical purposes, 1 minute of angle is considered to be 1 inch at 100 yards, 2 inches at 200 yards, 3 at 300, etc.

Sight adjustments are generally established and regulated in minutes of angle or fractions thereof. A sight described as having ¼-minute click or adjustment is one in which 1 click or graduation of movement will shift the line of sight—in relation to bullet impact—¼ inch at 100 yards.

Shot Pattern: The dispersion made by all of the individual shot pellets of a shotshell fired generally at the center of a large sheet of paper, or, in some instances, at a metal plate coated lightly with white lead.

Shot Placement: Placing one's bullet in the most desired portion of the target. When hunting big game or edible small game, proper shot placement consists of causing the bullet to strike in a vital area without producing excessive tissue destruction.

Snaphance (Snaphaunce): An early form of flintlock in which the steel or frizzen and the pan cover are separate parts rather than a single part as in later arms. Some variations required the pan cover to be opened manually before firing; in others it was driven clear as the cock fell. The snaphance is also distinguished by its lack of a safety or half-cock notch. Inadvertent firing was accomplished by moving the steel forward out of the flint's path.

There are many minor variations, the Dutch (introduced before 1550) being the most common. The name is believed to also be Dutch in origin, deriving from the similarity of the cock's action to that of a pecking rooster. Originally *Schnapp-hahn*, it was eventually corrupted to *Snaphance*.

Trajectory: The path of a bullet in flight. For all practical purposes, the bullet begins decelerating and falling toward earth the instant it leaves the muzzle, the rates of deceleration and fall continually increasing.

Trajectory is generally measured in two different ways but most often in terms of "midrange trajectory height," which is the distance between the bullet's path and the line of sight from the gun to its aiming point at a specific range. For example, a "200-yard midrange trajectory height" indicates the highest point the bullet's patch reaches above the line of sight when the rifle is zeroed at 200 yards. This point occurs approximately halfway.

Trajectory is also measured in terms of "drop." This is a measurement taken at right angles to the extended centerline of the bore down to the path of the bullet at any given point. Drop at 200 yards would be the distance below the bore's centerline to the bullet's path at the range.

Wildcat: Any cartridge not standardized within the shooting industry or not standardized domestically within the Sporting Arms and Ammunition Manufacturers Institute (SAAMI).

A wildcat cartridge is born when a gunsmith or gun enthusiast alters an existing cartridge case to suit his own particular needs. This alteration may consist of nothing more than shortening the case, or necking it down or up to use bullets of a different diameter.

Reprinted from Firearms Encyclopedia, *by George C. Nonte, Jr., Outdoor Life Books.*

---

the .30/06 case. Remington made the .35 Whelen, long a favorite wildcat, a factory cartridge this year.

24. b) and, possibly, d) The Hastings Paradox is one of several rifled shotgun barrels designed for accurate slug shooting, and Paradox was the name of a weapon with rifling only in the last few inches of the barrel. A rifled *smoothbore* would be an oxymoron.

25. True. The .250 Savage was originally known as the .250/3000 (which was Savage's way of bragging about the round's performance), and it is enjoying a revival in popularity as a deer/varmint load.

26. False. In some guns, with some loads, it may be. The only way to know is to pattern your gun with various buckshot loads.

27. b) and c) The load described gives a muzzle energy figure of about 665 foot-pounds, which is about right for turkeys (where legal) and coyotes, but too light for sure kills on deer. A lighter load—40 grains of FFFg—might give slightly better accuracy and would still be powerful enough for squirrels.

28. b) Clay-pigeon shooting—especially the less "programmed" forms such as sporting clays or handtrap games—is still the best off-season practice available; and it can help anyone become a better game shot.

29. a) and b) Remember that the bullet *never* rises above line of bore. Gravity makes that impossible.

30. e) In England, 2½-inch 12-gauge shells are common, and Federal is bringing out a 3½-inch 12-gauge for waterfowl and turkey hunting.

31. e) Unlike England and other European countries, we have no government proof testing of civilian weapons. That chore is handled by the firearms manufacturers.

32. e)

33. False. Ruger and Winchester both offer rifles in Weatherby Magnum calibers.

34. True. However, a proofed gun is no protection against overloaded shells, incorrect ammunition and plugged barrels.

35. a) Most hunters just shoot their muzzleloaders to unload.

36. a) The original .220 Swift, 1935, had a muzzle velocity of 4,110 fps with the 46- or 48-grain bullet.

37. False. Though the range of most scattergun shots is shorter, and wind, therefore, has *less* effect, a strong crosswind can still move a shot charge enough to turn a hit into a clean miss at 40 yards. If you needed another excuse for missing, this is a good one.

38. d) The rebated case simply means that the rim diameter is smaller than the body of the case. The .284 is a fine deer load for short-action rifles.

39. d) Most .30 caliber weapons take a bullet that is .308 inch in diameter.

40. True. The .30 Carbine is not powerful enough for big game.

41. True. Both take a .312-inch diameter bullet.

42. a) A hurried second shot is often a missed second shot, and rarely would you choose a tighter choke in thick stuff, but the shorter overall length of a double gun can be a real plus when you find yourself situated in cramped quarters.

43. True. Though some hotshots can hit reliably at twice that range with scoped handguns and a solid rest, handgun hunting remains a short-range proposition for most of us. That's what makes it fun.

44. False. Recoil is an "equal and opposite reaction" determined by the weight of the gun and the weight and velocity of the projectile and propellant. Gas-operated guns *delay* part of the recoil (lessening the impact to the shooter). Muzzle porting, incidentally, *diverts* part of the recoil. But in each case, the physical movement we all recoil is the same, given the same weights and velocities.

45. False. Hunters in states where only shotguns are legal could get into a *lot* of trouble choosing one of those cartridges, no matter how good they are for deer.

46. True. Integral scope bases have fewer screws to loosen or break. However, they may make the mounting of certain scopes on certain rifles impossible.

47. False. A minute of angle is ⅟₆₀th of a degree, or, roughly, 1 inch at 100 yards. There's no time limit on minute-of-angle accuracy.

48. True. It's a darned good thing, too, because most deer rifles aren't anywhere near that accurate. Varmint rifles should be that accurate, however, and often are.

YOUR SCORE

0-12: If you haven't already, subscribe to *Outdoor Life* right now, and make sure to read the Shooting Department religiously.

13-24: You should hang around more at the local range or sporting-goods store, but try to avoid getting involved in any firearms-related debates.

25-36: You've obviously done some shooting, but I wouldn't start handloading for brown bears just yet.

37-48: Okay, so you're loaded for bear. Feel free to shoot off at the mouth with the best of them.

PART 5

BIGGER GAME

Elk All Season Long

By Walter L. Prothero

Elk behavior changes markedly from early September to the late hunting season late in the fall. If the hunter isn't aware of these changes, hunting elk is likely to be confusing.

The most challenging and exciting time to hunt is during the rut. The earliest hunts generally begin at about that time, in mid-September or a bit later. Occasionally, during warm and dry weather, the rut may not get into full swing until early October.

One season, I was hunting elk in some high country adjacent to Yellowstone National Park. I'd seen elk the previous evening, the day before the season opened. They had fed out of the timber into a broad, open basin near timberline. Far down the drainage, a bull bugled. The herd bull, enraged, bugled a reply and then viciously hooked a stunted pine sapling, sending pine boughs a dozen feet into the air. Then, suddenly, it was dark. The two bulls bugled from time to time throughout the night. It was difficult to sleep, and I tossed and turned in my tiny tent.

At dawn, as the first dim light filtered into the meadow, elk bugles floated on the icy breeze. The band of elk was feeding toward the pine saplings they had been in the previous evening. It was nearly a mile across the basin, and the elk could be in the timber, or at least into the thick saplings, by the time I could work close enough to shoot, but it was worth a try.

I must have set some sort of record for jogging across an alpine basin. I was gasping in the rarified, 10,000-foot air, when I found the place where the tracks led into the saplings. I followed slowly,

Bugled challenges, confrontations, and combat for harems usually cease when gun season opens. John L. Hautzinger photo.

watching carefully ahead. The wind was favorable. I hadn't gone 200 yards before I saw a tan movement to my left and then another ahead. There were other movements on the slope above me. Two cows were staring hard in my direction, obviously alarmed. Unexpectedly, I'd gotten into the middle of the band, but I had no idea where the bull was. Suddenly, elk were running in every direction. I caught a glimpse of great, ivory-tipped antlers disappearing into the pine scrub.

Even though bull elk are less cautious during the rut and have little on their minds but mating and fighting, the best bulls are invariably with cows during the initial two weeks or so of the rut, usually in late September or early October in "normal" Rocky Mountain weather—whatever that might be. So, instead of stalking one animal possessing keen eyes, ears and nose, you have to worry about several. It can be a tough proposition, but it is an exciting way to hunt elk.

I think that bugling is overrated when it comes to calling in good bulls. Trophy bulls usually have acquired a harem early in the rut. It happens before the rigors of herding, breeding and fighting have taken their toll, and long before these bulls are replaced by younger and fresher bulls. Big bulls therefore often move away from bugling. I spent eight autumns observing rutting elk in three western states and one national park for a graduate degree in wildlife biology, and about 80 percent of the herd bulls that I observed took their harems away from bugling. Most of the rest either did not move at all, occasionally answered the bugling or, in a minority of cases, approached tentatively. I was using a high-fidelity recording of a bugling elk instead of a blown call to eliminate any mistakes. I could legally use the recording because I wasn't hunting.

On one occasion, long before I became involved in elk research, I hunted elk along Beaver Creek in northern Utah. It was the first time that I'd hunted them; I had purchased an elk bugle and had practiced faithfully with a training record. I was bugling to a herd across the canyon early one morning before sunup. There was a good bull in the bunch. Occasionally, I could see antlers above the aspen scrub. He would bugle back to answer me and smash saplings fiercely with his antlers, but he would not come closer. At times, he disappeared into heavy timber, and I could hear the crackle of brush as the herd moved through it. At such times, I hoped that he was approaching, but he wasn't. Eventually, he was answering only infrequently. An hour or so later, when I heard the last of that bull, he was something like a half-mile away. He had herded his harem into the next canyon. I was to find out years later that his behavior was fairly typical. Bulls that already have a harem have little to gain by seeking a fight, so they seldom come to calling.

Bulls without a harem, often termed "outriders" by behaviorists, will approach an artificial bugle if it's done right. Don't bugle too often, though. It's

During the rut, outrider bulls are aggressive and highly visible, and even herd bulls answer calls.

difficult to say just what is too often. Probably the best advice is to bugle no more often than the bull you're trying to call. If he is approaching, bugle only often enough to keep him interested. The frequency of calling varies markedly from bull to bull. Smash and scrape brush with a stout branch. When the bull is close, bugle rarely, if at all, and at a much-reduced volume. Circle, if necessary, to keep downwind of the approaching bull, but do it silently. Usually, outrider bulls that are approaching artificial bugling will be searching for cows and not for a huge trophy herd bull. As a rule, these bulls, though they have smaller antlers, are much better eating than trophy bulls. They still have some fat and haven't started to metabolize muscle tissue.

I once shot a bull that had been the harem-master of a harem a week earlier. He had been deposed by a smaller and fresher bull and was hanging out with another bull that had probably suffered a similar fate. There wasn't an ounce of fat on him, and he smelled strongly of urine and musk. He had a good rack with six points to a side, but he sure wasn't tender, though there are many ways to tenderize elk meat. My method is to keep it moist with a gravy or juice of some sort, and to cook it at low heat, say, 275° to 300°, for four to eight hours, depending on the size of the roast. I prefer to cook in a Dutch oven or foil-covered cast-iron skillet. The best meat comes from yearling (spike or two-point) bulls that haven't as a rule even shed their velvet by the time the rut starts, or from two-year-old bulls (usually three to five points to a side). If you are hunting in late October or November, even herd bulls have started to put on weight again after the rigors of breeding, and taste much better than they would have if shot a month earlier.

In my experience, bugling is a good way to locate bull elk rather than to call them. This is especially true if you are after a huge harem-master.

One time, during the peak of the rut late in September, I was bugling to a bull across a canyon. Occasionally, I could see elk as they moved through the timber, and I saw the bull once. He was a good one. They were feeding slowly toward the top of a ridge. The bull would bugle in answer to my call often enough so that I could keep him located. I figured that if I hurried to the bottom of the canyon and then a few hundred yards up a creek, I could get to the mouth of a long ravine on the other side of the ridge toward which the elk were feeding. If they kept moving in the same direction, I could intercept them. I worked down to the bottom of the canyon. From time to time, I bugled and the big bull answered. Just before I started up the draw, I bugled one last time. He answered, and from the sound, he was still heading his band in the same direction. Once I started up the ravine, I didn't bugle again. I didn't want to risk spooking the elk. An hour later, they crossed the ravine just below where I was waiting. The one-shot kill was anticlimactic.

Another good way to hunt elk during the rut is simply to locate a place where a herd is living. If they are undisturbed, they often stay in a small area, feeding out into an open meadow or basin in the evening and back into the timber at first light. The colder it is, the longer they are apt to feed. Although it is one of my favorite methods of hunting elk, it is increasingly impractical because there are fewer and fewer undisturbed places. And once an elk is badly frightened, he is likely to move five, 10 or even 20 miles away. I was once hunting elk near the headwaters of Montana's Hellroaring Creek when a group of hunters opened up on a herd of elk 500 yards away across the canyon. The bull had the top of one antler shot off but was otherwise unhurt. I was packing out my elk at the time. The next day, as I drove south through Yellowstone National Park, I spotted that bull along the Gardiner River, nearly 20 miles from the place where the hunters had shot at him.

Occasionally, though, a hunter is fortunate enough to find a canyon or basin that is undisturbed. In Montana one September, I was hunting several adjacent basins off the Buffalo Plateau that had, for some reason, been overlooked by hunters. In each basin was a herd of elk, with a good harem bull, and several outrider bulls, but I'd had no luck getting close enough for a shot. It would have been an easy matter to shoot one of the outriders, but the herd bulls were unapproachable. I didn't want to spook the elk because I knew that they'd leave the country, so I was being careful. If I'd been more concerned with meat, I would have dropped one of the younger, more tender outrider bulls. For one reason or another, I had not had the right circumstances to try a stalk on a big bull. Once, the wind was wrong. Another time, the elk didn't move into the open until nearly dark and there wasn't enough time for a stalk. Still another time, there were cows scattered all through the ravine I had to climb to get a crack at the herd bull. And so it went. I'd been tantalized by the sight of one big, barrel-chested, heavy-antlered bull, but there had been no way to get close enough for a shot.

I was becoming desperate, but then thought of something that might work. As the elk fed out of the timber one evening, I made a rapid circuit through the timber behind them. I was in the timber where they'd bedded earlier, and there was the strong, musky odor that often lingers for a surprisingly long time in an elk bedding area. I moved cautiously through the pines toward the mile-long basin where they grazed each night. When I was nearly to the edge of the trees, I unfortunately jumped two outrider bulls. They crashed off through the blowdowns—nothing is noisier than frightened elk—toward the herd. That was the last I ever saw of those elk.

Many open seasons occur after the rut has ended. By mid-October, adult bulls have pretty well ended all rutting activity, though they may still bugle from time to time. Yearling bulls and two-year-olds may still act a bit rutty on into November, but virtually all cows have already been bred.

By that time, adult bulls often hole up in the densest tangles and most inaccessible country they can find. This is almost invariably true if they have been hunted at all. There, they can rest up from the rigors of the rut, eat and put on weight. By the end of the rut, adult bulls have changed from noisy and aggressive to shy and secretive.

One November, I was hunting deer in the mountains east of Cokeville, Wyoming. The weather was cold, I'd been hunting for about a week, and the elk season was open. Most of the elk hunters were local citizens who drove out in their four-wheel-drives and hunted country along the road. The road ran up the bottom of the big canyon I'd been hunting toward the canyon head, and then climbed onto a broad ridge 2 miles above and about 2,000 feet higher in elevation. I'd often run into hunters during my ramblings. They'd ask whether I'd seen any elk, commenting that they hadn't. I always said, "No," lying through my teeth. I never did have much affection for that kind of hunter. Although I didn't have an elk tag, I still enjoyed seeing the huge bulls that lived in a steep and extensive stand of lodgepole pines below the ridge and road, and I didn't want them to stir up "my" deer country. Almost every day, I'd see elk there, and some of them were trophy bulls. They were all living in the very thick timber. Only the most soft-footed hunter stood any chance at all of approaching them. Only the most dedicated elk hunter would even try. That part of the canyon was incredibly steep, rugged and thick, and it would have been very difficult to get horses in to pack out if a hunter did score.

One day, I'd been following a large deer track through the pines, moving slowly and quietly. I'd been following the track all morning and had gone no more than a half-mile. I nearly stumbled over a big six-point bull that was lying among three or four blowdowns. He was up and over one of the downed trees in the blink of an eye. I could hear him crash off through the timber long after he'd disappeared. The next day, I jumped three bulls from a thick tangle of pine saplings and aspens. They crashed off through the brush. The first two were six-pointers, the last a massive seven-pointer, the largest I'd ever seen outside of Yellowstone and undoubtedly a record-class bull. Right then, I'd have given my left leg for an elk tag. I saw those three bulls again several days later. They were grazing in a small meadow in the center of that big, thick stand of pines. With the feed in that meadow, they didn't have to move outside the pines, even at night. And even though I had previously frightened them, they knew that stand of pines was still the safest place in a big stretch of country.

After the rut, it is fairly common for a big bull to go off by himself and find a small area where food is abundant and where he can rest and hide. He may not show himself again until he moves down onto winter range. These elk nests are usually in rough, secluded country and in thick timber or brush. Often, there are no elk tracks in the area except in the center of the hideout. One deer season in Utah, I found a typical elk nest while I was deer hunting.

I had decided to climb to a remote hanging canyon a couple of miles away across a deep gorge. After several hours of climbing, I looked over the knife-edge of the ridge. Not entirely to my surprise, two good bucks were browsing in the brush on the other side of the canyon. I picked the better one, held on the top of his back and squeezed the trigger. The buck dropped and rolled, thrashing down the steep slope until he disappeared into a small, thick patch of willows and maples. A second later, a six-point bull elk crashed out of the brush and ran up the canyon until he disappeared into the timber. From the tracks, the layers of droppings and the

way the beds had been packed down in that patch of brush, the bull had been staying in it for some time. A stream ran through the center of it, and there were still plenty of grasses and forbs. He'd been safe there, and he had no reason to leave. Over the years, I've found other such hideouts.

Undisturbed elk such as those in Yellowstone Park will occasionally move down onto upper winter range, even before the first heavy snow. As a rule, though, the lower country is too accessible to man. Elk in hunted country move down no earlier than they are forced to do so. It often takes 20 or even 30 inches of snow to force elk down to where most hunters are located.

It was November. The regular elk season had ended a month earlier, before the heavy snows. It was the first chance I'd had to try out my new cross-country skis. I'd skied up the long lower canyon in only 8 or 9 inches of wet snow on the lower reaches. I passed through armies of elk hunters who had been lucky enough to draw special late-season permits. They had heard that this was the place to go—the head of the canyon, almost 3,000 feet above. The snow was at least 30 inches deep there, too deep for the hunters. That was where the elk were staying. Most of them were in the timber—mixed stands of fir, spruce and aspen—or they were on the windswept ridges where the snow was not so deep.

The elk appeared to be waiting for the hunters to go home. There was enough browse for them to get by for a while. There were a few bulls in the head of that canyon, one a good six-pointer. Undoubtedly, he had earlier been a herd bull and had used up his fat reserve. Now, he was living well enough so that his stomach had begun to sag with fat once more. Two days after the late hunt ended, the elk were down on winter range, grazing in a rancher's field.

To increase his chances, the hunter must realize that elk behavior changes markedly throughout the season. It is almost like hunting completely different animals. During the rut, outrider bulls are aggressive and highly visible, and even herd bulls answer calls. Unfortunately, at this time bulls are seldom far away from herds of cows, so the hunter must contend with many keen noses, ears and eyes. Stalking one bull can be difficult.

Later, after the rut has wound down, usually by mid-October, adult bulls generally hole up in remote canyons or dense stands of timber to recuperate from the rigors of rutting. If a hunter is very careful, patient and quiet, he can often track a bull to his bed. It is a tense, exciting game.

Still later in the season, after the bulls have rested and put some weight back on, they may keep on the high country, despite severe November weather, to be safe from all but the most dedicated hunters.

If a hunter wants to improve his chances of taking a good bull elk, he has to hunt differently as the season progresses.

Wallowing in Elk

By Jim Zumbo

"That bull elk is crazy," my companion whispered. "What in the world is he doing?"

I watched, fascinated, as the animal rolled around and around in a mudhole, kicking mud and filthy brown water in all directions.

"I'm not sure," I said, "but he seems to be enjoying it."

Finally, the six-point bull climbed out and walked off, with a fresh coat of mud glistening on his hide.

That happened more than 20 years ago, when I was new to the West. I had been hunting blue grouse with a pal when the elk's splashing had caught our attention. We had walked over quietly, not knowing what to expect, and had been amazed at the sight.

I hadn't known it at the time, but the bull was behaving normally. As I've since learned, elk commonly wallow in mud during the late summer and early fall.

Biologists believe that elk use wallows for two reasons: to cool themselves, and to perform part of their breeding ritual.

Dr. Valerius Geist of the University of Calgary says that wallowing is done mainly by older bulls, but that wallows also attract yearlings. Geist, considered to be one of the world's top elk authorities, believes that bulls tend to return to the same wallows each year.

Other wildlife experts support Geist's contention that wallows are used primarily by mature bulls, and some scientists feel that the wallow is a mark of advertisement or a dominance display.

According to Geist, a bull will dig a wallow with his front feet, bugling and tearing at the ground with his antlers while digging. At the same time, the bull directs a spray of urine onto the underside of his neck and then rolls about in the wallow after it is dug, continuing to urinate in the wallow. As the bull rolls, he rubs his neck mane on the edge of the wallow and cakes his face, chest, belly, legs and sides with mud.

After wallowing, the bull often rubs his mud-caked neck on the trunk of a nearby tree. He may also thrash saplings and bushes with his antlers, stripping off bark and demolishing branches.

Although elk wallows have been noted by biologists for years, the ritual is not completely understood. Some scientists feel that a single bull will "own" a wallow, and if the bull is killed, another bull will take the wallow over.

According to another belief, the sudden absence of bulls at traditional wallows could indicate a serious reduction in the number of mature bulls in that particular area. Most biologists believe that wallows are not essential for breeding rituals, pointing to elk areas where there are few, if any, wallows. Those areas, however, are often in lowlands or arid locations where dirt habitat conditions prevent elk from digging wallows.

After watching the bull cavort in the wallow that first time, I began to pay attention to every mudhole and dug-up spot in moist ground that I found. If I hadn't observed the wallowing bull, I'd have continued to ignore those hotspots of elk activity, just as

I'd ignored whitetail scrapes in eastern woods those many years ago.

It's interesting how quickly we're learning about animal behavior. Whitetail scrapes, for example, weren't understood until fairly recently. Early books—classics in their day—on whitetail deer never mentioned scrapes. Now, everyone who hunts whitetails has heard about scrapes, and hunters who correctly utilize scrapes score more consistently than those who don't.

Modern wildlife scientists are unraveling amazing behavior patterns involving big-game species, and hunters are incorporating these discoveries into hunting strategies. Elk wallows are a good example.

It's obvious that hunting near wallows can be an effective technique, but most elk hunters are unaware of the possibilities. During my big-game hunting lectures each year, I ask the audiences a series of questions to determine their level of elk knowledge. On the question of wallows, many people have no idea of their importance, although most report seeing wallows while hunting.

When I was learning about elk hunting many years ago, an old-timer taught me some valuable lessons. He killed an elk every year, and he took most of them by hunting wallows. Although it might not seem unusual for a skilled hunter to take an elk every year, my friend did it in a state that had a poor elk hunting success rate. A spike bull was cause for celebration in that part of the country, and it would earn admiring glances as it was shown off.

My friend used a simple technique to take his elk back then. He would merely wait for a bull to show up at a beaver pond that had some active wallows and fresh rubs adjacent to it. He told me that most elk appeared during the hottest part of the day—between and 2 P.M. and 4 P.M.—and that an early snowstorm or cold front often resulted in little or no elk activity at the wallow.

Because wallowing usually occurs when temperatures are high, bowhunters who try for elk in the late summer can set up stands near active wallows. In states where bow seasons start in August and early September, hunting near wallows is often the only effective technique if bulls aren't responding to calls.

I've observed elk using wallows as early as mid-August. Once, when I was fishing for brook trout in August along a remote creek, I came to a beaver dam and noted fresh elk tracks everywhere. I investigated further, and found a mud hole 25 yards uphill from the dam where a seep moistened the fertile soil. Elk tracks were distinctly imprinted in the bottom of the wallow.

Several hours later, I hiked back down and heard a large animal crash through the timber somewhere near the beaver pond. I didn't see the animal, but

Biologists believe a bull elk will use a wallow for two reasons: as part of the breeding ritual, and to cool himself with a coating of mud. Bill McRae photos.

the wallow was muddy and freshly disturbed. I'm convinced that I'd spooked a bull elk that had been frolicking in the wallow.

Another time, while bowhunting for deer in late August, I watched a spike bull elk in a wallow. When I spotted him, he was standing in the middle of the wallow and sniffing the edges of the mudhole. He then proceeded to roll in the mud before walking off into the forest.

The wallow was in a limited-entry hunting unit that required a hunter to obtain a tag in a lottery draw. When a friend of mine drew a tag, I took him to the wallow. He killed a fine six-point bull on opening day as the animal was walking down a trail toward the mud hole.

The following year, another pal drew a permit, and it was a repeat performance. He took a big five-point bull on the second day of the season as the bull jumped out of its bed 75 yards from the wallow. The bull's flanks and mane were caked with mud.

Hunting wallows offer an obvious new dimension to elk hunting. The prime bugling period is generally from mid to late September. Bulls are often silent or only moderately vocal before the rut is in full swing, and they usually won't answer a call at this time. This is when hunting wallows pays off.

Bow seasons are typically held during the rut in the western states because hunters must get close to their quarry to score. Calling is almost mandatory for elk hunters, but early seasons that begin in August offer little opportunity to bugle in a bull. Most elk simply aren't interested. Other than trying to sneak up on a bedded or moving elk, hunting next to a wallow is about the only strategy that will allow a close-in shot.

Stalking close to a herd of elk isn't impossible. In fact, I've found it easier to sneak close to elk than to get near deer. I suspect the reason for this is that elk are noisy animals because of their large size, and they will tolerate natural noises, such as branches and twigs being broken, that are often made by stalking hunters. Metallic or obviously man-made noises, of course, won't be tolerated. But even though a bowhunter might be able to stalk close, it's another story to thread an arrow into a vital area of a bedded elk. Generally, an elk will be surrounded by brush or trees, and even if a clear shot is possible, the elk's position while bedded often offers a very small target area. A hunter using a rifle would have a better chance of scoring, and he wouldn't have to sneak so close.

Watching trails for elk is often an exercise in futility, unless you've found a well-used trail leading to the neck of an active wallow or a trail that's consistently used by elk simply moving from one area to another. Finding one of the latter type of trail, however, is a big order because elk normally travel in small herds over a vast area. You'll be looking for a group of animals in an enormous landscape, and most movement will be within an hour of sunrise and sundown. This doesn't leave you much time to hunt the trails.

I know several bowhunters who hunt wallows exclusively in August and early September because of the poor odds of stalking bedded or moving elk. Many hunters don't have the luxury of time, and they can't spend days merely walking through a forested area. They concentrate their efforts in high-use areas that attract elk. Wallows fill the bill nicely.

There's another major reason to consider hunting wallows an important strategy: For numerous reasons—including general weather patterns, local storms and heavy hunting pressure—elk will sometimes refuse to bugle or respond to a call, even during the peak of the rut. Many skilled hunters and outfitters believe that today's elk are bugling less than they used to. It's felt that the enormous increase in elk calling by hunters is having an effect on elk behavior. Bulls are getting wise to elk calls, and they are refusing to answer.

No experts believe that elk have completely quit bugling because calling is an important aspect of the breeding ritual. Instead, most feel that calling is now most frequently done at night. I've camped in elk country many times in the past, sleeping in a small mountain tent literally amidst elk herds. Night bugling by elk is routine, but in the past few years I've heard much more nighttime vocalization than I had in the past. I believe that this can be attributed to the fact that the area I hunt is public land where elk calling by hunters has increased a great deal in recent years.

Extremely dry, hot weather often has a negative impact on bugling, too, and under these conditions elk tend to become silent, refusing to call or respond to calls. The 1987 season was a good example. Balmy fall days with temperatures in the 80s were common throughout the West, and elk activity seemed to come to a halt. Even in the best elk country, it was tough to hear an elk bugle during the peak of the rut.

What all of this means is that elk bugling can't always be counted on. And when the bulls aren't bugling, wallow hunting offers another ace in the hole when conventional methods won't work.

The next logical question is, how does one find an elk wallow? Unfortunately, there isn't any sure-fire way, but there are some general rules that have the best potential. Wet places are obvious spots. Creek bottoms, especially those dammed by beavers, often are good wallow locations. When you walk the bottoms, crisscross the drainage if you can and look for elk tracks. An active wallow will have plenty of tracks around it, and there may also be a well-used trail leading to it.

A freshly rubbed tree is a good clue to a wallow's presence, too. Investigate the area around the tree closely, even if it means making an out-of-the-way crossing through a marsh or a brushy tangle.

Once when I was hiking along a steep mountain. I stopped in a small clearing and looked across the canyon. With my binoculars, I saw three saplings that had been recently demolished. The bark had been stripped away, leaving naked yellow wood

Bowhunters who try for elk in the late summer should try setting up a tree stand near an active wallow.

that was easily seen. I guessed that an elk had thrashed the trees, and I hiked over to look. I had to make a difficult crossing through a thick spruce blowdown, and then had to wade the stream at the bottom to get to the rubbed trees.

The trip was worth it, though, as a fresh wallow was located just 10 yards from the trees, and the size of the elk tracks in the area convinced me that the wallow was worthy of special attention. Shooting light was almost over, so I headed for camp, intending to hunt the area in the morning.

As luck would have it, I intercepted a good bull about 500 yards from camp at sunrise the next morning. When I fired at the elk, my pal heard the shot and walked over to help me field-dress and skin the bull. My companion had just left camp and was headed in another direction. Like me, he had discovered an active wallow and had figured on hunting it that day.

When the skinning chore was over, I suggested that my pal hunt the wallow I'd located because it was much closer to camp than the one he'd found. I insisted on quartering the carcass myself because my partner would lose too much hunting time if he stayed to help. As it was, the dressing and skinning job had taken up plenty of time, and there was only a half-day left for him to hunt. He agreed and headed out for the closer wallow.

I had just finished hanging the last quarter when my pal showed up. He was wearing a big grin, and he told me about the six-point elk he'd shot. The animal had been just leaving the wallow with a fresh coat of mud on when my buddy had spotted him.

Wallows are also common along mountainsides where underground springs and seeps emerge. You can spot these areas by noting the different forms of vegetation near the moist areas. Lush grasses and shrubs often grow in wet spots, and their foliage is distinctive compared with that of adjacent trees.

Although elk can come to a wallow at any time of day or night, I've found that the late afternoon seems to be a productive time. Most hunters experienced in wallow hunting agree. Bowhunters often either build a tree stand near a wallow or use a portable stand. Hunters using firearms normally find a vantage point within good shooting distance.

Some hunters—myself included—don't have the patience to sit for very long around a wallow, and they prefer instead to stillhunt in the vicinity of a mudhole. Elk country is usually so big that it's tough to cover it thoroughly. Knowing where wallows are helps pinpoint places being used by bulls. In one area I hunt, I know of four active wallow sites in a single drainage. I can visit the wallows in two hours' time if I walk steadily, but I usually spend the entire day just wandering about in the woods and brush around each of them.

Elk hunting is tough, and it makes sense to use every strategy you can to turn the odds in your favor. Wallows are foremost in my bag of tricks. The concept works, and that's good enough for me. Anything that puts me closer to a bull elk is worthy of my attention, and wallows do just that.

Quest for a Dream Bull

By Kathy Etling

It was still dark when the first, faint notes of the bulk elk's bugle carried across the sagebrush hills. The hunter looked at his companion, then brought his call up and bugled in reply. The bull answered immediately, even though he was still far away.

The two hunters started out, trekking across the sandy soil. In less than 30 minutes, they'd covered more than a mile. Dawn was breaking when they finally stopped to plan the final stalk. As they stood there, talking in low whispers, the magnitude of it all hit them. There they were, 1,200 miles from home, without a guide, hunting one of the world's premier trophies, the Rocky Mountain bull elk, on the first day of Colorado's early rifle season. And what's more, they were now so close to the bull that they could hear the guttural grunts he was using to conclude each bugle.

They'd seen a tremendous bull near the same spot two days before. He was a massive six-pointer, and he had stood and watch them for long minutes, his ivory tines seeming to glow in the evening light. Then he and his harem had high-tailed it across the sagebrush hills. Now, it was opening day. The two hunters wondered if it was the same bull bellowing his challenge just out of sight.

For many hunters, the bull elk epitomizes the glory of the West. They yearn for the chance at a real trophy, but feel that it is beyond their reach—at least financially. Many simply can't afford an outfitter, and they feel that's their best—maybe their only—hope. Though it's true that outfitters can and do often lead their clients to dream bulls, finding the right outfitter is never an easy—nor cheap—task.

Luckily, all over the West, quality elk areas are becoming more and more popular. Quality elk areas do two things. First, they limit the number of hunters allowed into the specific area; and second, they allow the elk herd in that area to be managed so that there's an excellent chance to see—and possibly shoot—a mature bull. One of the best examples of a successful quality elk area can be found in Colorado, where the opening scene occurred.

The two hunters in the story were my husband Bob and myself. And though both of us had gotten bull elk on our own before, neither of us had ever hunted during the bugling season, nor had we been close to a rut-crazed wild bull before. And *close* we were; so close, in fact, that we decided to split up, hoping to double-team the animal.

The fog lay like a thick cloak over charred junipers and sagebrush, which had been blackened by a recent range fire, but as each of us eased in the bull's direction, the burn gradually gave way to thick green junipers and shoulder-high rabbit brush and sagebrush. Bob stopped and bugled again. And furious now, the bull charged closer, hanging up at the last minute, just out of sight.

Bob Etling scored on this six-pointer in Colorado quality area.

The day after bugling in a six-pointer, the author took this fine 4×4.

Reaching up, Bob then started breaking dead limbs off the juniper above his head. That was all it took. The bull had finally had enough, and he charged into a small opening 20 yards away. Moments later, a shot from Bob's .300 Weatherby Magnum rang out across the plains.

Within 10 minutes—and following a heart-thumping bit of tracking—the two of us stood looking again at the biggest bull we'd ever seen in the wild. It was the same bull we'd spotted two days before—the dream bull.

His main beams measured just under 60 inches in length, and they were 9 inches in circumference.

The ivory brow and bez tines averaged 18 inches in length and the entire rack curved in perfect symmetry above the animal's head. After drying, the antlers' final Boone and Crockett Club score was 324 points.

Getting that bull wasn't a fluke, either. While I waited for Bob to get the backpacks from the truck, I bugled once while standing several yards away from the downed bull. I felt the ground shake as another, equally huge bull galloped to within 20 yards of my position.

The other bull couldn't have been hiding more than 100 yards from where we'd just field-dressed the first elk. And it also became very clear that *here* was the reason why Bob's bull had been so aggressive. Without realizing it. Bob had gotten between the two rivals, and he had goaded one into showing himself. Now, the challenger stood in front of me, looking at his fallen rival. He was somewhat off to my side and looking away, so I tried to ease my 7mm Weatherby Magnum off my shoulder while he gawked. I moved slowly, but not slowly enough. He saw me and took off. I tracked him to a wash full of elk sign, and then I lost his trail.

When Bob returned, he told me that he'd seen yet another monster six-pointer that had streaked past him within 50 yards of where he'd parked the truck. It seemed as though the hills were swarming with big elk.

It took us all day to cape, skin, quarter and pack out Bob's bull. And once we had it all stashed in our four-wheel-drive, we promptly ran over a sharp sagebrush stob and got a flat tire. It was dark before we finally turned onto the paved highway that would take us to Rimrock Taxidermy in Craig, Colorado.

When we got to the taxidermist's late that night, Rimrock owners Jan and Carol Roth told us about another super bull that had been taken on the last day of the bowhunting season close to where Bob had taken his bull. Glenn Pritchard, a local bowhunter, had scored on that tremendous bull with less than an hour remaining in the season. Pritchard had hunted long and hard before finally connecting with the elk, which scored 311⅛ points and easily qualified for the Pope and Young Club record book (which requires a minimum score of 260 points). What's more, during his time afield, Pritchard saw 16 big bulls—each with six points or better to a side!

All of this action occurred in Game Management Unit 2, which is located in the northwestern corner of Colorado and is one of the state's four desert-quality elk areas (the others being units 1, 10 and 21). The terrain in this area looks like something out of a Western movie. A creek that actually runs red like its name—Vermilion—cuts across the stark landscape. Douglas Mountain and two hills called the Bear's Ears are the predominant landmarks. To the west, the Green River flows through the incredible Canyon of Lodore.

The land is deceiving. Although it looks big and open and flat, it is actually cut up into gulches and swales where elk can disappear quite easily. Luckily, my husband and I had gotten to our hunt area four days early so that we could locate some bulls. It took a lot of glassing—about eight hours each day—but we'd located five good bulls before the season even started. Strangely enough, none of the bulls we found were where we had been told to look by game officials. That's not to say that elk hadn't been in the recommended areas, it's just to point out that elk can be almost anywhere.

Even after Bob got his elk, we still knew where three other bulls had been hanging out. And the big six-pointer that had charged my position was on my mind as well.

So, the next morning we went back to the same spot. The weather had turned ugly, and our time was getting short. We'd already been hunting mule deer for a week in Wyoming before coming to Colorado, and we were due back at work in St. Louis very shortly.

Fortunately, I shot a dandy four-pointer that very same day. We had jumped two bulls while stalking through the sagebrush hills. At first, they had taken off as fast as they could. But when they got about 200 yards away, curiosity got the best of them. They turned broadside and looked back. I shot once at what I thought was the biggest one, and he dropped in his tracks. Later, Bob told me that the other one had been a five-pointer.

There are 5,000 quality-area elk licenses for bow, muzzleloader and modern rifle hunts allocated each year in Colorado for 21 different areas. These licenses are distributed in no set percentage to residents and nonresidents alike, and this means that a nonresident's odds of getting a license are as good as a resident's.

"Quality elk areas were established in 1983 to provide a quality hunting experience by limiting the number of licenses," said Bob Hernbrode, program specialist with the Colorado Division of Wildlife. "Hunters won't run into lots of other hunters. And animals have a better chance of attaining both maturity and trophy size.

"Trophy animals can survive in fairly large numbers in three ways," Hernbrode continued. "One is by occupying private ground where landowners limit access. Another is by living in areas so rough and remote that people hesitate to hunt them. And the last is through the establishment of quality areas.

"You can choose any kind of area you'd like to hunt with the quality-area system," Hernbrode concluded. "There are mountain quality elk areas and desert areas; tough hunts and easy hunts."

Colorado operates on a preference-point system for all limited-entry elk licenses. Here's how it works: For every year that a hunter applies for a particular area (he may change areas at any time) and is unsuccessful in drawing a permit for that area, he gets a preference point. The next year, the applications that are submitted with the most preference points are the ones that get the licenses first.

It took my husband and me four years of applying and three preference points each before we both were lucky enough to be drawn for permits. We immediately started applying again. For the 1988 season, it took a minimum of five preference points to get a modern firearms permit of Colorado's Game Management Unit 2.

Our success on bulls isn't unusual, either. Hunters from all over the country are traveling to Colorado—and other states as well—to get trophy bulls

APPLYING FOR QUALITY ELK LICENSES

In **Colorado,** limited-area elk licenses are available for bow, muzzleloader and modern rifle hunts. Hunters do not have to apply for one specific hunt. The seasons typically begin in mid-August, and some run as late as January.

Only one limited-area elk license per hunter can be applied for in a year. And in some areas, only four-point or better bulls are legal.

Hunters who do get licenses might want to consider renting horses from local outfitters. Information is available from the Colorado Outfitters Association, Box 31438, Aurora, CO 80041.

Other invaluable aids are Bureau of Land Management maps, which indicate public and private blocks of land. Although my husband's and my bulls were taken on public land, we first got permission from all of the landowners in the area.

For more information about success rates in particular units, or which areas usually require the least number of preference points, contact the Colorado Division of Wildlife, 6060 Broadway, Denver, CO 80216.

In **Arizona,** residents and nonresidents have an equal opportunity to draw the quality elk licenses (for four-point or better bulls). For more information, contact the Arizona Game and Fish Department, 2222 W. Greenway Rd., Phoenix, AZ 85023.

In **Idaho,** for information, contact the Idaho Fish and Game Department, 600 S. Walnut, Box 25, Boise, ID 83707.

In **New Mexico,** for information, contact the New Mexico Game and Fish Department, Villagra Bldg., Santa Fe, NM 87503.

In **Oregon,** for more information, contact the Oregon Department of Fish and Wildlife, 107 20th St., La Grande, OR 97850.

In **Utah,** for information, contact the Utah Division of Wildlife Resources, 1596 W. North Temple, Salt Lake City, UT 84116.

In **Washington,** for information, contact the Washington Department of Wildlife, 600 N. Capitol Way, Olympia, WA 98504.

In **Wyoming,** for more information, contact the Wyoming Game and Fish Department, Cheyenne, WY 82002.

It's important to note that application deadlines, quality-area rules and fees change periodically, and anyone interested in pursuing a limited-entry hunt should contact the fish and game department in the appropriate state as soon as possible.

of their own *on* their own in quality areas.

Ronnie Ansley, a businessman from Albuquerque, New Mexico, hunted one quality area near Creede, Colorado, for three years straight. He was lucky, getting a license each time he applied, and he got a bull for two of those three years as well—a long spike in 1985 and a 4×5 in 1986. In 1987, two other hunters in his party were successful—one got a cow and the other took another 4×5.

"There are plenty of bulls there," commented Ansley. "I've seen several 5×5s, and in 1986, we got into a herd that had a real good 6×6. But then we got two feet of snow, and we couldn't get back to that group."

Ansley and his friends normally hunt during the second season (typically in late October), when snow is a real possibility. They leave their vehicles at 12,000 feet and ride in 15 to 20 miles on horses that they've trailered from Albuquerque. They hunt around 13,500 feet. A hunter has to be in darn good shape to be able to get around at that altitude. According to Ansley, the area is extremely scenic, with high mountain meadows, lots of aspens, and good-size streams rushing through deep canyons. "It's rough country," he said. "I like it because it really weeds out the other hunters. And it's great for elk, too."

Ansley took his 4×5 bull after an exciting stalk. "When we first spotted him, he was bedded down with some cows about 800 yards away," Ansley said. "I'll never forget it because it was snowing hard and we were lucky to see him at all. We worked our way to within 125 yards of him before he spotted us. When he did, I shot."

Yet another tale of trophy elk hunting success comes from Tom Shirley, a retired Florida game warden who now makes his living as an Everglades guide. Shirley, who lives in Fort Lauderdale, Florida, was hunting during the first rifle season while the bulls were still bugling.

"The area we hunt near Estes Park, Colorado, is mountainous and really rugged," Shirley said. "It's just full of dark timber. Climbing around can get pretty strenuous. Luckily, we'd brought horses with us on this particular hunt.

"We were prepared to stay out 10 days," he continued. "I didn't spot my bull until late on the seventh day. He was with a couple of cows on the side of a mountain, about 300 yards away. I could see that he was a big bull, and I was a little worried—one step and he'd be out of sight. If I was lucky, I'd have one chance for a shot.

"When I did shoot, the bull disappeared. My buddy asked me if I hit him, and I didn't really know. When I looked through the scope, I thought I could see his nose sticking out from behind a rock. Later, I discovered that I'd made a perfect heart shot with my .30/06 Remington pump.

"Walking up on that bull was the thrill of my life," Shirley said. No wonder. The tremendous six-pointer had extremely wide and heavy antlers. Shirley's hunting buddy also connected on a good 6×6 bull, making this a real hunt to remember for both of them.

We all have a few dreams that only we know about. If a trophy bull is one of yours, then a quality elk area just might be the ticket to make your dream a reality.

Collect Call
for Elk

By Jim Zumbo

It was hard to believe. I'd been hunting for six days in prime elk country during the peak of the bugle season, and I hadn't heard so much as a peep out of the bulls. I saw enough fresh sign to know that they were around, but they were silent.

As a wise elk hunter once told me, elk oftentimes have a good case of lockjaw. This obviously was one of those times.

The weather was unseasonably hot, reaching 80° even in the high country where I hunted. It was the third week of September, a time when elk should have been screaming madly on the mountain where I was hunting.

On the seventh day, I hiked down into the bottom of a canyon, where huge cedars and firs sent roots into earth that was continually dampened by a crystal-clear creek. My pocket thermometer showed the air temperature to be 66°, about 15° cooler than on the ridgetops and upper slopes.

I was about to sit on a log and eat an apple when a bull bugled so close by that I couldn't believe it. Bringing my rifle to shooting position, I gave a call on my bugle.

That was it. The elk emerged from the thicket, trotted to within 40 yards and never suspected that I was in his hideaway. Five minutes later, I tied my tag to the antlers of the five-point bull.

There are plenty of mysteries in the outdoors, and elk hunting is near the top of the list. Highly vocal during the breeding season, elk baffle even the most skilled hunters. A bull's seemingly whimsical man-

ner has no rhyme or reason. The big animals of the West are a curious enigma during the rut.

Every year, when the quaking aspens turn lovely hues of gold, yellow and orange, elk have romance on their minds. Bulls have already shed the summer velvet from their antlers and are ready to gather up all of the females they can acquire.

Rounding up a harem means that a bull will have to be tougher or a better bluffer than his competitors. Bugling serves as a warning to other bulls, but it also has other meanings. Some biologists believe that the bugle call is a reassurance to cows that their herd bull is strong and capable of tending to their needs. It's also thought that a bull bugles to assert his dominance—not only to caution other bulls but also to show off, much as a young boy does by beating his chest as though he were Tarzan.

Some inexperienced elk hunters believe that all you have to do to call in a bull is walk out on a ridgetop, blow the bugle and shoot the madly charging elk at 25 steps. Though that scenario happens every now and then, it's seldom that easy. Too many variables, such as climate, weather conditions, romantic status of the cows, status of the bull, time of year, time of day and other factors, have a profound effect on the bull's behavior.

One of the most frequently asked questions is, what gets the rut into full swing? Theories suggest the moon, first frost, the climate and other reasons.

There seems to be no argument among biologists. Elk start into the rut because of photoperiod, or di-

167

minishing daylight hours, regardless of all other external factors.

If this is so, why do elk seem to bugle with vigor and frequency at certain times, and stay quiet during others?

Dr. Gary Wolfe, who managed the famous Vermejo Park in New Mexico for many years and is now a top officer with the Rocky Mountain Elk Foundation, told me that a very cold weather front often results in more active bugling. On the other hand, hot weather seems to turn off elk calling.

I've seen this happen so often that I'm convinced it's true. The story I related at the beginning of this article suggests that warm weather indeed affects elk behavior.

During a Montana hunt a few years ago, bulls were notably quiet during the prime breeding period. The weather was unseasonably hot, but the situation changed immediately when the temperature plunged to 20° during the night. The next morning, a layer of ice coated a bucket of water outside my tent, and the grass was glazed with heavy frost.

The woods seemed to be alive with elk. It was difficult to believe that I was hunting the same drainage that had appeared barren and lifeless the day before. I heard five different bulls that morning, and killed a decent elk the following day.

Though it seems that elk aren't in the rut when they're silent, evidence proves otherwise. Bulls are as active as usual; they're simply not vocal.

It's believed that most breeding activity takes place at night. Don Laubach, who lives just outside Yellowstone Park and is a noted authority on elk, thinks that most bulls are actively pursuing cows and challenging other bulls in the dark.

For many years, I backpacked for elk solo, camping just at the edge of a drainage inhabited by a good herd of elk. It was common to hear bulls bugle all night long. Generally, they stopped bugling as the sun rose above the ridgetop, but occasionally they'd call during the daytime.

Elk are originally animals of northern latitudes. According to some scientific theories, they crossed into North America across the Aleutians from Siberia. Being hardly animals that are tolerant of cold weather, elk seek cool environments when the weather is warm. It makes sense that they're uncomfortable during hot weather, which could explain why they're inactive until nightfall, when the temperature drops.

During warm weather, the best strategy is to look for elk in cool areas. In much elk country, that means deep in canyon bottoms where there are no pack trails or roads. Elk will remain in an area if they feel secure, but will usually move out if they detect human activity.

Many factors determine when the rut—and a bull's accompanying strange behavior—will take place. Rich Kirchner photo.

Getting to the dark recesses in drainages is often a major physical undertaking. In prime elk areas, there are no horse or hiking trails. You'll be fighting underbrush most of the way, and when you get to the bottom of the canyon, you're apt to find blowdowns of timber crisscrossed every possible way. In the best country, you'll be crawling as much as you'll be walking upright.

It seems impossible for elk to live in these jungles, especially big-racked bulls, but they do. These are their most secure sanctuaries.

When you work your way down the slope, watch the wind, and stop often to listen for bugling elk. In dense timber, an elk's voice doesn't carry over a long distance.

Don't worry about making noise as you travel. It's practically impossible to move silently, and elk will tolerate the sounds made by branches breaking and twigs snapping. Elk are big animals, and make plenty of noise themselves as they slip through heavy timber. If they hear you, they're often inclined to believe that you are another elk.

It's common for a bull to bugle if he hears noise in timber. He assumes that another elk is approaching, and he gives notice of his presence.

Once, when I was doing preseason scouting in elk country, I rode my horse through fairly heavy cover. We broke large branches constantly, and I'm sure that we could be heard by any animal for several hundred yards.

Suddenly, an elk bugled from about 100 yards away. I halted my horse and waited quietly. I could hear the elk crashing toward us, and he bugled again, this time much closer. I had no call, but whistled naturally, imitating his call as best as I could. The bull reacted instantly and ran toward us until he finally spotted us. Then, he whirled and disappeared into the sea of timber. I sat on my horse, amused, taking note of the location for the season that was yet two weeks away.

Some hunters who know that elk hang out in timbered canyon bottoms try to coax them uphill by bugling from a ridge. This method seldom works. During hot weather, elk are reluctant to leave their hiding spots and won't move far to meet a challenger.

A herd bull will be doubly hard to call out of his lair. He isn't about to leave his harem unguarded, and at best he'll merely bugle and hold his ground. Most of the time, he won't bugle at all. By penetrating his hiding spot, however, you're invading his territory. Suddenly, you become a bold adversary that must be dealt with.

Rainy weather can turn elk off as much as heat does. Jack Wemple, an outfitter in Idaho's Selway Wilderness, says that rain and snow tend to quiet bugling bulls. When that happens, the best option, once again, is to head for pockets that might hold elk and move into their territory.

A few years ago, when I hunted with Wemple, we fought our way through soggy underbrush on a gloomy opening day. The elk were holding tight, so

A herd bull is tough to call out of his lair unless you penetrate the territory. Len Rue, Jr. photo.

we headed for Wemple's favorite area, known as The Hole. After working our way through dense brush, we were able to get an elk to answer our call, but he wouldn't come toward us. We worked him for an hour, but he held his ground.

Rather than make a move forward, we backed off and decided to try another area. Later in the day, we heard a bull bugling and grunting nonstop. He sounded plenty upset and was traveling up the mountain far above us. By his constant bugling, we were able to determine that he was moving around the mountain on a uniform contour.

Instead of bugling, we hastily hiked up the mountain, and I ambushed him as he made his way toward us. He was a dandy bull, with six long, heavy tines on each antler. As we approached him, we saw a fresh wound between his eyes and figured that he'd been gored by another bull. That was obviously the reason for his anger.

Many hunters believe that the moon phases affect elk hunting because the animals feed throughout

full-moon nights and are back in cover before daylight. I haven't seen this theory proved by biological studies, but the idea might have some credibility after the elk rut is over.

When breeding season is done, elk go about their business as usual and stay in heavy cover. This is especially true when crowds of hunters head for the woods during the general firearms season, which usually occurs after the rut has passed.

During the bugling period, however, I don't think the moon has that much effect. Regardless of the brightness of the evening, elk still want to breed. Hunting them in hidden pockets will still work no matter how active they may have been during the night.

It's been proved that bulls are much more active when one of their cows is in heat, or when they scent a cow in heat being tended by another bull. This situation almost always stirs bulls up enough to increase their bugling frequency. This could explain why bulls often bugle throughout the day.

Crowds of hunters in the woods could possibly turn off elk, causing them to bugle more at night. If hunters are bugling so much that elk begin to associate excessive calling with humans, the animals could quiet down and shun bugle calls.

My pal Mike Perry had an interesting experience in Utah a few years ago. He was in a popular area crowded with plenty of other hunters when he heard a bugle in the quaking aspen forest where he was walking. Thinking that it was another hunter, Mike stood still, listening to the sounds come closer and closer. Mike was astonished to see a bull elk traveling toward him, bugling madly every few steps, even though hunters were everywhere. Mike raised his rifle and neatly claimed the bull.

Many hunters feel that bugling reaches its greatest intensity before the peak of the rut, when bulls are actively gathering cows. This is when competition among bulls is keenest.

The rut generally begins in early September and runs into October. I've heard elk bugle as early as August and as late as December, but I've pinpointed the first day of fall to be the peak.

In many western states, bugle hunts open in mid-September in backcountry units. Several hunters and outfitters I know say that the second week of the season, starting on September 22 or 23, provides the most bulls.

I've had good luck during various parts of September, but would choose the first week because I feel that elk are more active then.

There are no hard rules regarding elk bugling. Every hunter has opinions, just as he has opinions on firearms, automobiles and TV sets. Opinions are formed by experiences webbed together by common threads.

The best advice is to try all the options. If you head into elk woods with an open mind, and are prepared to hunt hard in places where few other hunters go, you'll be far ahead of the game. The only thing predictable about elk is their unpredictability.

Moose of a Lifetime

By Don Blake

The disappointment of not having filled my moose tag was weighing heavily on me as I walked near the treeline of a logged-off area 20 miles up the Caribou Trail. A bright sun shone in my face, and there was a gusty wind. Suddenly, out of the corner of my eye I noticed something white on black floating above the 7-foot poplar brush about 200 yards out. I grabbed my binoculars for a better look. It was the biggest bull moose that I had ever seen in the five years that I had been hunting grouse in this area of the Superior National Forest. Seeing me, he trotted off. Starting to get the shakes, I ran up a hill to get above him.

Here it was, day 13 of the 16-day moose season in Zone 77 of northeastern Minnesota. For 11 of those days, I had been hunting harder than I ever had in my life; I had blown stalks on two bulls, passed up an easy shot on a cow, and had seen or heard two other moose.

I had been introduced to the area by a friend, Glen Kvelland, who had been hunting grouse there since childhood. This has come to be my favorite part of the state. I have seen numerous moose during my many trips to the area. I usually see moose when I am grouse or bear hunting, but now that I was moose hunting, the reverse was true.

Minnesota's Canada moose are not well known. The herd numbers about 10,000 animals, and the hunts are scheduled every other year. In 1985, when I received my license, the state's department of natural resources held a lottery drawing for 1,068 moose tags. This allowed a party of four the privi-lege of taking one moose; the odds of being drawn are about one in 25. The success rates have run around 85 to 92 percent. If your application is drawn, you cannot apply again for five seasons.

When I called the DNR (Department of Natural Resources) during the summer and learned that our party had been drawn for a moose license, I could not believe it. This was the third time that I had ap-plied for a moose license. My three hunting part-ners were my wife and two friends.

I chose to use my .30/06 Remington 700 with a Redfield 2×-to-7× scope for long-range shots, and my Remington 870 12-gauge shotgun with a slug barrel and Brenneke slugs—a gun that can shoot a clover leaf at 50 yards—for hunting in the thick brush and bogs.

During the late summer, I developed a handload for the Remington 700 that consisted of 4064 Du Pont rifle powder, Federal large rifle primers, Hor-nady 180-grain Spire Point bullets and once-fired Federal cases; it gave me ¾-inch patterns at 100 yards off the bench.

During two scouting trips with Darlene and one of my hunting partners, we looked for moose and moose sign so that we could determine the best hunt-ing spots. This area is almost totally unsuitable for tracking because the ground is very hard and rocky, but we did see moose tracks around watering holes and rain puddles. In the end, we saw no moose but did find evidence of moose calfing areas, droppings, and feeding and bedding areas. The beds were usually on south-facing slopes in brushy areas or on the edges of wooded areas. We checked, but did not see, moose in lakes and marshes—probably because the vegetation they like to feed on had already died at that point in the season. We also saw five black bears, and during the evenings, while sitting around a warm blazing campfire, we heard wolves howl in the distance.

While preparing for the hunt, I got the bad news that the fourth man on the license was sick and could not go. The third man could only go for the first weekend. If the three of us didn't fill by the end of the first weekend, it would only be Darlene and me hunting for the next seven days before we had to leave the fulfill a prior commitment, so we hoped for the best.

Opening day was rainy and miserable, without much time spent in the field because of the weather. No moose were seen or heard. The next day, I found two wallows that were all dried up. The wallows were on trails leading from bedding to feeding areas. They measured about 8 feet across and had a weak urine smell; this indicated to me that the moose were not using them any longer. A wallow that moose are using can be smelled 100 yards or more away. English Leather for moose! I was beginning to wonder whether the rut was over.

We drove to the moose registration station on Route 61 in Tofte, Minnesota, on Monday to find out the status of the hunt. While there, we found out that the rut was over. This was determined by DNR tests for semen content in the testicles of moose taken by other hunters.

This called for a change of hunting plans. My original plan had been to look for the dominant bulls defending their territory. My thoughts shifted to looking for bulls laying up and feeding to recover from the rut. Darlene and I started to do stillhunt/ drives through the bogs and the islands in the swamps, paying special attention to the short poplar stands.

Tuesday dawned dark, cold and windy with occasional snow flurries. Returning to our truck later that day after making some short stillhunt/drives toward each other, we arrived at a T intersection of two trails. As we turned the corner, Darlene suddenly grabbed me and began breathing as though she had just had a glass of cold water thrown into her face. I looked out in front of us and saw two large bulls trotting down the road side-by-side.

The two bulls did not seem overly concerned by our presence—they just continued to trot off around the corner.

Between Darlene's excitement from never having seen a moose before, and my own amazement at finally sighting one, we must have looked like two of the Keystone Kops. By the time I reacted, the bulls were out of sight. They had nice racks, too, about 50 to 55 inches wide.

I ran after them and could just make out their forms across an alder swamp in the corner of the next woodlot, about 200 yards away. As I moved closer, I could see that they had started to feed. One

Charles Denault illustration.

was behind brush that was covering all of his vital areas. The other bull was head-down, and all I could see was his spine; but which end was which? I did not want to try for a glancing shot on a spine.

After watching the bulls for about five minutes, I decided to stalk in closer. With the wind quartering me as I faced them, I tried to sneak through the swamp. Coming out on the other side of the swamp 25 yards from where I had last seen the moose, the two bulls were not there. Disappointment!

Wednesday started out with the same weather we'd had during the previous day. Unfortunately, Darlene had developed a bad cold that prevented her from giving me much help that day. While still-hunting, I found a dropped antler in the middle of a bog. Guessing from the antler's size, I thought that the bull must have had a rack that was about 50 inches wide. I decided to try the horn against brush and rocks to see whether it would raise up the two bulls that we had seen the day before. We set up an ambush, with me doing the rattling behind some car-size boulders and Darlene sitting on some high ground. We tried the rattling off and on for more than two hours without any success.

During the next four days, we encountered two more moose. One was a cow that watched us from 25 yards inside the woods for about 20 minutes, then slowly crashed off through the brush. The other close encounter was when a moose snorted at me in a thick bog; all I found was a steaming pile of scat.

Returning home on Sunday night, Darlene and I reviewed what had happened. One of our thoughts was that perhaps the grouse hunters, who were scattered throughout the zone and driving their three-wheelers on the trails, had spooked the moose into deeper cover.

I decided to return, by myself, on Wednesday. My wife was concerned about my hunting alone, but I was starting to get compulsive about filling the tag.

On Thursday, I went down to the registration station to find out how many moose had been taken in my zone and where. Fourteen of the 16 parties had been successful.

Leaving the registration station, I decided to go to a large clear-cut 20 miles up the Caribou Trail from Lutsen. At the registration station, I had noticed that no moose had been registered from this area. I also knew that this spot was at least 10 miles from the nearest campground, which diminished the chances of the moose being spooked. Darlene and I had spent a few hours scouting this clear-cut, but we had decided that it was too far from our base camp at Baker Lake.

After I reached the area, I hiked up a hill. There had been little action up to this point; now, too much would happen at once. Coming over the crest of the hill, I spotted a bull just inside the treeline 75 yards away, staring at me. I threw my Remington to my shoulder and pulled the trigger when the Redfield 4-plex crosshairs passed through the heart area

of his chest. I heard the bullet hit the animal. Two giant steps later, the bull disappeared into the woods behind him.

Running down after him, I went through a small creek and into the woods, which were thinner than the treeline had indicated. About 100 yards later, I saw the bull standing about 50 yards from me.

Shaking, I drew up the gun and, as before, fired when the crosshairs passed through the chest. The bull ran off limping, favoring the right front leg. This time, I could hear him crash through the woods as he headed away from me. The noise filled the forest for a few seconds, and then suddenly the woods were quiet.

Very slowly approaching where I had last heard his noises, I began to hear the rasping breath of a dying animal. By climbing up on a tree stump and standing on tiptoes, I could see the bull 30 yards away, lying on the ground.

I circled around and approached the bull from his back side, away from his legs. Seeing the hair rise and fall along his back, I put a round into his spine. Walking around him, I poked his open eye with my rifle barrel to ensure that he was dead.

Stopping now to look at this magnificent creature, it started to dawn on me just how large this animal was, and how hard a job it was going to be to get him out of the woods. I couldn't help squatting down and affectionately petting the bull.

Returning to my four-wheel-drive pickup, I drove as close to the moose as I could, which was one-eighth mile from the kill site. Gathering up my butchering equipment, rope, flashlight, lantern and other tools, I noticed that it was 3:30 P.M. Going back to the site where the moose lay, I tried to move him out of the depression where he had died by using two one-ton block and tackles. After breaking both block and tackles, and getting blisters on my hands, I gave up on that idea.

As I dressed the moose out, I was able to determine the track of two of the bullets. The first bullet had hit a rib, blown up the heart and shattered the leg bone that attached to the shoulder blade. The bullet had then stopped just below the skin. It had perfect expansion. The path of the second shot was unclear. The last round had not penetrated the spine at all!

The most difficult part of dressing out the moose was getting the stomach up and over the side of the stomach cavity. The stomach was the size of a small coffee table, and removing it took about 45 minutes.

By midnight, I had dressed the moose out, skinned half of it, removed the front leg with the shattered bone, and wiped down the cavity as best I could.

Exhausted, I crawled back to my truck. When I tried to sleep, though, my mind kept replaying not only the day but the entire 13 days of the hunt. I finally fell asleep, awoke briefly just before sunrise and fell back to sleep again.

Suddenly, around 8 A.M., I was roused by wolves howling about 100 yards from the truck. I had never

A mature bull with huge antlers is an impressive sight. James Keith Rue photo.

heard them that close before, let alone in the daylight. I was almost hoping that they might help themselves to some meat, saving me a lot of the work that I knew lay ahead that day.

Working against the deadline of the registration station closing at 6 P.M., I began to bone out the meat into manageable sizes so that I could carry it out on my pack frame. It took 16 trips to bring out all of the meat. The only bones I brought out were the T-bones and the section of leg bone needed for my possession tag.

The hide was the next load after the meat. All tied up on my pack frame, the hide weighed 150 to 175 pounds. It was all I could do to lift the load. Straining, I stood up and wobbled my way to the truck. Halfway there, I heard a ripping noise, and one of the straps was suddenly lying in my hand. Nothing to do but keep on going.

Carrying the skull out was much easier, though it was a bit unwieldy going through the trees and brush. The rack only weighed 55 pounds.

With my tail dragging, I had to force myself to pack my gear and remove the signs of my presence. The only breaks I took were for a little canned fruit to give me quick energy, and for a cup of coffee every three or four trips out. I didn't finish until 5:30 P.M.

During the drive out of the forest, I knew that I could not make the registration station by closing, but I hoped that someone would be there late. Arriving there at 6:30 P.M., the lights were out, but luckily a person from the DNR stepped out of the shadow of a building and asked, "Do you want to register a moose?"

The DNR measured the antlers, following a Boone and Crockett Club scoring sheet for Canada

moose. The green score given at that time was 229 points. I really didn't know where this would put my moose in the club's standings, though I did know that the minimum Boone and Crockett score at that time was 195 points.

A U.S. Forest Service employee and his wife came out to watch the registration and commented that these were the largest antlers they had seen that year. The full meaning of the score and the statements still did not register in my mind. I was the last party to fill: Zone 77 had a 100 percent success rate.

On the drive home, I alternated between euphoria and exhaustion. I left the windows open and put the stereo on full blast. My arms and legs shook from exhaustion.

About an hour from home, I called my wife and told her about the moose. She was very happy for me. Now she could stop worrying; I was on the way home.

When I arrived home at 11:30 P.M., I carried the antlers to the front door and called upstairs to Darlene for some help. I just felt too tired to get them through the door by myself. Seeing the antlers, Darlene exclaimed, "Oh, my God!" She had been thinking that the rack was the size of the antler I had found in the bog, but the size of this set shocked her.

The next morning, Darlene and I took the meat to the butcher, and the hide to Mid-America Taxidermist in Savage. The meat packages almost filled a 22-cubic-foot freezer. We had the hide tanned with the hair on for a rug.

While at the taxidermist, I compared the Boone and Crockett green score against the Safari Club International book. My set of antlers, according to that book, would be number three. Now I was starting to get an idea of just how large the antlers really were.

After the required 60-day drying period, the antlers were scored by Bernie Fashingbauer, an official scorer for Boone and Crockett. The final official score was 229 Boone and Crockett points, with a spread of 59⅝ inches. When I called Boone and Crockett, I found out that in the 1981 *Records Of North American Big Game* and the 1984 update, my moose antlers would hold the number-five position. I also found out that my moose was the number-one Minnesota rack. (Since then, however, a larger Minnesota moose has been taken, so my bull has dropped a notch in both listings.)

After finding out about my moose's standings in the Boone and Crockett and Minnesota record books, I decided to invest in a full-head mount. My taxidermist had to buy the cape from an Alaskan moose to fit the large skull and huge rack. Without a place in the house to properly display the trophy, Darlene and I have decided to build a house with a vaulted ceiling and a stone fireplace, proving true the axiom that it is not the cost of the hunt that is the greatest expense involved in taking and displaying a trophy animal.

PART 6

PREP AND COOKING

How Big Is That Buck, Anyway?

By Jeff Murray

From my deer stand, I could hear the hunters yakety-yakking as though they were just over the hill. Ordinarily, I'd rather have listened to the woods talk during the deer season; you know, the soothing language in which leaves rustle, birds sing and squirrels bark. But this time, I was thankful for all of the racket.

It was one of those still, cloudy nights—the kind during which voices carry as though they were in a telephone wire. And I remember the conversation all so well because it was the hunters' chatter that helped me get from my deer stand to the tote road that November evening. I had lost my compass and couldn't see a thing in the dark.

Their conversation was a common one, no doubt one carried on over many a plate of deer-shack stew. It seems that one of the hunters had nailed a decent buck, and while the two were dragging it out, they ended up arguing over how much it weighed.

"This monster's gotta go at least 220," I overheard one of them say triumphantly.

"Wanna bet?" replied the other. "More like 250!"

When I came upon them at this point, we exchanged pleasantries with the usual congratulatory fanfare that accompanies the taking of a thick-necked, 10-point buck. And though most argu-

Deer vary in weight from year to year. When nuts are abundant, a buck like the one at right may accumulate three or four inches of fat on its back. Leonard Lee Rue III photo.

176

ments of this sort die shortly after they begin, this one grew and grew. Not only that, but somehow I found myself the appointed arbitrator of the dispute. So rather than merely guess the buck's weight with a stab in the dark, I simply did what any well-equipped deer hunter would do: I pulled from my pack a little gizmo tailor-made for the situation.

"I'd say that this buck should go about . . . 190, give or take 5 pounds,"

"One ninety?!" they shrieked in unison. Before we separated, I handed my business card to the teenager who had shot the buck. "If you get it weighed on a good scale," I said, "give me a call and let me know what you find out."

"Sure, be glad to," he replied.

A full year went by before I got the call. A shy

voice explained that it was "the guy with the deer." I'd seen lots of guys with deer that year, I told him; could he refresh my memory?

"Well," he began sheepishly, "my deer ended up having a little weight problem."

Turns out that his buck didn't weigh 250 pounds, or 220 pounds—or even 200 pounds. It weighed 192 pounds.

How is it that my estimate was so close? Well, I used a little formula. You see, a number of researchers at various conservation agencies, colleges and institutes throughout the country have been studying whitetail body conformities. And in the process, a lot of research has led to several formulas for determining a deer's body weight. All are derivatives of a time-honored method of estimating cattle weight based on a heart-girth measurement.

Which formula is the most accurate? Now, that's a darn good question. Unfortunately, there isn't a simple answer. To make matters worse, there are a variety of "deer tapes" sold commercially that only add to the confusion. These devices are tape measures that help you calculate everything from a deer's dressed weight to how much meat you should get back from the butcher. Some are fairly accurate (for a specific locale), but most are not.

W
hy? In the words of Bob Giles, professor of wildlife management at Virginia Tech, "There are big local differences, and each person ought to develop an equation for his area." The reason for all of the differences is the wide range of body conformities among whitetails. Part of the problem is brought out in E. Raymond Hall's *Mammals Of North America*. According to the author, there are 30 distinct subspecies of whitetail deer. So, you could develop a formula that might work well for one subspecies but not so well for another subspecies not too far away. As a matter of fact, there are even variations of subspecies within individual states. For instance, in my home state of Minnesota, there are three subspecies—the huge *borealis*, the western *dacotensis*, and the southeastern *macroura*.

Another bugaboo is the overall condition of a particular deer herd. In years of mast-crop abundance, the deer will have as much as 3 or 4 inches of body fat on their backs. In lean years, 1 or 2 inches of fat may be common.

So, what's the answer? Simple. Use an equation that's best suited for the deer you hunt. I've already done the legwork by carefully comparing several formulas from a number of areas throughout the country and tossing out the ones that produced the widest extremes. By using one of the resulting formulas, you should be able to come up with something that is close enough to at least settle an argument or two.

But you should still fine-tune your formula on the local level. To do this, contact your state fish and wildlife department or conservation agency, and ask officials which formula they use. Then, compare the formula they give with the ones listed below.

Take things a step further and have your deer weighed to confirm the reliability of your equation.

To make your own "deer tape," all you need (besides the correct formula) is a tape measure. Go to the nearest fabric store and purchase an ordinary yellow cloth tape measure. Then, scribble the appropriate formula on the tape with a permanent-ink pen as follows:

- If you hunt in the South (including Texas), write: C (which stands for the deer's chest circumference) times 5.6, minus 94, equals field-dressed weight. (Note: A southern deer that looks as though it will dress out at 200 pounds or more is most likely one that was transplanted from, or is the progeny of deer that were transplanted from, Wisconsin; because of this, the midwestern formula should be used to calculate the dressed weight.)
- For most of the rest of the country, especially the East, Professor Giles suggests this formula: C × 6.5 − 120 = dressed weight.
- Deer hunters in the Midwest, particularly Minnesota, Michigan and Wisconsin, should consider the following formula developed by Minnesota Department of Natural Resources officials in Grand Rapids: C × 7.7 − 178 = dressed weight.

Rather than carry a calculator along with the tape measure in your fannypack, I'd suggest multiplying through the normal range of measurements ahead of time. Then, inscribe the calculations on the tape.

The most reliable formula in the country won't do you a bit of good if your in-the-field measurements aren't accurate. Pat Karns, a research coordinator with the Minnesota DNR, told me that even trained officials can come up with different heartgirth figures if they're not careful. He suggests that you observe three rules when taking a chest measurement with the tape.

First, always place the tape directly behind the animal's front leg while the animal is on flat ground. Second, run the tape around the chest in a uniformly snug manner, perpendicular to the back. And third, make sure that the chest cavity is neither compressed nor enlarged (some hunters prop it open with a stick after evisceration for better cooling; the animal may stiffen in this position and inflate the chest measurement accordingly).

In addition to the field-dressed weight, suppose you want to know how much your deer weighed on the hoof, and how much freezer meat it will yield. No problem. There are formulas to arrive at these figures, too, though they're not quite as accurate.

If you hunt in the East, to get your deer's live weight, simply multiply the dressed weight by 1.25 and add 4 pounds. For the Midwest and West, multiply the dressed weight by 1.25 and add 2.6 pounds. Southern deer hunters should multiply the dressed weight by 1.17 and then add 5 pounds.

And the "freezer weight"? From an honest butcher, you should get back roughly one-half of the dressed weight of the deer, provided that you didn't order a lot of sausage or hamburger.

Stew:
Feast in a Pot

*By Angus Cameron and
Judith Jones*

Autumn breezes are blowing, and you can feel a nip in the air. At home or in hunting camp, those rumblings in your stomach could be calling for a steaming kettle of venison stew—or any other game you were lucky enough to bring back from your last hunting trip.

Whether you prefer a meat-and-potatoes stew or a French bourguignon, the recipes in The L.L. Bean Game & Fish Cookbook will help keep you warm on a chilly fall afternoon.

Authors Angus Cameron and Judith Jones offer the following tips on how to prepare a stew from the game of your choice. They've also found recipes from around the world for big game, small game, upland gamebirds and waterfowl.

There are a number of special ingredients that can enhance the flavor of your stew, including the animal's innards and bones. Kidneys heighten the meat taste without giving a kidney flavor to the stew. Simply stew the kidneys in the broth, cutting them into large chunks so that they can be easily removed before serving.

When butchering deer and larger animals, the lower legs, which are normally discarded, can be saved and used later as marrow bones to enhance the flavor of the stew. Just skin them out, saw them up into marrow-bone size (3- or 4-inch pieces), then package and freeze them at the time the meat is frozen. You can also save the bones left over after boning out the meat.

Wine, cognac and other brandies are standard ingredients used to flavor stews, but the use of beer, whiskey, rum, gin and other liquors is not as well known. When it comes to the practice of using spirits in game cookery, we recall how the late Jack O'Connor, *Outdoor Life's* legendary Shooting Editor, used gin to enhance the flavor of gamebirds.

Some cooks may be unaware that they regularly use lilies in their recipes—namely garlic, chives, shallots, onions and leeks. When preparing big-game stew, we recommend using stronger herbs such as onions and garlic, while the more delicate leek or shallot suitably seasons a gamebird. To give a stew a more pronounced flavor, add crushed garlic near the end of the cooking along with the additional vegetables.

We also strongly recommend using all members of the lily family *fresh* whenever possible, not in powdered or salt form. Garlic particularly leaves an unpleasant aftertaste when it has been dehydrated. Look for bulbs with plump, firm cloves.

We think that the stew recipes that follow will be sure hits in camp or at home.

In camp or at home, delicious stews can be made from venison, moose, elk, caribou, and antelope. Rabbit, squirrel, muskrat and beaver make fine stews, too! Carl Doney photo. Photo stylist: Kay Lichthardt.

Stove-Lid Stew

This stew is really a basic camp stew, and I've made a lot of them on an old lumber camp stove on Horseshoe Lake in the Ontario bush. A nice thing about a wood range is that you can be boiling something over one stove lid, simmering something over another and keeping something warm over still another, all at the same time and with the same fire. It's just as good at home, where I usually use half beef broth and half red wine for the liquid.

This is a one-dish meal in camp with a large can of peaches for dessert; at home, serve with a salad and French bread. Beaujolais goes well with this dish. Serves 6.

3½ pounds venison, moose, elk or other stew meat, cut
 into 1½-inch cubes
Flour
5 tbsp. lard or oil
2 large onions, chopped
1 rib celery with leaves, chopped
1 green pepper, chopped
2 cloves garlic, crushed or thinly sliced (or 5 cloves gar-
 lic, unpeeled, to be taken out later)
1½ cups game or beef broth (canned will do)
1 cup tomato sauce, canned or homemade*
1 tsp. Worcestershire sauce
2 sprigs parsley, chopped (or 1 tbsp. dried)
1 tsp. thyme
½ tsp. savory
4 to 5 bay leaves
2 tsp. salt, at least
Pepper
Vegetables: Use potatoes (5 quartered), carrots (4
 scraped and cut into thick slices), onions (2 to 3
 small ones), 1 turnip (diced)
1 tbsp. blackstrap molasses

½ pound kidneys of game, veal or lamb, cubed (optional)
1 dill pickle, chopped (optional)

Roll meat cubes in flour and brown them in lard or oil in a Dutch oven, deep metal casserole or electric skillet. Don't crowd the cubes, but rather brown them in relays so that they do not touch each other in the pan. When one batch is browned, take it out and set aside while you do next batch. This will take 20 to 25 minutes.

Add chopped onions, celery and green pepper, and saute until tender (not brown), 6 minutes or so.

Return meat, add whole garlic cloves,** broth, tomato sauce (or tomatoes), Worcestershire, parsley, thyme, savory, bay leaves, salt and pepper, and bring to quick boil. Cover, turn down heat and simmer (if you use electric skillet, simmer at 250°) for about an hour. Stir occasionally.

Add vegetables, molasses and kidney cubes (optional), cover again and continue to simmer for another 1 to 1¼ hours.

If the flour on the browned meat has not thickened the stew sufficiently, mix 1 tbsp. flour with a little water and stir into stew gradually. Let it simmer (along with the optional chopped pickle) a bit longer to thicken.

*In camp, maybe 1 small can (11 ounces) tomatoes.

**If you use crushed garlic, add it when you add vegetables.

Venison Stew Paprika D. D'A
Serve with egg noodles or spaetzle, salad and hot Italian bread. Serves 6.

2½ to 3 pounds venison stew cut into 1½-inch cubes
½ cup flour
3 tbsp. paprika
Salt and pepper
2 tbsp. butter or margarine
2 medium onions, chopped
2 cloves garlic
1 tsp. marjoram
1 small can (11 ounces) tomatoes (or 1 can tomato sauce)
½ cup wine
½ cup sour cream, at room temperature (optional)

Shake meat cubes in paper bag with flour, 1 tbsp. paprika, salt and pepper.

In Dutch oven or fireproof casserole, melt butter and saute coated venison cubes until nicely browned. (You may have to brown the cubes in stages. Do not crowd them but leave space between them; otherwise, they will steam, not brown.)

Remove cubes to warm dish. In same casserole, saute until soft the onions and garlic with 2 tbsp. paprika, then add marjoram, tomatoes and wine. Cover and cook under medium heat for 20 minutes.

Add browned venison cubes and simmer over low heat for 1½ to 2 hours or until meat is tender.

Just before ready to serve, stir in, if you wish, ½ cup sour cream.

Moose (Elk, Caribou, or Venison) Bourguignon
This is the game stew deluxe and deserves its reputation as queen among stews. I believe that the glazed vegetables and the kidney endow this stew with its especially marvelous flavor. When made this way, it has that "best of French restaurants" taste.

Serve with noodles, homemade spaetzle or rice. Serves 6.

¼ pound salt pork, diced
½-pound slice of ham, diced (or 3 strips bacon, diced)
Flour
Salt and pepper
3 pounds round or rump, cut into 2-inch cubes
1 game kidney, sliced (if moose or elk; both if deer), or beef kidney
1 tbsp. brown sugar
1 tbsp. currant or beach plum jelly
1 tsp. Kitchen Bouquet
2 bouillon cubes
24 small or pearl onions (if unavailable, quarter 3 medium onions)
5 carrots, sliced
3 cloves garlic, sliced
2 cups red wine
1 can cream of mushroom soup or 1 cup beef broth*
1 tbsp. Worcestershire or Harvey's sauce
3 bay leaves
2 tsp. thyme (or 1 tsp. thyme and 1 tsp. crumbled rosemary)
½ pound mushrooms, sliced
Butter
¾ cup cream
3 tbsp. chopped parsley

In skillet, try out the salt pork and frizzle the ham cubes (or bacon). Reserve cracklings and ham.

Roll or shake meat chunks in salted and peppered flour. Same for the kidney slices. Brown the meats in the salt pork fat on all sides, making sure that you do not crowd the pieces, i.e., brown one batch of pieces, remove to casserole, then brown the next batch.

Stir sugar, jelly and Kitchen Bouquet into skillet, then smash in 2 bouillon cubes and melt, stirring to blend over low flame. Glaze onions, carrots and garlic slices until sticky but not caramelized. Remove to casserole. Stir in red wine, then can of mushroom soup, if you are using it; otherwise, add beef broth. Stir in bay leaves and thyme and smooth out the liquid. Set aside.

Cover and simmer for 2 to 2½ hours, adding water if stew thickens too much. Add vegetables to casserole for the last 30 to 40 minutes of cooking. If you didn't use canned mushroom soup, saute mushrooms in butter for 2 to 3 minutes, then add the cream. Cook down until the cream has thickened—about 5 minutes. Add cracklings and ham to the mushroom mixture just long enough to warm them, and add to stew along with parsley.

*Use canned mushroom soup if you're in camp or anywhere that fresh mushrooms are not available.

Flemish-Style Antelope Stew With Beer

A Flemish stew known as carbonnade uses dark beer as a braising liquid and lots of onions. The same savory treatment can be given to any red game meat; only the cooking time will vary, depending on the toughness of the meat. So, be sure to start testing after 1½ hours of cooking. Serves 6.

3 pounds antelope stew meat
4 tbsp. pork fat
6 medium onions, sliced
4 large cloves garlic, smashed and chopped
Salt and freshly ground pepper
2 cups dark beer, or 1 cup regular beer and 1 cup stout
1 cup game or beef stock
½ tsp. thyme
2 tbsp. brown sugar
2 bay leaves
About 8 sprigs parsley
2 tbsp. arrowroot or potato or cornstarch
2 tbsp. red wine vinegar

Cut antelope meat into pieces approximately 1½ to 2 inches square and one-half inch thick.

Heat 2 tbsp. fat in large, heavy skillet. Pat pieces of meat dry and brown them, not too many at a time so that they don't crowd each other, over high heat, turning until all sides are seared. Remove pieces as they are done and continue with the rest.

Add remaining fat to skillet and saute onions until they are lightly browned all over. Add garlic and saute gently, stirring, for a minute more.

In casserole of about two-quart capacity and not more than three inches deep, arrange layer of meat, salt and pepper well, spread half of onion mixture over it, add another layer of meat, season, and finish with onions.

Heat beer and stock in skillet, scraping up any good browned bits. Stir in thyme and brown sugar, then pour this over meat and onions. Lay bay leaves and parsley sprigs on top. Cover with foil and casserole cover, and bake in preheated 325° oven anywhere from 1½ hours to as much as 2½. Check carefully and remove when tender; don't overcook so that meat gets stringy.

Mix arrowroot with vinegar and a little cold water to get smooth paste. Pour liquid out of casserole and into saucepan, stir in paste and bring to boil, whisking to make smooth. If sauce seems a bit thin, let it boil down for a few minutes.

Remove bay leaves and parsley sprigs and pour thickened sauce over meat. Reheat if necessary.

Elk Stew, Peruvian Style

For the cook who might wish to give a Latin American touch to a game stew, here is a recipe converted from Elisabeth Ortiz for beef (Seco de Carne) in her *Book of Latin American Cooking*. Serves 6.

4 tbsp. lard or vegetable oil
4 cloves garlic, finely chopped
1 medium onion, finely chopped
1 tsp. hot ground pepper or cayenne*
3 pounds elk or moose, etc., cut into 1-inch cubes
2 cups beef stock
Salt and freshly ground pepper
2 tbsp. chopped fresh coriander (cilantro or Chinese
    parsley) or 2 tsp. ground coriander
Juice of 1 lemon
2 pounds potatoes, boiled and halved

Heat lard or oil in casserole and saute garlic, onion, hot pepper and meat cubes until cubes are lightly browned.

Add beef stock, salt and pepper to taste, and coriander. Cook partially covered over low heat until beef is tender, 1½ to 2 hours. Liquid should be reduced so that sauce is quite thick and not very abundant.

Just before serving, stir in lemon juice and cook one or two minutes longer. Heap stew on warmed serving platter and surround with freshly cooked, hot potato halves.

*If you are able to buy small, hot dried chilies, just crumble in fingers to get "ground" pepper called for in recipe. But if you do crumble chilies, be sure to wash your hands in warm, soapy water.

Game Meat Goulash With Noodles Or Spaetzle

Because stew meat makes up a fair proportion of butchered game, the cook with game in the larder will want to vary its use. Game Hungarian-style is a tasty variation. Round of game can be used, too. This dish is made in Hungary with red deer as the meat. Elk meat would be the New World version. Try to use real, sweet Hungarian paprika. Serves 6.

3 pounds stew meat or round cut into 1½-inch cubes
Flour
4 tbsp. lard or butter and oil
2 large onions, chopped
2 cloves garlic, smashed
2½ tbsp. sweet Hungarian paprika
1 rib celery with leaves, chopped
½ tsp. thumb-and-finger-crumbled savory
¾ cup red wine
1 cup game or beef broth
Salt and pepper
1 cup tomato sauce or puree, or 4 tomatoes from a can
*1 cup sour cream**
Noodles or spaetzle

Roll meat cubes in flour and brown in lard as in recipe for Stove-Lid Stew.

Add and saute onions and garlic. When soft, add paprika, mix thoroughly and cook for another minute or so.

Return all meat to pan and add celery, savory,

wine, broth, salt, pepper and tomatoes. Cover and simmer over low heat for 1½ hours or until meat cubes are done (taste one). If you use electric skillet, simmer at 250°. When meat is tender, check to see whether flour on meat cubes has given you the right consistency for the sauce. If too thin, mix flour and a little water and stir in, simmering 3 to 4 minutes longer to thicken.

Stir in sour cream and serve with noodles or spaetzle.

*If made in camp where sour cream is scarce it will still be good without it.

Squirrel Stew With Black Olives
Ripe olives, especially if they are those wrinkled, ill-tempered-looking oil-cured olives from France or Greece, have an affinity for game. Any black olives will do, but if they are unpitted, you must pare off the flesh ahead of time to extract the pits.

Of course, you can also use this recipe for rabbit, two pheasants, four grouse or four or five partridge. All gallinaceous gamebirds are delicious prepared this way. Serves 6.

1 tbsp. oil or lard
¼ salt pork or enough cubed to make ⅔ cup
2 squirrels, cut up as you would a frying chicken
Juice of 1 lemon
¾ cup flour
1 tsp. thyme
1 tsp. rosemary
Salt and pepper
3 onions, minced
1 small carrot, sliced very thin
½ cup dry white wine or dry vermouth
½ cup giblet stock or chicken broth*
3 cloves garlic
3 bay leaves
2 tbsp. tomato paste
½ cup pitted black olives
Chopped parsley

In big skillet or casserole, put 1 tbsp. or so of oil or lard, and when hot try out the salt-pork cubes in it until they are crisp. Remove and reserve these delicious cracklings.

Moisten squirrel pieces with lemon juice, and then roll or shake in paper bag with enough flour mixed with thyme, rosemary, salt and pepper to use up all of this flour/herb mixture. Reserve remainder.

Next, saute floured pieces in fat. Do this over medium heat, and try to stand over skillet or casserole with fork or kitchen tongs, turning pieces until golden.

Remove squirrel pieces, and saute onions and sliced carrot slowly for 8 to 10 minutes. Now, add wine, stock, garlic cloves and bay leaves and meld in tomato paste. Simmer together for five minutes.

Put squirrel pieces and salt-pork cracklings in and cover. Simmer for 30 minutes.

During latter process, you may need to check for moisture. If needed, add stock or half stock/half

white wine. The browned flour pieces should cook off enough flour to thicken sauce some. If in your ministrations it becomes too thin, swirl some of reserved flour/herb mix in a little water and stir into sauce. Simmer a few minutes more to phase out the raw-flour taste.

A few minutes before serving, fish out the gum-cutting bay leaves, and stir and work in the olives. Garnish with parsley. *If you have made the giblet stock yourself, dice cooked squirrel livers, then squash and add to other ingredients later.

Brunswick Stew
Technically, this stew is always made with squirrel, but it can be made with other meats—rabbit, musk-rat, beaver or combinations. Here's the stew for four made from one squirrel. Very slow simmering is the trick. Serve this stew in soup bowls with corn pone or hushpuppies. Serves 4.

1 squirrel, cut into 6 to 7 pieces
Flour
Salt and pepper
3 tbsp. butter
8 cups boiling water
1 tsp. thyme
1 cup fresh corn
1 cup lima beans
3 potatoes, quartered
¼ tsp. cayenne
2 onions, sliced
2 cups canned tomatoes with juice

Roll squirrel pieces in flour, salt and pepper. Brown butter. Add squirrel and all other ingredients, save tomatoes, to boiling water, cover and simmer for 1½ to 2 hours.

Add tomatoes and continue to simmer for another hour.

Jan Herbert's Rabbit Stew, Maine-Style
Jan Herbert, a Bean staff member, likes the way her sister, Helen MacDonald, makes a rabbit stew. "Good with dumplings," she writes.

1 to 2 rabbits
8 carrots
2 large onions, cut up
6 ribs celery and leaves, cut up
6 to 8 boiled potatoes, cut up
1 tbsp. salt
Pepper to taste
Flour

Dress rabbit and wash. Put in kettle with lightly salted water to cover, and cook until just tender.

Remove rabbit, take meat from bones and put back into cooking water. Add carrots, onions and celery. Add potatoes last when other vegetables are tender. Season with salt and pepper. Thicken stock with thin paste of flour and water.

Index